Books are to be returned on or before
the last date below.

7 – DAY
LOAN

Media and Male Identity

Media and Male Identity

The Making and Remaking of Men

J. R. Macnamara

First published 2006 by
PALGRAVE MACMILLAN
Houndmills, Basingstoke, Hampshire RG21 6XS and
175 Fifth Avenue, New York, N.Y. 10010
Companies and representatives throughout the world

PALGRAVE MACMILLAN is the global academic imprint of the Palgrave
Macmillan division of St. Martin's Press, LLC and of Palgrave Macmillan Ltd.
Macmillan® is a registered trademark in the United States, United Kingdom
and other countries. Palgrave is a registered trademark in the European
Union and other countries.

ISBN-13: 978–0–230–00167–1
ISBN-10: 0–230–00167–X

This book is printed on paper suitable for recycling and made from fully
managed and sustained forest sources.

A catalogue record for this book is available from the British Library.

Library of Congress Cataloging-in-Publication Data
Media and male identity : the making and remaking of men / J.R. Macnamara.
    p.   cm.
  Includes bibliographical references and index.
  ISBN 0–230–00167–X (cloth)
  1. Men in mass media.   2. Men—Identity.   3. Mass media—Social
aspects.   I. Macnamara, Jim.
  P94.5.M44M43 2006
  302.23081—dc22   2006046018

10   9   8   7   6   5   4   3   2   1
15   14   13   12   11   10   09   08   07   06

Printed and bound in Great Britain by
Antony Rowe Ltd, Chippenham and Eastbourne

For men; for those entrusted with boys growing up seeking their identity; and for the many women who care about, befriend and love boys and men. With special thanks to my wife, best friend and muse, Gail Joy Kenning.

Contents

List of Tables

List of Figures and Illustrations

Acknowledgements

Research on the scale reported in this book cannot be completed without assistance from many people, too many to name them all individually. However, I would particularly like to acknowledge Dr Peter West from the Research Group on Men and Families at the University of Western Sydney, and Associate Professor Bob Perry and Professor Mike Atherton, Associate Dean (Research) at the University of Western Sydney. Others who were very helpful in providing information and whom I wish to acknowledge are: Paul Nathanson and Katherine Young from McGill University, Canada, whose research published in *Spreading Misandry: The Teaching of Contempt for Men in Popular Culture* (McGill-Queen's University Press, 2001) provided a sparking point for debate on this subject; David Gauntlett for his research in *Media, Gender and Identity* (Routledge, 2002); Kimberley Neuendorf and Cleveland State University for the excellent references and materials on content analysis made available online and in *The Content Analysis Guidebook* (Sage Publications, 2001); Chris Newbold, Oliver Boyd-Barrett and Hilde Van Den Bulck for their text *The Media Book* (Arnold/Hodder Headline, 2002); Professor Kenneth Clatterbaugh, Professor of Philosophy at the University of Washington for papers kindly provided; and Bruce Hawthorne from the Family Court of Australia for research data made available. A special thank you is due to Amanda Hellmund who assisted in coding around 2,000 media articles. Also, I would like to thank my publisher, Palgrave Macmillan, for their support and assistance, especially Jill Lake. Collectively, I would also like to express appreciation to the many other academics, authors, media, journalists and columnists cited and quoted with in text acknowledgement in this book.

Introduction

A half-century of research has identified that mass media portrayals of women are influential in shaping their self-image and self-esteem, as well as men's and societies' views of women. Comparatively few studies have examined mass media portrayals of men and male identity, and gender studies have mostly assumed these to be predominantly positive and unproblematic. But, in a post-industrial era of massive economic, technological and social change, research shows mass media are projecting and propagating new images of male identity from 'Atlas Syndrome' workaholics and 'deadbeat dads' to 'metrosexuals' and men with 'a feminine side', all with potentially significant social implications. This book presents a landmark, in-depth study of how mass media contribute to the making and remaking of male identity.

Mass media have been identified as primary sites of discourse which influence individuals, culture, social structures and political policy and also reflect social, political and intellectual views and attitudes. This multidirectional cause-and-effect relationship is what makes mass media so significant in modern societies, and media representations of men and male identity are explored from both perspectives.

Research cited in this book looked at 650 newspapers, more than 100 magazines and more than 330 hours of television. A total of over 2,000 media articles and segments were analysed using in-depth quantitative and qualitative content analysis methodology.

While part of the research was conducted in Australia, a number of international media were analysed including the television programmes *60 Minutes*, *Oprah* and *Queer Eye for the Straight Guy*, as well as magazines such as *Cosmopolitan* and *FHM* and news, including numerous US, UK and European wire services and syndicated newspaper and magazine articles. With major news, current affairs stories and programmes

1

published and broadcast globally, the findings have international relevance.

There is ample evidence that all is not well in the world of men and boys. Male suicide rates are four times the rates of female suicide in most Western countries; boys are failing and dropping out of school at an alarming rate; male health and longevity are deteriorating, while women's are improving; an increasing number of men are electing not to marry or have children; groups such as Fathers-4-Justice are forming and launching protests such as climbing the London Eye and the walls of Buckingham Palace to bring attention to men's concerns; and a record number of submissions and complaints are being made by men to advertising standards bodies and to child custody and Family Court inquiries as cited in this book.

While the subject of this book is men and male identity, it is not only a book about and for men. It is also a book for women. What is happening to men has an impact on the women who raise them, care about them, love them, marry them, create families with them, and dwell and work alongside them. In many ways, women will care about the issues discussed in this book as much as men because of their interest in the health, welfare and happiness of their husbands, partners, brothers, male friends and sons growing up and seeking their role and identity in a changing world. It is also a book for educationalists, health workers, social institutions, policymakers and anyone interested in a healthy society.

The approach is not to present men as victims. It is freely noted that in most societies, men still hold most positions of power and authority. But many do not. And even those who do are not necessarily immune to emotional damage by erosion of and attacks on their identity.

Also, the extensive data presented and an inclusive approach strived for in this text should render it beyond dismissal as a 'backlash', as alternative or even slightly divergent views on gender are often dismissively categorized. This book is not anti-feminist. To the contrary, it supports and draws on feminist theory. But it advocates that gender as a concept, gender identity and the roles of men and women in societies should not be formulated in feminist terms alone. In particular, the nature of men, male identities and men's roles should be subjects in which a range of men (not only pro-feminists) are engaged and given space. Discussion on a topic as important as gender which goes to the heart of human identity should be able to be conducted inclusively, in an open, frank and constructive way. The widely used term 'gender war' is a misnomer. Despite much disputed ground, men and women are not on opposite sides, and it would be sad for societies if they ever became so alienated.

As a fellow Australian who was a pioneer in gender studies said: 'Wars cannot be won . . . Women who adopt the attitudes of war in their search for liberation condemn themselves to acting out the last perversion of dehumanized manhood' (Germaine Greer, 1999, p. 354).

1
Why Study Mass Media Portrayals of Men and Male Identity?

In traditional (pre-modern) societies, identities, along with roles and modes of behaviour, were largely prescribed by tradition, including myths and narratives handed down from previous generations. Philosophers, anthropologists and sociologists have concluded that when tradition dominates, individual roles and actions do not need to be analysed and thought about very much because choices are already prescribed (Gauntlett, 2002, p. 96).

Identity first appeared as a term during the Enlightenment around the sixteenth century, according to Davies (1993, p. 8). However, the concept of identity became important in modernist thinking and even more so with postmodernism. With modernism, tradition, myth and religion, while remaining influential in human identity and modes of living, were largely overtaken by science, technology, law and other disciplines based on rational thinking and reason as the basis of knowledge and 'truth'.

Marxism further attacked beliefs and worldviews implanted by traditional institutions such as the Church and economic systems such as capitalism, labelling them 'false consciousness' and advocating new strategies for achieving self-consciousness.

With postmodernism, all established pillars of social identity, including traditions and modernism's scientific 'truths', were questioned and cast aside. Lyotard (1979, p. 37) advocated 'incredulity towards meta-narratives'. Master narratives or scripts for living provided by traditions, religion and science were replaced by a new cultural self-consciousness. In this environment, Giddens (1991, p. 53) says, 'the self becomes a reflexive project'.

In modern societies (i.e. societies where modernity or postmodernism is established), Gauntlett (2002, p. 96) says self-identity is 'an inescapable issue', that through a self-discovery process 'we create, maintain and revise a set of biographical narratives – the story of who we are, and how we came to be where we are now . . . ' (p. 99). Giddens (1991) refers to this process as constructing 'narratives of the self'. These narratives are not created once early in our lives, but are ongoing constructions. Gauntlett says: 'To believe in oneself, and command the respect of others, we need a strong narrative' and this 'needs to be creatively and continuously maintained' (2002, p. 100). Hall (1990) also sees identity as an ongoing 'project of the self': 'instead of thinking of identity as an already accomplished fact . . . we should think, instead, of identity as a 'production' which is never complete, always in process . . . ' (1990, p. 222).

There are a number of ways individuals and groups construct and maintain their 'narratives of the self'. Marxist philosophy viewed class and economic factors as key determinants of identity. As shown by Faludi (2000) in her examination of working-class men, *Stiffed: The Betrayal of Modern Man*, work continues to be a key component in constructing the identities of men in late industrial and post-industrial societies.

In postmodern cultures, lifestyle has emerged as a key element of self-identity. Lull (2000, p. 157) says Bourdieu's concept of 'habitus', which he defined as 'a system of socially learned cultural predispositions and activities that differentiate people by their lifestyles', provides a lens through which we can view and understand modern communities. Bourdieu (1990, p. 110) argues that people, individually and collectively, 'internalize their position in social space'. Giddens (1991) also sees lifestyle as significant in modern identity, asserting that everyone in modern society has to select a lifestyle. Lifestyles are described by Gauntlett (2002, p. 102) as 'ready-made templates for a narrative of self'. Movements such as hippies, punk, grunge, the 'camp' gay community and the back-to-nature eco-trend are examples of lifestyles that carry with them identities for individuals and groups. But, equally, corporate executives, warehouse-living inner-city dwellers, suburban quarter-acre block owners, farmers, rock stars, youth and retirees choose and closely conform to lifestyles. Modern marketers identify and target groups based on lifestyle factors such as Yuppies (Young Upwardly Mobile Professionals), DINKS (Double Income No Kids), Generation Xers and Generation Ys.

But identities are determined by more than class, economics and lifestyle. At a deeper level, identities are also derived from nationality, ethnicity, social class, community, gender and sexuality (Woodward, 1997, p. 1).

The important role of gender in human identity – for men and women

From the beginning of the twentieth century, sex and sexuality have been identified as fundamental elements of identity. Freud and the movement of psychoanalytic thinking that he spawned focused attention on sex and sexuality as key determinants in a wide range of human behaviour and perceptions (Connell, 1995a, pp. 8–21). 'Sexual development and sexual satisfaction... became bound to the reflexive project of the self' (Giddens, 1991, p. 164).

The terms sex, sexuality and gender are used in various ways throughout the extensive literature in this field, as are the terms masculinity and femininity. Their meanings will be discussed and clarified as far as possible in relation to specific usages in this book, rather than attempting to state definitions in advance, as there are no single, agreed interpretations. Some writers use the terms interchangeably, while others continue to dispute their meaning. Gauntlett (2002, p. 34) notes that the nature of sex and gender has been the subject of long debate among psychologists and sociologists.

Freud and Jung, while differing on a number of issues, both saw gender as 'rooted in timeless truths about the human psyche' – i.e. biologically determined or innate (Connell, 1995a, p. 13). This perception of gender dominated thinking about the sexes for the first half of the twentieth century.

Jean-Paul Sartre in *Being and Nothingness* (1958, originally published in 1943) saw the Freudian school of psychoanalysis as too rigid and overly focused on sexual desire as a principal factor influencing the human condition. His partner and noted feminist writer Simone de Beauvoir (1997) drew on Sartre's existential psychoanalysis which moved beyond the static typologies of Freudian psychology in her landmark book *The Second Sex* (first published 1949) and explored gender as 'an evolving engagement with situations and social structures' (Connell, 1995a, p. 19).

Weatherall (2002) attempts to summarize thinking and draws a distinction between sex and gender based on the influential work of the anthropologist Gayle Rubin (1984) who proposed sexuality and gender as 'two distinct systems', although Weatherall also uses the terms in varying and somewhat contradictory contexts. She says, 'Since around the 1960s an important distinction has been drawn between sex as biological and gender as social' (Weatherall, 2002, p. 81). Then, on the next page, Weatherall states: 'The simple belief in two and only two *sexes* can be understood, not as a biological given but as a normative social construction, a product of *gender* discourses' (2002, p. 82).

Davies (1993, p. 10) notes sex/gender theory that claims 'sex' refers to biological characteristics while 'gender' denotes social characteristics, but says that 'the boundary is now so blurry that the distinction is no longer a meaningful one'. In examining male and female identity, one has to negotiate both concepts, she concludes.

The nature of gender and its relationship to biology and social conditioning are explored in more detail in Chapter 3. For now, the important point is that philosophers, psychoanalysts and gender studies academics agree that sex and gender are important components of human identity and that we each have a gendered identity – an imprint made on us or a mould which shapes us by virtue of our being male or female. 'Gender roles are like scripts', Nathanson and Young (2001, p. 61) say. Grbich (2004) cites gender as the third dimension of social space, after race and class.

Feminism has applied considerable study to the relationship between gender and identity and concludes that gender is central to self-identities and identity of women as a class. In introducing a poststructuralist discussion of identity and subjectivity, Davies (1993, p. 7) writes: 'The division of people into male and female is so fundamental to our talk . . . and to our understanding of identity'.

If it is true that gender is fundamental to the identities of women as more than half a century of feminist theory has argued, it is fair to conclude that gender is also an important element in the identities of men and boys both individually and collectively. Study of men and boys and how their identities are shaped by their gender and perceptions of their gender is, therefore, of social significance. But such research is seriously lacking in some respects, as we shall see.

By way of clarification, it is noted that poststructuralist theory questions the term 'identity'. Sarup (1988) points out that the preferred poststructuralist term for the individual is 'subject' and, emphasizing the non-fixed, fluid, ongoing, highly personal process of understanding one's self and others, poststructuralist thinking replaces the term 'identity' with 'subjectivity'. Notwithstanding, the poststructuralist concept of subjectivity is largely understood to be a parallel – albeit for some a preferred replacement – for what others term identity and is constructed and constituted in postmodern societies through the same processes and influences. In this book, references to the constitutive forces of identity can be read as applying to the poststructural notion of subjectivity. Reflecting the similarity of these concepts, Mac An Ghaill (1994, p. 9) uses both terms, referring to 'subjective identities'.

Social scientists and feminists widely agree that self-identity, or subjective identity, are important to individuals' self-esteem and their approach to life, as well as to society's perceptions of individuals and groups.

The role of discourse in constructing identity – how we are made by 'talk'

Discourse, in a simplistic sense, is what people are saying on a given subject. But it is more than random talk or unconnected fragments of speech or text. Discourse refers to dominant ideas and viewpoints that emerge and become worldviews and consensus of knowledge and, in turn, form groundswells and tides of opinion that influence social and political landscapes. Importantly, in addition to comprising discussion describing or reflecting existing conditions, discourse includes ideas and viewpoints that influence and create social, political and economic conditions – i.e. it can define what ought to be and exert influence in bringing that about. It is what poststructuralist thinkers call a 'constitutive' force in societies.

Definitions of discourse in social sciences literature, ranging from the complex to the simple, include:

> Discourses are 'practices that systematically form the objects of which they speak... discourses are not about objects; they do not identify objects, they constitute them and in the practice of doing so conceal their own invention. (Foucault, 1972, p. 49)

> Discourse is a language or system of representation that has developed socially in order to make and circulate a coherent set of meanings about an important topic area. These meanings serve the interests of that section of society within which the discourse originates and which works ideologically to naturalize meanings into common sense. (Fiske, 1995, p. 14)

> Discourse is a body of ideas, concepts and beliefs which become established as knowledge or as an accepted world view. These ideas become a powerful framework for understanding and action in social life. (Bilton et al., 1996, p. 657)

> Discourses are not just 'a bunch of words' – they determine our social responses. A discourse does not represent what is 'real' – it actually

produces what we come to understand as real. It determines what can be said and even what can be thought. (Woods, 1999)

A discourse is the way objects or ideas are talked about publicly that gives rise to widespread perceptions and understandings. (Lull, 2000, p. 173)

Discourse is variously used in the gender and language field. It may be used in a linguistic sense to refer to language beyond that of words. Or it may be used in a poststructural sense to refer to broad systems of meaning . . . discourse is not restricted to spoken language but also refers to written language, (Weatherall, 2002, pp. 76–7)

Discourse is, in fact, the story of reality as it is presented to us through media or other cultural texts. (Newbold et al., 2002, p. 85)

Both structuralism and poststructuralism recognize the constitutive force of discourse in shaping social structures and identities (or subjectivities). Structuralist views maintain that people are socialized into the world by social structures such as policies, mores, institutions and laws, and by other individuals and groups such as family and peers. While also believing that identity is constituted by structures and discourse, poststructuralism differs in that it disputes the structuralist view that socialization is imposed on individuals. Rather, poststructuralist theory argues that each person goes through a process of *subjectification* in which they actively 'take up the discourses through which they and others speak and write the world into existence as if they were their own' (Davies, 1993, p. 13). Thus, the potential power or influence of discourse is even greater in a poststructural view of society than its already important role identified in structuralist theory.

Foucault made a major contribution to understanding the relationship between identity and discourse with his concept of the 'technologies of the self'. Foucault supported the view that identities are constructed from the materials available to people and advanced the idea that one of the key 'technologies of the self' is discourse. He proposed that discourses shape the way we perceive the world and our own selves (Gauntlett, 2002, p. 133). In his earlier writing, Foucault suggested that discourses constrain people (i.e. prevent them from saying or doing things they otherwise might do), while in his later work he proposed that discourses act more subtly by causing people to 'police themselves' (Gauntlett, 2002, pp. 116, 125). In simple terms, Foucault suggested that discourse does not exercise a direct, overt influence on members of a society, but has a hegemonic power that causes them to conform to certain modes of thinking and behaviour.

Conventional social psychological research viewed language as a medium or mode of expression related to, but existing independently of, identity. It was assumed in this view that language and interaction reflect gender identities. However, poststructuralist thinking has led to a starkly contrasting view. Discursive psychology follows what Weatherall (2002, p. 75) calls 'the discursive turn' in the humanities and social sciences, moving away from earlier essentialist and structuralist approaches to focus on language and discourse as a constitutive or creative forces. In a discursive psychology view:

> identities are produced and negotiated in the ongoing business of social interaction. In this view, identities do not have predefined, essential characteristics. Rather, identities emerge from the actions of local conversations... Thus, identity is not viewed in essentialist terms as something that people 'are'. Rather, identities are progressively and dynamically achieved through the discursive practices that individuals engage in. (Weatherall, 2002, p. 138)

Edwards (1997) summarizes this as a shift in emphasis and focus from 'cognition' to 'talk'. Talk in this sense is used broadly. As shown in the definitions of discourse, Weatherall notes that 'discourse is not restricted to spoken language but also refers to written language' (p. 77) and it reasonable to conclude that this view equally applies to visual language. Thus, books, newspapers, magazines, movies and television form part of the 'talk' or discourse in modern societies.

As well as considering its role in shaping identity, discourse is also important in noting the Foucauldian focus on the power effects of discourses – i.e. the effects that various discourses have in society in shaping social and political agendas and even government policy. The types of knowledge discourses produce and institutionalize 'shape the creation and sustenance of political decisions, policies, social norms, practices and institutions', Woods (1999) notes.

Constructionist views of gender in particular cite discourse as a central element in the process of creating gender identity. Weatherall (2002, p. 82) states that construction of gender is 'a product of gender discourses'. Davies (1993) says 'gender is constituted through the discourses with which we speak and write ourselves into existence'. She adds:

within poststructuralist theory, it is possible to see human subjects as not fixed but constantly in process, being constituted and reconstituted through the discursive practices they have access to in their daily lives. The tensions and instabilities in each person's subjectivity become visible... through an examination of the discourses and practices through which our subjectivities are constituted. (1993, p. 11)

Mass media as primary sites and propagators of discourse

In modern and postmodern societies, mass media are considered to play a key role in discourse, although precisely what part and effects they have are subjects of some debate and will be reviewed in detail in Chapter 4. Media representations – some call them re-presentations – refer to more than the physical presentation of information to readers, viewers and listeners. According to the media researchers Newbold et al. (2002, p. 261), media representations refer to 'the media's construction of reality... the relationship between the ideological and the real'.

In discussing how identity is produced, Stuart Hall (1990, p. 222) says identity is 'always constituted within, not outside representation' – in other words, we cannot escape the representations of our gender and form our gendered identity framed within representations of it. De Lauretis (1987, p. 5) agrees, saying 'the construction of gender is both the product and the process of its representation'. Saco (1992) makes similar observations.

Representation is defined by various media researchers and feminist writers. Two examples highlight the key elements pertinent to this study.

Representation refers to the process by which signs and symbols are made to convey certain meanings. Importantly, this term refers to the signs and symbols that claim to stand for, or re-present, some aspect of 'reality', such as objects, people, groups, places, events, social norms, cultural identities and so on. (Newbold et al., 2002, p. 260)

The feminist writer Judith Butler (1999, p. 3) says there are two meanings or uses of the term 'representation' – one denoting an operative or functional process, the other suggesting a normative function:

Representation... serves as the operative term within a political process to extend visibility and legitimacy... on the other hand, representation is the normative function of a language which is said either to reveal or to distort what is assumed to be true.

Mass media and their impact on societies have been studied intensively since the 1920s. In public debate on racism, mass media were cited as 'a central means of creating, reproducing and sustaining racial ideologies', Newbold et al. (2002, p. 311) say. They comment:

> Psychologists, criminologists and others continue to be concerned about such matters as the implications of exposure of children and adults to programmes containing scenes of violence; educationalists are concerned with the potential of the media for education; social anthropologists, who are most foremost among those staking out new questions in audience research, are interested in the ways in which people use, experience, relate to, live around and take meaning from the media. (2002, p. 15)

Many researchers point to the key role and effects of mass media in contemporary societies. Some examples are cited in the following:

- 'Without communication there can be no such thing as society. How communication is mediated is therefore a matter of singular social importance' (Beavis, 2002, p. 10).

- 'Media remain central to most people's lives... next to sleep and work, our next most time-consuming activity is attending to media' (Barr, 2000, p. 16).
- 'Today, popular media are obviously primary channels for the dissemination of prevailing discourses... The news and factual media inform us about the findings of lifestyle research and actual social change... Information and ideas from the media do not merely reflect the social world, then, but contribute to its shape, and are central to modern reflexivity' (Gauntlett, 2002, p. 98). Media are key to 'propagating modern lifestyles which are templates for narratives of the self' (Gauntlett, 2002, p. 103).

- 'In a contemporary society, the media are probably the most important producers of meaning, when they make claims about the way the world is, they become powerful ideological institutions' (Grossberg et al., 1998, p. 182).
- Specifically in relation to identity, Grossberg et al. say: 'The media's ability to produce people's social identities, in terms of both a sense of unity and difference [is] their most powerful and important effect' (1998, p. 206).
- Baudrillard claims that mass media generate what he calls 'hyper-reality' which dominates people's primary consciousness. He says

that in postmodern societies much of what audiences experience is defined for them by mass media and what is 'real life' is indistinguishable from its 'simulation . . . some fictional simulacrum of the real conjured up by the media' (Windschuttle, 1998; 2000).

- Gauntlet (2002) comments further: 'with the decline of traditions inherent in modernism and postmodernism, identities in general – including gender and sexual identities – have become more diverse and malleable . . . mass media suggest lifestyles, forms of self-presentation, and ways to find happiness (which may or may not be illusory) . . . individuals construct a narrative of the self which gives some order to our complex lives. This narrative will also be influenced by perspectives which we have adopted from the media. Our relationships with our bodies, our sexual partners, and our own emotional needs, will all also be influenced by media representations' (Gauntlett, 2002, p. 113).

It is sometimes claimed that mass media content is 'simply entertainment' and that, by implication, socially significant meanings cannot be read from it and significant effects on individuals or society are unlikely. However, Marxists, feminists and social researchers argue and present considerable evidence that media content is never 'just entertainment', that it is never politically or ideologically 'innocent'; rather mass media send 'messages' to viewers about the way things are, can be or should be (Nathanson and Young, 2001, p. 189). Nathanson and Young conclude: 'The [mass media] productions . . . cannot be dismissed by anyone with moral and intellectual integrity as 'nothing more than entertainment' (2001, p. 136). And further: 'there is nothing trivial about popular culture. It is the folklore, the conventional wisdom, of an urban, industrial society' (2001, p. 81).

Lull (2000, p. 171) cites empirical studies conducted by two American communication researchers which 'show that it certainly does matter what people see at the movies and watch on television and that people do not, perhaps cannot, maintain much distance from their mediated communicative interactions'.

Feminists have extensively cited the role of mass media representations in shaping gender identity in relation to women. For example:

- Weatherall, in her studies of gender in language and discourse, concludes: 'A context where sexist discourse is rife is in linguistic representations of women in the media' (2002, p. 76).

- Tuchman examined portrayals of women in mass media and concluded that women are 'symbolically annihilated by the media through absence, condemnation or trivialisation' (1978, pp. 3–17).
- Humm, in *Feminism and Film*, begins with the assertion: 'Film... often and anxiously envisions women stereotypically as "good" mothers or "bad" hysterical careerists... today, every Hollywood woman is someone else's Other' (1997, p. 3).
- Seger (2004) reports from her studies of women in film and television in the 1970s that 'many women featured in movies and TV programs were usually flat, shadowy figures, someone's wife or girlfriend. Or they were stock figures of fun: the mother-in-law, the kid sister, the old maid... most of the images of women are not just restricted, but negative'.
- Nathanson and Young observe: 'Feminists have long pointed out that the way women are represented in movies or on television can have profound effects on the way men see women in real life and – even more important – on the way women see themselves in real life' (2001, p. 18). They also comment: 'Feminists... have made popular culture one of the chief battlegrounds in their struggle for women' (2001, p. 244).
- Newbold et al. report from their studies of mass media: 'From very early on, feminist analysis attempts to uncover the constructed messages behind the representations of women in the media, attributing to these images a crucial role in the perception of real-life women and thus the maintaining of a social status quo' (2002, p. 269). They also comment that 'hegemonic discourses on women have been reinforced by mass media as a prime instrument' (2002, p. 85).

Feminist concern with the mass media continues in the so-called Third Wave of feminism. Baumgardner and Richards (2000, p. 93), in reviewing modern feminism, comment: 'It's clear that women get a bum deal in the mainstream media', and argue that this affects women's identity and position in societies.

A number of researchers contend that the role and effects of the mass media are increasing. According to Chaney (1994, p. 58), 'traditionally, social institutions such as family and religion have been seen as the primary media of [cultural] continuity. More recently... the role of ensuring continuity has increasingly been taken over by... forms of communication and entertainment'. Beck (2002, p. 26) says that in modern societies 'inherited recipes for living and role stereotypes fail to function...we have to make our own patterns of being and...it seems clear that the media plays an important role here'. Gauntlett (2002, p. 1) states in the introduction to *Media, Gender and Identity*: 'Media and communications are a central element of modern life, whilst gender and sexuality remain at the core of how we think about our identities. With the media containing so many images of women and men, and messages about men, women and sexuality today, it is highly unlikely that these ideas would have no impact on our own sense of identity'.

As well as representing female gender identity in various ways, mass media also extensively represent men and male identity. Connell (2000, p. 151) notes that 'mass media are crammed with representations of masculinities – from rock music, beer commercials, sitcoms, action movies and war films to news programs – which circulate on a vast scale'. Schirato and Yell (1999, p. 84), in a discussion of men's life-style magazines, comment: 'It is interesting to consider how this change in the profile of men's magazines impacts on discourses of masculine subjectivity. Magazines certainly constitute a significant site within the culture for the discursive production of subjectivity...changes in the market and profile of magazines indicate shifts in the "available discourses"...for constructing identities'. Nathanson and Young (2001, p. 295) conclude:

> It is true that adults should be able to read books or see movies without feeling threatened enough to fall apart. It is true also, however, that adults should be able to acknowledge the link between their own feelings and the cultural forces that induce them. Women are not merely childish for doing so. And men are not merely childish or (unduly) threatened for doing exactly the same thing.

Study of mass media representations of gender is also important as they provide a window to examine identities in a community and even global sense, rather than only on an individual basis or in small groups as occurs with social research such as ethnographic and other types of in-depth qualitative studies. Feminist writers and researchers have increasingly focused on the global position of women and the gender implications stemming from international trade, politics and the 'culture industry'. Connell (2000) says 'we must think about how masculinities are constructed by global forces and how men, in all their diversity, are positioned by global society' (p. 33). Mass media provide an opportunity to identify some of the global forces and global dimensions of men and masculinities. Connell states: 'The growth of global mass media, especially electronic media, is an obvious vector for the global-isation of gender' (2000, p. 44).

Why more study of gender and mass media?

While there have been numerous studies of mass media representations of gender, as with gender studies generally these have focused predomin-antly on women. Mass media representations of men and male identities have been comparatively little studied and some research that has been conducted, while valuable, is dated (e.g. Busby, 1975).

Nathanson and Young's *Spreading Misandry: The Teaching of Contempt for Men in Popular Culture* was a controversial attempt to examine how men are portrayed in mass media today. The authors comment in their introduction: 'By the 1980s, the word "gender" was routinely used as a synonym for "women". To study gender is still, by implication, to study women' (2001, p. 8). They add:

> our society was androcentric until recently (focussed on men), at least to the extent that it focussed on gender – although we do not agree with many feminists on how or why androcentrism came to prevail. But conditions have changed . . . by the 1990s, androcentrism was increasingly being replaced by gynocentrism in popular culture. (2001, p. 5)

As reflected in the title of their book Nathanson and Young identify misandry – contempt for males – and note in their preface that 'no systematic study of misandry in popular culture has been produced' (2001, p. x).

Kimmel (2002) savagely criticizes Nathanson and Young, describing the book as 'astonishingly selective, simplistic and deeply shallow' (oxymoron intended) and labelling it a work of 'their fevered imagin-ations'. There are limitations to the study of mass media portrayals of men by the two Canadians in relation to sample size and depth of analysis as acknowledged in this text and by the authors themselves, but these do not, as Kimmel suggests, warrant dismissing their text outright. The outraged and emotional tone of Kimmel's criticism itself departs from academic objectivity and his suggested readings of media texts are themselves questionable.

A number of scholars have cited how dominant groups are often ignored in societies and comment that men fall in this category. Katz

(1995, p. 133) refers to the lack of scholarly attention paid to men and masculinities as consistent with the 'lack of attention paid to other dominant groups'. Newbold et al. (2002, p. 287) note that this was the case in discussion of race which, for a long time, did not deal with whites and whiteness. Winter and Robert (1980, p. 250) observe that 'ruling groups are often the last to be scientifically studied, and men appear to be no exception'. An assumption is inherent in many public discourses that allegedly dominant or pre-eminent groups do not have issues worthy of consideration.

Brod (1987, p. 19) makes a telling and highly relevant observation in relation to men and women: 'While women have been obscured from our vision by being too much in the background, men have been obscured by being too much in the foreground'.

Seidler (1994, p. 113) argues for attention to men and men's issues saying: 'While it is crucial for men to recognize what women have been obliged to put up with for years, this should not discount what men have to share about their experience'. Newbold et al. (2002, p. 287) comment specifically in relation to mass media portrayals of men and male identity: 'media representations of men and masculinity (or, more precisely, masculinities) should not be perceived as unproblematic . . . as might have been implied by early feminist writing'.

When men have been studied, often there has been an assumption that feminism provides the only valid framework and approach to study gender, including male gender identity. In reviewing a number of texts on men and gender, Bankart (2005) notes that 'the scholarship in these books rests on a number of assumptions that may or may not with-stand close scrutiny'. He says: 'Foremost among these is that academic feminism has identified pretty much all the vital core issues, questions and challenges that confront men and the study of men in the twenty-first century' 2005, p. 434). Bankart challenges this view, as does this author.

A further factor supporting the need for more research is that in the limited studies of mass media representations of men and male iden-tity that have been conducted, as in studies of mass media portrayals of women, the focus has been primarily on advertising and enter-tainment media such as movies and TV drama. Newbold et al. (2002, p. 272) say: 'it is worth noting that one of the most widely studied areas of women's representations has been and still is advertising'. Van Zoonen (1994) comments that advertising has an 'obsession' with gender and sexuality – and gender studies seem to have an obsession with advertising.

Gauntlett (2002, p. 77) also questions the preoccupation with advertising in media research: 'Sometimes it is unclear why gendered messages in advertising are singled out for particular attention by researchers... when TV series take up more of our time and attention than ads'. As noted by the Third Wave feminists Baumgardner and Richards (2000, p. 103): 'critiquing ads is not critiquing the media but only going after something that is already 'reader beware', because it is labelled 'advertising'. It is the editorial content that needs to be read and analysed with a gender lens, they argue.

In the case of media advertising, its presentation within designated TV programme 'commercial breaks' and print media layouts separated from editorial, and production techniques such as voiceover, provide clear signals that the content is not reality reported and photographed. Similarly, with TV and radio comedy and drama, devices such as 'canned' laughter and music interspersed within dialogue signal that the presentation is a media product and not reality – although 'suspension of disbelief' can often circumvent these signals.

Conversely, news, current affairs, talk shows and non-fiction articles in newspapers and magazines are presented as if they are 'real' and 'true'. In fact, many programmes and publications in these genre make explicit claims to present the 'truth' and reality with slogans such as 'the one you can trust' and 'the way it is'.

Media researchers point out that all media representations are selective, limited or framed, and 'mediated' (Grossberg, Wartella and Whitney, 1998; McQueen, 1998; Newbold et al., 2002). Newbold et al. (2002, p. 264) state: 'news, current affairs programs, documentaries and similar seemingly 'real' representations of reality can represent but a version of 'reality'... news is just as mediated and constructed as any other content...'. However, as Newbold et al. warn: 'when it comes to non-fiction programs, like documentaries and news, it is more likely that audiences believe the information they are getting is 'true' and are less aware of these programmes being mediated' (2002, p. 262). In studying media portrayals of racial minorities, Gilens (1996) notes that 'because consumers of news look to this source for accurate information and knowledge about the social world, the types of images... that are highlighted are consequential'. However, news and news-related media, which are often consumed uncritically as 'reality', have been comparatively little studied in relation to gender and warrant close attention.

A third reason that more study needs to done of mass media portrayals of gender, and men in particular, is that many of the studies, while making valuable contributions to understanding, have been based on small samples and sometimes flawed methodology; as a consequence, their findings are questionable. Gauntlett (2002, p. 31) refers to 'reckless abuse of research procedures' which 'seems to be acceptable when people are pinning blame on "media effects"'. Details of the weaknesses in some media research, and how they were avoided as far as possible in research reported in this book, are outlined in Chapter 6.

In summary, this book contributes to understanding of how mass media represent men and male identity in contemporary societies in three important ways:

1. While numerous studies of the role of mass media representations in discourse on gender and alleged effects have been conducted, most gender-related media research has focused on women. Comparatively few studies have examined the treatment and representations of men in the mass media. There is a gap in gender studies in this regard which this book seeks to help fill. Seidler (1994, p. 112) argues that 'intellectual issues about the place of men's studies cannot be settled by saying it is for feminism to set the agenda while it is for men to work out their response'. Limited recent studies that have been conducted, such as research by Nathanson and Young (2001) and Faludi (2000) show that men and masculinity are often presented in highly negative ways in mass media. Given the impact of mass media as discussed in this study, these emergent findings and their possible implications warrant further exploration.

2. Some analyses of mass media content, particularly in relation to gender, have been based on small samples and unscientific method- ology. Nathanson and Young (2001, p. x) acknowledge in the preface to their study that their method was 'not scientific'. To draw conclu- sions that are 'generalizable, objective and summarizing', an aim of formal quantitative and qualitative research as opposed to more subjective idiographic investigation, requires a sufficiently large and representative sample and rigorous methodology (Neuendorf, 2002, p. 11). Research reported in this book studied an extensive sample of mass media using research methods designed to achieve a high level of reliability and validity in its conclusions, as well as qualitative methodology for in-depth insights into likely interpretations and meanings.

3. Most media content studies that have been conducted in relation to gender have focused on movies, entertainment programmes and advertising. As noted by Newbold et al. (2002) and others, few studies have focused on news, current affairs and other media genre

purporting to present 'facts' and 'truth' such as talk shows and life-style magazines and programmes. Research presented here analyses these less studied genre, an important step as a number of researchers suggest that these genre may have a greater impact than obviously mediated content such as films, TV drama, comedy and advertising.

2
How Feminism Shapes Academic and Media Discourse on Men and Male Identity

While men are the subject of this book, gender studies have mostly originated from and been heavily influenced by feminist theory. Kidder (2004) in *American Masculinities: A Historical Encyclopaedia*, says that study of men and masculinities 'are indebted to the academic framework of women's studies which created the vocabulary of gender-based discrimination and social constructs'. As well as providing an overall framework for study of gender, Seidler (1994, p. 112) says, 'feminists have . . . set the agenda of men's studies'. Therefore, any study of gender identity has, as its theoretical foundation and starting point, feminist gender theory. Also, at a practical level, it must consider how feminism has shaped gender debate on women *and* men.

Feminism has impacted on the study of men and male identity in three important ways. First, as Kidder notes, it has established the language and vocabulary which is used to discuss men as well as women. Second, even where feminism has focused primarily on identifying and advancing the roles and identities of women, its attacks on patriarchy and its redefinition of the identities and roles of women in relationships and in society have inevitably included considerable discussion of the identities and roles of men. This continues today. Contemporary debate concerning the pressures on working women with children are inextricably bound up with discussion of the roles and identities of men in relation to work, fatherhood, and domestic and family involvement. A by-product of much feminist discussion of women's issues is discourse on men. Third, some elements of feminism have advanced specific views on men and male identity, as we shall explore later in this chapter.

As discussed in Chapter 1, feminism has identified mass media as primary sites of discourse on gender identity, and feminists have actively targeted mass media to communicate messages about gender – men as well as women – as will be examined in following chapters.

Sex and gender – biology versus social construction

One of the fundamental issues concerning gender that has intrigued scientists and psychoanalysts for a century and which provides much of the vocabulary and language in which gender – male and female – are defined and described, is whether gender is biologically determined or socially and culturally constructed, or a combination of both. The view taken on this key point frames all ensuing discussion. If, as some say, gender in innate, determined by biology, then the nature of men and women is predetermined and relatively fixed by genes and hormones, with minimal or no change able to be effected socially and culturally. However, if gender is a social and cultural construction that a male or female sexed body adopts, as argued by many involved in gender and cultural studies, then the characteristics and manifestations of gender and roles assigned on the basis of gender are changeable and open for negotiation.

While a biological basis of gender has seemed self-evident in popular discourse, the basis of gender and the roles and rights assigned to people based on their gender have come under sustained attack in academic and intellectual discourse in postmodern societies – particularly within feminist-oriented gender studies.

Gender was traditionally viewed as principally biologically determined, a factor of genes and hormones which were seen to influence behaviour, attitudes and even mental capacity. Perceived innate gender differences ranged from physiological factors such as male muscular strength and female reproductive capabilities, to claims of psychological differences. Men were arguably more rational and logical. Women were claimed to be more emotional and empathetic.

Belief in innate biological characteristics of men and women led to gender roles and formed the foundation of individual and collective human identities for men and women over several centuries. Women's traditional roles and identities were based on mothering, nurturing and home-making, and largely on their reproductive biology. Men's traditional roles and identities were based on their being protectors and providers (hunters in early societies and then 'breadwinners' in waged work in industrial societies). The terms masculine and feminine were used throughout the nineteenth and first half of the twentieth century to describe gender traits and were seen to be primarily influenced by biological factors.

Influential in this view of sex and gender as synonymous and innate was the psychologist John Money, who drew on embryologists' research which, as early as the 1920s, identified that foetal development involved a single embryonic promordium or gonad which gave rise to either an ovary or testis, and hormones which triggered the development of male or female genitalia from a single set of structures. In the 1950s, Money extended this concept of separation from a single structure into two distinct genders to psychological development. Anne Fausto-Sterling (1995, pp. 128–9) describes Money's influential theory as a 'fork in the road' which occurs early in human development and lists Money's 'road signs' which signal male or female as:

1. chromosomal sex (denoted by the presence of an X or Y chromosome);
2. gonadal sex (when the X or Y chromosome instructs the foetal gonad to develop into a testis or ovary);
3. foetal hormonal sex (in which the embryonic testis produces hormones which influences following events);
4. internal morphologic sex (development of internal organs such as the uterus);
5. external morphologic sex (development of genitalia;
6. brain sex (discussed later in this chapter);
7. sex of assignment and rearing;
8. pubertal hormonal sex (when another emission of hormones occurs triggering developments such as hair growth, breast enlargement, etc.);
9. gender identity and role;
10. procreative sex.

On the face of it, Money's list of differences does not rule out exceptions, such as a person having an XXY or XYY chromosomal structure, thus opening the door to possibly more than two genders, although this thinking was not engaged seriously for almost half a century and remains controversial. Nor does it preclude social and cultural influence on gender. But his theory positions sex and gender as fundamentally determined by biological differences.

Summarizing essentialist views on gender, Garfinkel (1967) posed eight 'rules' which, he argued, determine 'natural attitudes' towards gender. Kessler and McKenna (1978, pp. 113–14) summarize these:

- Female and male are the two and only two genders.
- Gender is stable and enduring, assigned at birth or before.
- Genitalia are a fundamental aspect or designator of gender. Females have a vagina and males have a penis.
- Anyone who does not clearly belong to one of the two genders is abnormal.
- There are no transfers from one gender to another.
- Everyone belongs to one of the two genders. There is no such thing as someone without a gender.
- Two and only two genders are a naturally occurring fact.
- Membership of one of the two genders is natural and inevitable.

E. O. Wilson (1975) is another who claims that differences between the sexes are determined principally by biological factors. Rejecting Locke's notion that minds are a blank slate, Wilson argues that genes create characteristics which he calls 'universals' which in turn lead to some human behaviours being 'hardwired' into the brain during aeons of evolution. In these biological concepts of gender differences, males and females are seen to act in accordance with 'sex roles' – genetic scripts based on innate characteristics of gender.

However, sociologists attacked biological determinism, or essentialism, as it is termed. Joseph Pleck, an influential writer on the subject, criticized the sex role identity of men in his book *The Myth of Masculinity* (1981), pointing out that biological determinism and functionalist sex role discourse were based largely on assumptions with little empirical evidence of innate biological or psychological differences between the sexes (Pleck, cited in Connell, 1995a, p. 25).

Certainly some of the early claims of biological determinism, particularly those applied to women, lacked scientific evidence and earned a bad reputation for this school of thought. Views such as those by the philosopher Immanuel Kant that women were ethically inferior to men (Hoff Sommers, 2000, p. 91) and that women were too emotional to hold positions of authority or own property, even subject to hysteria, were indefensible in the face of expanding knowledge and, understandably, caused and continue to cause outrage among women (Kaplan and Rogers, 1990, p. 206).

The unscientific basis of early claims of biological determinism in gender, and the increasing study of gender within the social sciences during the late twentieth century, saw a shift in thinking on the nature of gender. In the late twentieth century, poststructuralist theory dominated the social sciences. Poststructuralists stressed the discursive and textual nature of social life – what Weatherall (2002, pp. 75–6) terms 'the discursive turn'. This prompted a shift from essentialist (innate biological) thinking to constructionist approaches for understanding gender. Over the past few decades, academic discourse, particularly in the social sciences, has been strongly biased towards a view of gender as mostly, if not totally, socially and culturally constructed (e.g. Brod and Kaufman, 1994, p. 3; Bibler, Sears and Trudinger, 1999, pp. 1–16; Connell, 2000, p. 28; Tacey, 1997, p. 47). Paglia (2003a) notes: 'in the last quarter century of mandarin theorizing, 'gender' has been revised to mean society's 'inscription' on the human mind and body'.

Vance (1995) traced the development of construction theory of sexuality and gender between 1975 and 1990 and comments that it 'drew on developments in several disciplines: social interactionism, labelling theory and deviance in sociology; social history; labour studies, women's history and Marxist history; and symbolic anthropology, cross-cultural work on sexuality, and gender studies to name only the most significant streams' (1995, p. 39). Vance notes a range of different and even conflicting views within gender constructionism and differentiates between radical constructionist arguments which maintain that there are no essential sexual differences and what she terms a 'cultural influence' model in which sexuality is seen as 'the basic material – a kind of universal 'Play-Doh' – on which culture works' (1995, p. 44).

A number of writers have attempted to differentiate between sex and gender, including the anthropologist Gayle Rubin in her widely quoted essay 'The Traffic of Women: the Political Economy of Sex' (1975, reprinted 1984). Rubin (cited in Butler, 1999) asserts a distinction between sex and gender which assumes the discrete and prior ontological reality of a 'sex' which is 'done over' in the name of the law and transformed subsequently into 'gender' (p. 94). Butler notes that 'distinction between sex and gender serves the argument that whatever biological intractability sex appears to have, gender is culturally constructed' (1999, p. 9). However, Butler makes it clear that she sees cultural construction as the primary influence and goes as far as suggesting that 'perhaps the construct called "sex" is as culturally constructed as gender' (1999, p. 10). Butler argues that the body cannot be sexed prior to constructed gender since it is precisely gender that provides the conceptual framework for reading the body's biological determinations. Weigman (1994, p. 5) supports this view, arguing for 'the impossibility of maintaining a separation between sex and gender'. So attempts to separate sex and gender lead the argument back to constructionism.

The pro-feminist writer Bob Connell is one who has particularly advanced the notion that gender is socially and culturally constructed. He states (1995a p. 35): 'That gender is not fixed in advance of social interaction, but is constructed in interaction, is an important theme in the modern sociology of gender'. Elsewhere, Connell comments specifically in relation to male gender:

> Masculinities are neither programmed in our genes, nor fixed by social structure, prior to social interaction. They come into existence as people act. They are actively produced, using the resources and strategies in a given social setting. (2000, p. 12)

> Masculinity is 'implanted in the male body, it does not grow out of it. (1995b, p. 126)

Kimmel and Messner (1995, p. xx) also support a constructionist view: 'our identity as men is developed through a complex process of interaction with the culture in which we learn the gender scripts of our culture... men make themselves, actively constructing their masculinities within a social and historical context'.

Bob Beale, the author of *Men: From Stone Age to Clone Age* (2001), comments that 'the 'gender revolution' movement that emerged in Europe and the US in the 1980s went beyond destabilizing traditional essential views of gender and pointing out the importance of social and cultural influences and argued that 'the entire gender system is an oppressive and divisive piece of social engineering, a human invention that has little to do with biology' (2001, p. 28). For instance, Elizabeth Grosz (1994, p. 143) says in her examination of male and female bodies and sexuality: 'There is no "natural" norm; there are only cultural forms of body, which do or do not conform to social norms.'

Some sociologists and psychologists suggest that a combination of biological factors and social construction constitutes gender. Jungian psychological literature notes that masculinity is, in large part, a result of social conditioning, but also recognizes a biologically inherited element. Betcher and Pollack (1993) argue that men's aggressiveness is, in part, biologically driven, but they add that cultural factors which restrict men's expression of emotion and lead them to anger makes them far more aggressive than nature destined them to be (1993, pp. 256–7). Goodwin (1992), in a speech to the American Psychiatric Association on the causes of violence, posed what he termed a 'reasonable' position between the extreme poles of environmental and biological determinism, saying 'Biology versus psychosocial is anachronistic. The question is how do psychosocial forces and biological factors interact with each other?'

However, Connell (1995a, p. 46) dismisses a 'common-sense compromise' between the 'nature versus nurture' poles of opinion. 'If biological determinism is wrong, and social determinism is wrong, then it is unlikely that a combination of the two will be right,' he says somewhat intractably (1995a, p. 52).

Mariani (1995) mounts an even more strident attack on a middle-ground position. She labels Goodwin's view 'a rhetorical dodge typical of biobehaviouralists' and says of his claim that psychosocial forces and biological factors interact together to form gender identity '. . . all of this is so much hot air' (1995, p. 142).

Connell (1995a), drawing on 'communities of practice' thinking from anthropology advanced by Eckert and McConnell-Ginet (1992, pp. 461–90) and discussed by Weatherall (2002, pp. 123, 135), goes on to argue that gender is 'a structure of social practice' which he posits is the everyday conduct of life organized in relation to a reproductive arena. He says this is not the same as posing a biological base to gender – 'we are talking about an historical process involving the body, not a fixed set of biological determinants. Gender is social practice that constantly refers to bodies and what bodies do [which he calls "gender projects"], it is not social practice reduced to the body' (1995a, p. 71). Connell elaborates on this in *The Men and the Boys* where he writes: 'when we speak of masculinity and femininity, we are naming configurations of gender practice' (2000, p. 28). Eckert and McConnell-Ginet describe gendered practices as constructing members of a community *as* women or *as* men, and argue that this construction also involves constructing relations between and within each sex. Relevant to this study, a feature of the discursive psychology approach to gender is that it recognizes the influence of discourses as well as social practices in the construction of gender identities (Weatherall, 2002, p. 145). In the constructionist view of gender, male-sexed humans *do* masculinity and female-sexed humans *do* femininity as a practice learned from social interaction and discourse.

Connell (2000) states further, in opposition to considerable scientific evidence: 'The embodiment of gender is from the start a social embodiment' (p. 59). 'From the start' in human development is surely the point of conception and growth of a foetus in the womb and this stage of human development involves no social interaction, yet considerable biological forces are at work. This is not argued to support a biological determinism view of gender, but claims that gender is totally a social and cultural construct have to be questioned.

While social sciences have widely promoted and accepted a social construct concept of gender, popular discourse has continued to take the view that maleness and masculinity are largely innate. Best-selling books such as Robert Bly's *Iron John* (1990) and Steve Biddulph's *Manhood* (1994) argue that men are 'suffering' and address this by seeking to help men rediscover their 'true self' – i.e. their biological or innate elements (Tacey, 1997, p. 13).

However, considerable debate continues within academia, mainly outside the social sciences, on what are loosely described as 'nature versus nurture' concepts of gender. Camille Paglia (2003a) notes that: 'The overwhelming majority of today's gender theorists belong to humanities departments and have made little or no effort to inform themselves about anatomy, physiology, endocrinology or evolutionary biology . . . ' She controversially advocates that teachers need to 'steer psychology of gender courses back toward scientific and historical rigor'.

While advancing a constructionist view of gender, Weatherall recognizes a biological element as well, describing a constructionist position on gender in the following terms:

> Instead of viewing sex as primary and biological while gender is secondary and social, the order is reversed and the boundaries made less distinct. A constructionist view is that social and cultural beliefs are primary and cannot be separated from biological 'knowledge'. (2002, p. 81)

Psychological, medical and endocrinal studies point out and continue to discover significant differences between men and women. *Scientific American* reported studies by the Simon Fraser University, Vancouver psychologist Doreen Kimura (1992; 1999), who concluded: 'It appears that perhaps the most important factor in the differentiation of males and females is the level of exposure to various sex hormones early in life' (p. 26). Kimura's findings, published in 'Sex Differences in the Brain' in *Scientific American*, substantially contradict social constructionist theories advanced by academics in the humanities and social sciences.

Wilber (1996) says biology plays a part in the differences between genders, especially the potent hormone testosterone, and notes that certain gender characteristics appear cross-culturally, referring to work by Carol Gilligan who suggests men tend towards individuality and autonomy, whereas women tend to focus more on relationships (1996, p. 304).

Hoff Sommers (2000, p. 89) cites research by Laura Allen, a neuroanatomist at the University of California, Los Angeles, which found that at least seven out of ten structures measured in the human brain are different between men and women. Research does not suggest that male or female characteristics are superior in any sense; only that they are different and distinct in a majority of cases.

Studies published in *Molecular Brain Research* in 2003 report that 54 genes with different levels of activity in the developing brain of male and females have been discovered in mice. A research team at the University of California, Los Angeles led by Professor Eric Vilain believes the study is likely to have applicability to humans. Whereas genetic research since the 1970s has focused on testosterone and oestrogen as responsible for differences between men and women (testosterone 'switches on' the male gene SRY which sits on the male Y chromosome), Vilain's team report that other genetic factors are at work well before SRY is hormonally triggered. They found 18 genes were more active in the brains of male mouse embryos and 36 were more active in female mouse embryos. 'If the same applies to humans, then sexual identity is rooted in every person's biology and springs from variation in our individual genome,' Vilain (2003) says.

In a significant study of autism, the director of the Autism Research Centre at Cambridge University and author of *The Essential Difference: Men, Women and the Extreme Male Brain*, Simon Baron-Cohen (2003a) discovered major psychological differences in the brain structures of men and women. In a summary, Baron-Cohen (2003b) identified the male brain as more oriented to systemizing, which he defined as 'the drive to analyse and explore a system, to extract underlying rules that govern the behaviour of a system'. The systemizer figures out how things work, he says, and terms this the type S brain. 'Systems can be as varied as a vehicle, a plant, a library catalogue, a musical composition, a cricket bowl or even an army unit. They all operate on inputs and deliver outputs, using "if X is true, then Y must follow" correlational rules,' he explains (2003b, p. 4). According to Baron-Cohen, the male brain is less oriented to 'empathy' – the 'drive to identify another person's emotions and thoughts and to respond to these with an appropriate emotion', which he terms a type E brain. This research will resonate for proponents of popular culture views that men are better at reading maps, fixing cars and doing practical things, while women are purportedly better at understanding emotions and communication – although such conclusions represent simplistic interpretations of these findings and cannot be applied to all men and women. As Baron-Cohen says, 'not all men have the male brain, and not all women have the female brain' and argues that his theory is not a return to stereotyping. 'I would weep with disappointment if a reader took home from my argument the message that all men have lower empathy and all women have lower systemizing skills'. He says, however, 'on average, more males than females have a brain of type S, and more females than males have a brain of type E'. Baron-Cohen further clarifies that his theory does not suggest the male brain is more intelligent, or vice versa; 'both processes give rise to different patterns of intelligence' (2003b, p. 6).

Baron-Cohen makes the interesting observation that 'society is less tolerant of a poor empathizer than of a poor systemizer. Someone with empathizing difficulties may end up isolated, ostracized, teased or even bullied, and with no simple strategy for how to circumvent their problem. In contrast, someone with systemizing difficulties can pick up the telephone and call for help when a system or machine needs fixing' (2003b, p. 5). The extreme type S brain, capable of meticulous systemizing but no empathy, exhibits the characteristics known as autism, according to Baron-Cohen, drawing on brain theory first developed by Hans Asperger working in Germany in 1944. Asperger's brain theory was not translated into English until 1991. His monumental idea therefore went unnoticed for nearly 50 years. Baron-Cohen says, 'those with the extreme male brain . . . experience a disability, but only when the person is expected to be socially able. Remove this expectation, and the person can flourish'. However, 'Systemizing gets you almost nowhere in most day-to-day social interaction' (2003b, p. 5). This proffers some explanation of why many men have excelled as soldiers, business executives, builders, explorers and inventors, but experienced difficulties in social relationships, including with women and their children.

There is no doubt that Baron-Cohen's research will create controversy. In fact, he reportedly postponed publishing his book because he was 'unsure whether a discussion of psychological differences could proceed dispassionately' (Das, 2003). But it and other evidence points to substantial biological differences between men and women.

Leonard Sax, a physician and psychologist, and author of *Why Gender Matters*, is another who has reported scientific evidence of significant biological differences between men and women. Sax reports that differences occur not only inside the brain but in the senses as well. He says women can see colours and textures that men cannot see and hear and smell things men cannot, while male retinas are better able to detect motion. In a major review of scientific findings in relation to male and female brains in *TIME* magazine (28 March 2005), Sax said the research may explain UK experiments that found newborn boys are much more likely than girls to stare at mobiles above their cribs and why boys prefer to play with moving toys such as trucks, while girls favour richly textured dolls and draw with a wider range of colours. The review also quoted Richard Haier, a psychology professor from the University of California at Irvine, who claims that men and women have different brain architectures. He says while both sexes process emotions using the area of the brain called the amygdala, women seem to have stronger connections between the amygdala and regions of the brain that process language, while men process their thoughts in more focused regions of the brain (Ripley, 2005).

In a 2005 review of gender studies texts, C. Peter Bankart (2005, p. 435) from Wabash College said: 'As a psychologist and a practicing clinician . . . I find that I require at least some minimal recognition of the contribution of biology in the creation of gender'.

A full review of gender differences research is not possible here, but it is important to note that considerable scientific evidence suggests that there *are* fundamental biological and psychological differences between men and women, while recognizing that many aspects of gender are socially constructed. Consequently, many contemporary educationalists and psychologists support the 'common-sense compromise' dismissed by Connell. The American developmental psychologist Eleanor Maccoby, author of *The Two Sexes: Growing Up, Coming Together* (1999), says that 'while gender is largely a product of cultural forces, those forces come into play so early in childhood and are so universal that they must be deeply grounded in our biology'. In her influential *The Psychology of Sex Differences* (1974), which was based on a review of more than 1,600 studies of gender differences, Maccoby posed that parental influence on children's socialization into a particular gender role and sexual preferences was not the primary influence. According to Carpenter (2000), Maccoby found biological influences and social environments jointly influence gender development.

There is support for both biological determinism (essentialism) and social construction theory in feminism. While Second Wave feminist theory, rooted in sociology and psychology, has mostly advanced the view that gender is socially constructed, Third Wave feminism has returned, to some extent, to a biological determinism view. Third Wave feminists such as the 'Girlie' movement seek to celebrate the differences between women and men, as well as the differences among women. From their study of mass media representations of gender Newbold et al. (2002, p. 251) conclude: 'There is a fundamentally essentialist element to postfeminism [Third Wave feminism], that significant biological, "natural" differences exist between genders and transcend "social constructionist" arguments'.

However, a constructionist approach is still advanced by many feminist and pro-feminist writers, and it needs to be said that this often conveniently suits feminist argument. If gender is largely or even partly biologically determined, being a man and being a woman – and masculinity and femininity – are at least partly programmed genetically and, therefore, limited in the degree to which they can be changed. But, under a constructionist approach, women can be anything they want to be, and men can be anything they (or women, or the media) want them to be. Seidler (1994, p. 100) says of the 'pervasive social constructionist view' of gender that it 'helps foster a form of rationalism that gives the idea that our lives are within our rational control, and that through will and determination alone we can determine our lives', and warns of the danger of social constructionism (and feminism) reinforcing a particular moralism in relation to how men should be (1994, p. 114).

First, Second and Third Wave feminism

One of the key challenges in discussing feminism is that it is not a single, homogeneous movement, but a collection of varied elements (Baumgardner and Richards, 2000). Whittier (1995) provides a comprehensive sociological study of the evolution of American feminism from the 1970s to the 1990s which chronicles the 'continuities' and 'discontinuities' of feminism and the 'transformation' of early radical thinking into new models.

Feminism is generally regarded to have grown out of *feminisme*, an intellectual movement in nineteenth-century France (Baumgardner and Richards, 2000, p. 51). The term entered the United States in 1906 (Baumgardner and Richards, 2000, p. 325), although feminism is considered to have begun in the US in 1848 with the launch of the women's suffrage movement. In the period 1848–1920 feminism was focused largely on the struggle for the right to vote – finally won in the US in 1920. This was followed by a campaign for the Equal Rights Amendment (ERA) to the American Constitution and other basic rights in other countries, such as the right to own property. This early phase, focused on institutional inequities in society between men and women and individual human rights, is widely referred to as First Wave feminism.

Kristeva (1981), in an analysis of feminism over the past 150 years, describes three periods of feminism distinguished by their evolving philosophical and political focus. The first she terms Liberal feminism. Kristeva's Liberal feminism closely correlates with what others call First Wave feminism, as she describes Liberal feminism as focused on rights and individualism.

With the right to vote won in the US and many other countries (Australia granted Federal and State voting rights to women twelve years before the US in 1908), the focus of feminism from the 1920s onwards turned to job equality (equal pay for equal work) and reproductive freedom (Richards, 2000, p. 20). This new focus has been termed Second Wave feminism by a number of feminist writers, although the phase covers a relatively long period (more than 60 years) and embraces a number of changes in focus and philosophy.

The early stages of Second Wave feminism were strongly influenced by Marxism and humanist and existentialist philosophy, particularly as advocated by Sartre (1958) in *Being and Nothingness* (first published in 1943).

A further significant Second Wave shift was influenced by structuralists such as Louis Althusser, who proposed that ideology was 'not the result of a conspiracy or collusion of those in power. Nor was it a function of alienation specific to capitalism that would somehow disappear after the revolution like a veil being removed to reveal the real object underneath'. Althusser believed that ideology was a 'product of institutions, practices, and value systems that produce and validate some ideas and denigrate or exclude others. What the subject believes are products of his or her own thoughts are in fact produced elsewhere... and serve political and class interests in obscured but unconscious form' (as cited in Grosz, 1990a, p. 68). Althusser's thinking directed feminists away from humanist and liberal philosophies towards a more structural account of oppression.

Another key influence on feminism was the French psychoanalyst Jacques Lacan, who drew heavily on the Freudian theory of the unconscious and sexuality. Many aspects of feminism resonate with Freudian theory, including Freud's account of the construction of sexuality involving the Oedipus complex and castration fear. For Lacan, the phallus is the key signifier of the symbolic order (patriarchy) which oppresses or ignores women. Elizabeth Grosz (1990a, p. 75) summarizes

Lacan: '[Woman] is positioned in the symbolic order as a spoken exchanged object, not as a subject who is a partner within exchange'.

In Kristeva's (1981) analysis of three stages of feminism, the early period of Second Wave feminism broadly correlates with what Kristeva terms Radical feminism, which focused on redressing the secondary role of women (the Other) and attacking patriarchy. Radical feminism celebrated womanhood and the feminine – and why shouldn't it? But, in this context, early Second Wave and Radical feminism viewpoints were based on binary structuralist thinking about gender and power. Radical feminism promoted women against men (eg. goals to attack and break down patriarchy). Whereas Liberal feminism operated within the existing social and political institutions and sought to win rights for women based on rationalist debate (eg. equal pay for equal work), Radical feminism sought to overthrow patriarchal systems and replace them. It proposed that, in order to empower women, power had to be taken from men.

A further significant evolution in Second Wave feminist thinking was triggered by poststructuralist theory in relation to power, especially the work of Michel Foucault and Jacques Derrida. In *History of Sexuality* (1978), Foucault questioned the major features of psychoanalysis. Whereas liberal political theorists (e.g. Hobbes, Locke and Mill) maintained that power is a social and legal right established through social contract in which individuals agree to give up some personal power for the good of society, and Marxism claimed that power is a property or right of one class over another to keep it subjugated, Foucault proposed that 'power is not possessed, given, seized, captured, relinquished or exchanged. Rather, it is exercised. It exists only in actions' (Grosz, 1990a, p. 87). Furthermore, Foucault argued that power is distributed unevenly over a 'grid' and that the grid creates points of resistance which interact with power. While he accepted that power could cause individuals or groups to self-regulate, he rejected universalized views of power as something that one group (eg. men) hold permanently and others (eg. women) do not have.

Notwithstanding Foucault's poststructuralist view, many feminists, including modern feminists, hold to dated Marxist concepts, describing patriarchal power as 'something that men, as individuals or as a group, exercise over women' in a conscious and intentioned way (Grosz, 1990a, p. 87). Simplistic universalized understandings of power have permeated much feminist thinking and literature. Mansbridge (1995, p. 29) defines feminism as 'the commitment to ending male domination'. The Redstockings Manifesto, developed in 1969, two years after the first Women's Liberation convention in Ann Arbor, Michigan, echoed this simplistic, universalized view of power and propelled feminism from its early liberal origins to a more radical stance. The Redstockings Manifesto stated:

> We identify the agents of our oppression as men. Male supremacy is the oldest, most basic form of domination. All other forms of exploitation and oppression (racism, capitalism, imperialism, etc.) are extensions of male supremacy; men dominate women, a few men dominate the rest. (Castells, 1997, p. 178)

Castells reflects this generalized and universalized feminist doctrine of male power. He says: 'Patriarchalism is a founding structure of all contemporary societies' and goes on to claim that 'interpersonal violence and psychological abuse are widespread precisely because of male anger, individual and collective, in losing power' (1997, pp. 134, 136).

Late twentieth- and early twenty-first-century feminism has been labelled post-feminism by the media and some academics. However, many feminists reject the term, arguing that it suggests that feminism has ended, or that in deriving the term from postmodernism, it implies that feminism has been or can be deconstructed to a state where it has no clear meaning or identity. Some media have directly suggested that feminism has lost its way, failed or even died. For example, *TIME* magazine ran a controversial June 1998 feature titled 'Is Feminism Dead?'

Baumgardner and Richards, in *ManifestA: Young Women, Feminism and the Future*, admit Third Wave feminism 'doesn't have an easily identifiable presence' but point to 'hubs' unique to the new generation of feminists (2000, p. 79). They say that in the 1990s, feminist attention turned to new issues (new in the sense of focus, not occurrence) including sexual abuse, violence against women, HIV/AIDS awareness, eating disorders, body image and access to technology such as the Internet (2000, p. 21).

In terms of its central philosophy, Third Wave feminism has involved a ground-shift away from the view of women as the same or equal to men and towards a celebration of 'difference' but with equality (Newbold et al., 2002, p. 250). In an attempt at a definition, Newbold et al. say:

> The third wave of feminism . . . accepts sex-positive attitudes, the celebration of previously taboo areas such as sexual attractiveness, fashion and pro-capitalist ideologies; perhaps partly inspired by the 1980s role models such as Madonna. It can be seen as a backlash

against writers such as Andrea Dworkin – postfeminism sees woman as equal but different, and that they can 'have it all'. (2002, p. 423)

The evolution of feminism has not been a smooth transition or even an entirely agreed change of focus and position. Third Wave feminism has within it divergence referred to as the 'feminisms of equality' and the 'feminisms of difference' (Grosz, 1990b, p. 333), and a wide range of sub-movements from Riot Grrrls and 'lipstick feminists' to opposing views influenced by Naomi Wolf's *The Beauty Myth* (1991). Many argue that the goals of feminism are far from achieved and that there is still much to do to liberate women – and that may well be true and an important ongoing sphere of activity. However, within Second Wave or Radical feminism, and continuing in many elements of Third Wave feminism, is discourse on men and male identity that warrants examination for what it says about and to modern societies and the influence or 'power effects' that it has in those societies.

Ideological and 'superiority feminism'

A number of researchers and writers dispute the equality goals of First, Second and Third Wave feminism and pose another type of feminism. Fuss (1989, p. 2) discusses essentialism in feminism, pointing to feminist 'appeals to a pure or original femininity, a female essence, outside the boundaries of the social and thereby untainted (though perhaps repressed) by patriarchal order'. Irigary (1977, pp. 210–17) also advocates an essentialist feminism in her early texts. A common feature of this discussion is a focus on the positive traits of women compared with the negative traits of men. Weatherall (2002, p. 79) describes, without substantiation, women's interactional style as 'co-operative' while men's is 'competitive'. In discussing research methodology, Warren (1988, p. 64) says 'the focal gender myth of field research is the greater communicative skills and less threatening nature of the female fieldworker.

Castells (1997) poses two broad types of feminism, which he terms 'cultural' and 'essentialist'. According to Castells, cultural feminism is focused on building space for women within existing culture. It includes 'feminism of difference' but in a benign coexistence sense, and may involve separatism, but not to the extent of sexual separatism through lesbianism. 'Essentialist feminism goes a step further, and proclaims, simultaneously, women's essential difference from men, rooted in biology and/or history, and the moral/cultural superiority of womanhood as a way of life' (1997, pp. 196–7).

From their research, Nathanson and Young (2001, p. 199) also identify two types of feminism – one based on equality and one advocating superiority – referring to the latter as 'ideological feminism' and also as 'superiority feminism'. They point to nine characteristics of ideology and argue that a number of these apply to feminism, particularly 'dualism', 'essentialism', 'hierarchy', 'collectivism', 'utopianism' and 'quasi-religiosity' (2001, pp. 200–13). They argue that the rhetoric of 'difference' turns to the rhetoric of hierarchy in much feminist philosophy – what they call 'feminist triumphalism' (2001, p. 62). They say this line of feminist philosophy and discourse suggests 'male sexuality is innately evil, but female sexuality is innately good' (2001, p. 214) and conclude that 'after several decades of "identity politics" on behalf of women, feminists have convinced many people that women are somehow superior to men' (2001, p. 50).

Further research reported in this book substantiates the existence of this reverse sexism and raises important issues in relation to men and male identity. While mainstream feminism has addressed specific objectives related to the emancipation and welfare of women which are widely supported by women and men, some aspects of academic and intellectual feminism have undermined men collectively and individually in two ways. First, a corollary of some feminist progress has been regression of men's roles and identities. Nathanson and Young say:

> Men in our time in fact have good reason to fear that feminist ideology leaves them with no basis whatsoever for a healthy identity. A fundamental premise of feminism is that women can do, and should do, everything that men do. That leaves precisely nothing on which to base masculine identity except for those immoral things that women, unlike men, are allegedly immune to. In other words, men can make no distinctive, necessary, and valued contribution to society as *men*. (2001, p. 231)

This aspect of male disadvantage and loss of status at the hands of feminists, to be fair, has been largely accidental – what the American military would call collateral damage.

However, a more sinister element of feminism, often advanced by intellectuals and invisible to mainstream feminism, has been explicit and sometimes quite vitriolic attacks denigrating men and generalizing women as superior. Even though the pioneering American feminist Betty Friedan (1963) declared 'man is not the enemy' and warned that 'female chauvinism is highly dangerous and diversionary', some elements of feminism have criticized her for being too conservative and waged a campaign against men.

Extreme examples of early feminist attacks on men and superiority feminism include Valerie Solanas' *SCUM Manifesto* (SCUM – the Society for Cutting Up of Males) and her various writings calling for the castration and/or killing of all men. While Solanas was widely regarded as mentally unstable and was eventually confined to an institution, similar attacks on men have been made by other feminists and research shows that these are continuing in contemporary discourse.

Andrea Dworkin also made it clear in numerous writings that she wanted as little to do with men as possible, describing heterosexual intercourse as an 'invasion of female bodies'. Effectively, she accused all heterosexual men who have relationships with women of being rapists. In other words, all heterosexual men are criminals. Dworkin also advocated that women become vigilantes and murder the men who afflict them (Nathanson and Young, 2001, p. 249).

Mary Daly (1984) had this to say in *Pure Lust: Elemental Feminist Philosophy*:

> The weapons of Wonderlusting women are the Labryses/double axes of our own Wild wisdom and wit, which cut through the mazes of man-made mystification, breaking the mindbindings of masterminder double think... Recognising that deep damage has been inflicted upon consciousness under phallocracy's myths and institutions, we continue to name patriarchy as the perverted paradigm and source of other social evils. (Nathanson and Young, 2001, p. 212)

Despite its emotional and convoluted style of expression, it is clear that Daly blames men for most or all of society's evil and sees women as innately superior.

A number of scholars, including feminists and profeminists, recognize this aspect of feminism. Segal (1987) says that feminism is often sharply critical of men and little inclined to make distinctions between groups of men. Citing Segal, Connell (2000, p. 170) notes 'the damaging effect of a certain kind of feminist criticism which lumps all males together and relentlessly blames them' and acknowledges: 'The man reading feminist writing is likely to encounter pictures of men as rapists, batterers, pornographers, child abusers, militarists, exploiters, and images of women as targets and victims' (2000, p. 144). He also reads in feminist and profeminist literature a narrative of men as part of an organized patriarchy, intentionally subjugating and oppressing women in their unrelenting quest for power of which, allegedly, all men are beneficiaries (eg. Daly, 1984; Connell, 1987; Butler, 1999). Paglia, sometimes branded a traitor by feminists because of her man-positive statements, says: 'A major failing of most feminist ideology is its dumb, ungenerous stereotyping of men as tyrants and abusers' (Paglia, 2003b).

Ideologically motivated feminist attacks on men cannot be dismissed as things that were done in the distant past by early radicals. From their North American study, Nathanson and Young (2001) cite the declaration in 2000 of Valentine's Day, traditionally a day of celebrating heterosexual love and romance, as V-Day to draw attention to violence against women by men and the staging of Eve Ensler's play *The Vagina Monologues*, with its 'poisonously anti-male sub-text' (2001, p. 250).

On the other side of the world, on the sensitive and tragic issue of increasing male suicide attempts, the Australian feminist writer Eva Cox wrote in the *Sydney Morning Herald Good Weekend* magazine (26 August 2000): 'Maybe men's incompetence in this area should make them feel better'. She later apologized, but her statement demonstrates a disturbing tone in contemporary discourse. Also in Australia, Virginia Haussegger, a presenter for ABC TV news in Canberra at the time, commented in the *Sydney Morning Herald*, on the breakdown of marriages and relationships:

> For men in particular, such 'permanent temporariness' might seem a pretty good place to be, while they drag their adolescence well into their 30s and even their early 40s. With plenty of guilt-free sex readily available, and the ties of commitment and responsibility pretty thin on the ground, men really are 'having it all'. (Hausegger, 2003)

This statement provides a goldmine for text analysis and discourse analysis. Its language is couched with sarcasm and condescension, evidenced by terms such as 'drag their adolescence well into their 30s or even early 40s' and in two sentences it refers to no fewer than four common criticisms by women of men – never grow up; won't make commitment; screwing around/promiscuity; and the age-old feminist claim that 'men have it all'. Such invective could be accepted as an individual woman's viewpoint based on her experience, but Haussegger was writing as an allegedly 'objective' journalist employed by the publicly funded national broadcaster in a leading quality daily newspaper.

Generalizations that men are innately violent, warlike, sexually promiscuous (a pejorative term which women sought to escape from in favour of sexual freedom and choice), insensitive, commitment-phobic and even innately evil are common in gender discourse. Feminist literature has even ventured as far as suggesting that men are not necessary to society at all. Such claims have not been isolated or made frivolously. De Beauvoir (1997, p. 36) noted: 'In many species the male appears to be fundamentally unnecessary'. Modern science is finding and promoting ways for women to reproduce through insemination from sperm donors and an increasing number of women are demanding access to this technology. (This is further discussed in the next chapter.)

Meanwhile, superiority feminism promotes claims that women are better communicators than men; that women are more empathetic and caring and even more ethical than men; that women make peace rather than war; and a host of other universalized views. For instance, under the heading 'Women Mean Good Governance, Which Means Good Business', Margot Cairnes (2003), an author and consultant honoured as one of the '2000 outstanding intellectuals of the 21st century', wrote in a major 'op ed' newspaper opinion column: 'Women can often help build more trusting environments because they are naturally gifted in the areas of intuition, emotional intelligence and relationship building'. In the same column she commented: 'It is certainly true that the widely recognized aspects of good corporate governance – transparency, integrity and accountability – cannot thrive in the boy-dominated sameness of . . . boardrooms'.

An example of the oft-quoted claim that the world would be peaceful if women were in charge appeared in an editorial column in Sydney's *Daily Telegraph* in which the journalist Caroline Regidor (2003a, p. 30) stated:

> If women ruled the world it would be more peaceful because women's experiences cause them to think differently about the value of human life . . . if women ruled we would benefit from women's ability to listen and compromise.

Clearly, Regidor believes women are superior to men in a number of respects and would make better political and world leaders *per se*. But, as is common in such claims, she fails to cite any empirical evidence. In fact, she ignores historical evidence to the contrary – for instance, the exploits of Cleopatra or the more contemporary track-record of Margaret Thatcher in taking Britain to war against Argentina in the Falklands and waging industrial war against the unions in England and Wales.

In a twist of logic and irony, Weatherall (2002, p. 127) says women such as Thatcher 'disassociate from other women and use men as their reference group...to all intents and purposes "becoming men"'. In other words, when men do wrong, it is because they are men. When women do wrong, it is because they have become men or like men!

International media reporting of terrorism has exposed widespread superiority feminist views. Commenting on the case of Lynndie England and other US military women charged with abusing Iraqi prisoners, Melissa Embser-Herbert, an associate professor of sociology from Hamline University, Minnesota, wrote in the *Washington Post*:

> What motivated the young women seen in these photos to participate in such degrading acts? Were they trying to be accepted as 'one of the boys'? Was this a way of fitting in? (Embser-Herbert, 2004)

Embser-Herbert's comments exhibit superiority feminist views in that they imply that the women's behaviour was not natural to them as women, but was caused by pressure on them from men to fit in and be accepted. Furthermore, this statement, like others cited, imputes violence and aggression to men as a generalized attribute.

In analysing the seizing of children at a school in Beslan by Chechen terrorists in 2004, the newspaper columnist Miranda Devine wrote in the *Sydney Morning Herald*:

> [O]ne of the most unfathomable aspects of Beslan is that some of the terrorists who took over the Russian school were women. How could any person inflict such torture on innocent children, you wonder, but especially how could a woman whose earthly purpose is to create and nurture life?
>
> We have always thought of women as the gentler sex, the protectors, the nurturers. While men might wage war and commit atrocities against one another, women protect the children, laying down their own lives without question, if necessary. It was innate, we thought. Many a utopian has talked of how gentle and peaceful the world would be if women were in charge. (Devine, 2004, p. 15)

Her comment 'we have always thought of women as the gentler sex', claims to women's propensity to protect children as 'innate', and her statement that 'men...wage war and commit atrocities' are examples of widespread discourse that demonizes men and lauds women as innately superior in many aspects of humanity.

On the charging of Lynndie England with 19 counts of abuse of Iraqi prisoners at Abu Ghraib prison, the trial of Pauline Nyiramasuhuko for Rwanda's 1994 massacre and suicide bombings by Chechen and Palestinian women, Devine asks: 'Are the Lynndies and Paulines and suicide bombers "pawns in a man's game"'? In a strikingly similar tone to Weatherall's comments on Margaret Thatcher, Devine seeks to lay the blame for 'a new unleashing of female violence' at the feet of men.

Nathanson and Young (2001, p. 237) conclude: 'Either directly or indirectly, ideological feminism has resulted in the teaching of contempt for men'. The two Canadian researchers reported from their study numerous examples of feminists (and often the media and others following feminist thinking) laughing at men; looking down on men; blaming men; dehumanizing men; and demonizing men. They summarize: 'the worldview of our society has become increasingly both gynocentric (focussed on the needs and problems of women) and misandric (focussed on the evils and inadequacies of men)' (p. xiv). Examples of mass media content analysed by Nathanson and Young are discussed in Chapter 5.

While its efforts to raise awareness among women and in societies of the rights of women and gain political action to redress institutionalized inequities and injustices suffered by women have been among the most significant social developments of modern times and worthy of support by men and women, feminism has negatively framed and contributed to discourse on men and male identity. As well as occurring in academic and intellectual discourse, this has permeated public discourse including mass media representations of men and male identity and will be examined in following chapters.

3
The New Focus (or Lack of Focus) on Men and Masculinity

It has been only relatively recently that gender discussion has begun to focus on men other than as targets of feminist ire and campaigns – as gendered individuals in their own right – and on the related but significantly different subject, masculinities. Kristen Kidder, in *American Masculinities: A Historical Encyclopaedia* (2004), notes that men's studies first emerged during the late 1960s and early 1970s.

Early men's movement texts included Warren Farrell's *The Liberated Man* (1974) and Jack Nichols' *Men's Liberation* (1975), as well as 'men in distress' books such as Herb Goldberg's *The Hazards of Being Male* (1977), which referred to men living their lives 'in harness' (see Faludi, 2000, p. 14).

The fledgling men's movement

A small Men's Liberation movement was established in the United States in the mid-1970s, formed largely as a response to Second Wave American feminism (Connell, 1995a, p. 24). This evolved into disparate movements over the following two decades. Kidder (2004) identifies four major men's movements in the US during the 1980s and 1990s: 1) the mythopoetic movement influenced by the poet Robert Bly, which agreed with feminist opposition to patriarchy and traditional masculinity and promoted new age self-help therapy for men; 2) the Promise Keepers, a right-wing evangelist group which urged men to remake themselves spiritually through devotion to God and the family; 3) pro-feminist men who emerged in academia; and 4) a men's rights movement focused on men's legal rights in areas such as divorce and child custody.

Eugene August's annotated bibliography *Men's Studies* contained around 600 entries in 1985 and this grew to over 1,000 entries by 1995 when it was updated (Kidder, 2004). More recently, Flood (2004) has compiled *The Men's Bibliography: A Comprehensive Bibliography of Writing on Men, Masculinities and Sexualities*, which provides an extensive list of texts describing the evolution of men's movements and philosophies on men and masculinity. These and other texts, such as Brod (1987) and Brod and Kaufman (1994), are informative references for those wanting to study the men's movement and the evolution of men's studies.

Much of the focus within the mythopoetic movement, the Promise Keepers and among pro-feminist men has been on changing men – often in line with feminist prescriptions (Connell, 1995a, p. 220). The tellingly named National Organization for Changing Men founded in the 1980s, later renamed the National Organization for Men Against Sexism (NOMAS), is an example of new ways of thinking about men and exploring new masculinities. Precepts put forward urged men to escape from traditional hegemonic masculinity and adopt new ways of thinking and behaving. Often it was suggested that this required men to feminize themselves and emphasize their 'feminine side' (Nathanson and Young, 2001, p. 344).

As well as intellectual debate on men and male identity, the 1990s saw increasing popular discourse reflected in and stimulated by books such as Robert Bly's *Iron John* (1990), which was on the *New York Times* bestseller list for twelve months, and Steve Biddulph's *Manhood* (1994), which sold over 100,000 copies and made him a celebrity reported in mass media worldwide.

Notwithstanding the growth in study and discussion of men and masculinities, the men's movement has remained fragmented in most countries and many elements have had a chequered and sometimes infamous history. In the UK, the Lads and New Lads have sought to preserve traditional hegemonic modes of masculinity. In the US, a number of men's groups have adopted initiation ceremonies, drum-beating and back-to-nature forest excursions to recapture what they see as the primal nature of man (Faludi, 2000, p. 228). Kipnis (1991, p. 164) criticizes such groups, commenting that it is inappropriate for men in contemporary Western societies to adopt the rituals of primal cultures. In Australia, a group called The Men's Confraternity, which led a march on West Australia's Parliament House in 1992, was described in the media as 'a crusade of angry dads with an extreme right-wing view that feminism and the Family Court are undermining men' (Guilliatt, 2001). More recently, a militant men's group, The Blackshirts, has been likened to the Klu Klux Klan (Van Tiggelen, 2005). In the UK, Fathers-4-Justice conducted a high-profile campaign for 'truth, justice and equality in family law' (http://www.fathers-4-justice.org), which involved men dressing up in superhero costumes and climbing public buildings such as The London Eye, Buckingham Palace and the Houses of Parliament as publicity stunts. The group has spread to a number of countries, including Canada, the US, Ireland, the Netherlands and South Africa. However, in January 2006, when it was revealed that radical elements allegedly part of the group were plotting to kidnap the youngest son of the British Prime Minister, the founder, Matt O'Connor, closed down the organization in Britain, saying it was acting contrary to its founding principles. The organization continues to operate in some other countries, including the United States and Canada

But despite various men's movements and the formation of men's organizations – or perhaps because of the activities of some – men's studies remain an academic backwater and discussion of men, other than in feminist terms, is stifled. Nathanson and Young (2001, p. 67) claim that 'men are silenced now...just as women were silenced in the past'.

It is beyond the scope of this book to investigate fully the alleged loss or lack of men's voice and its causes, but there are a number of obstacles and objections to studying men that need to be recognized and overcome or side-stepped to enable this discussion to proceed and have validity and the attention it deserves.

The barriers and challenges to talking about men

Men's own reticence has been cited as one barrier to a better social understanding of their concerns and views. For instance, a number of texts and media articles comment that 'men just won't talk' (see the research findings on men's health reported in Chapter 6). Also, the lack of attention paid to majorities and groups with perceived power or advantage, as discussed by Katz (1995) and Winter and Roberts (1980) cited in Chapter 1, has undoubtedly reduced societies' willingness to engage in consideration of men. There remains a view in many societies that men have it all, so what could they have to complain about? However, scholars' capacity to talk about men and men's capacity to communicate their views are also impacted by two specific challenges – one intellectual and one political – which need to be addressed.

The first has to be dealt with because it disputes that any generalized group called 'men' exists. Unless put to the sword, this argument invalidates any discussion of men collectively or as a category, thus confining men's issues to the narrow domain of individual case studies and personal anecdotes.

Definitional issues and language barriers

While talking about 'women' and 'men' as identifiable categories seems self-evident in popular discourse, these generalizations or 'universalities' (terms applied universally to groups with differing constituents) are challenged by some academics. Feminism has grappled with this issue of language and terminology for some time. Moi (1985) criticizes feminists who advocate 'difference feminism' – views that women have innate differences from men – arguing that 'to define 'woman' is necessarily to essentialize her' – that is, group all women into a single category as if they have a single essence or set of characteristics, which she argues is not the case (1985, p. 139).

Connell (2000. p. 16) applies the same thinking to discussion of men as a category: 'To talk at all about a group called "men" presupposes a distinction from and relation with another group "women". That is to say, it presupposes an account of gender.' He notes that masculine conduct or masculine identity can go together with a female body and vice versa This may be true. But Connell's argument becomes circular and self-defeating. If, as he says, we cannot engage in a discussion of men as a category distinct from women without entering the territory of gender characteristics and behaviour, and that gender is socially constructed and not consistent within categories of men or women, then, under Connell's rules of debate, we cannot engage in a discussion of men at all.

Further, Connell says that not only is masculinity and his preferred term 'masculinities' a gender concept, but that the term 'man' is inextricably linked to masculinity/ies. Elsewhere, he rejects biological (innate) elements of gender, arguing that gender is a construct or, as he calls it, 'a configuration of gender practice' (2000, p. 29). Thus, Connell seems to be saying that 'man' is simply a product of socially constructed behaviours and that there are no common biological elements of men which bind them as a category or by which they can be identified as a category of a species.

Irigaray (1996), in her argument for 'difference feminism' which opposes claims of equality and sameness as man, says that denying discussion of women in specific terms and subsuming them into an abstract human universal is 'suicide' from an identity point of view. She adds: 'Aside from her own suicide, she thus deprives man of the possibility of defining himself as man, that is a naturally and spiritually sexed person' (1996, p. 27). Irigaray, as many feminists have done, argues that 'women' as a category can be studied and discussed, despite acknowledged differences between individuals within that category. Elisabeth Grosz (1990b, p. 341) also points to the paradox that feminism faces if it denies the practice of identifying women: 'if women cannot be characterized in any general way... if we are not justified in taking women as a category, then what political grounding does feminism have?' Indeed. As outlined in Chapter 2, feminism has extensively discussed 'women' as a group with shared characteristics despite significant differences between individuals, and feminism could be seen to be founded on the principle of rights for 'women' universally rather than some women as individuals. Suggestions by some feminists and pro-feminists that similar study of men and men's issues cannot be undertaken are self-contradictory, with their implication of 'close the gate after we're in'.

As with feminism's focus on women, studying men as a category is not to deny differences, even wide differences, between men and forms and expressions of masculinities, as well as similarities between men and women – or, as Connell says, masculine conduct and identity by female bodies and feminine conduct and identity by male bodies. Argument over what can be discussed as a generalized category seems to revolve around the terms 'men' and 'masculinity' or 'masculinities' and 'women' and 'femininity/femininities'. A useful exit from this definitional dilemma is provided by Clatterbaugh (1998), who suggests that 'talking about men seems to be what we want to do'. He adds: 'talking about masculinities... simply imposes a layer, a very confused layer, between ourselves and the social reality that we want to discuss'. He notes that the terms 'masculinity' and 'masculinities' 'carry a lot of historical baggage' and are 'extremely ill-defined' (1998, p. 41). Furthermore, Clatterbaugh notes that writing by women, in contrast to much of the writing by men, talks about men, not masculinities and argues, 'we are more likely to maintain our bearings by... talking about men, male behaviours, attitudes and abilities, on one hand, and images, stereotypes, norms and discourses, on the other' (1998, p. 43). Sedgwick (1995, p. 12) strongly supports Clatterbaugh's differentiation between discussion of men and masculinities, arguing, 'it is important to drive a wedge in, early and often and if possible conclusively, between the two topics, masculinity and men whose relation one to the other is so difficult not to presume'.

This text adopts Clatterbaugh's approach and focuses on men and the images, stereotypes and discourses concerning men and representing male identity, rather than the widely divergent concept of masculinities. With relatively rare exceptions, men are identifiable in societies and in texts with a high level of accuracy – certainly with sufficient accuracy to meet the criteria for systematic study.

'Backlash' politics

A second challenge thrown up to limit discussion of men – one could provocatively say a 'strategy' of gender discourse in some cases – is the tendency to label attempts by men to express their concerns or discuss gender issues, particularly those that involve any level of disagreement with feminist doctrine, a 'backlash' against women. Men's views are often claimed to be part of a sinister organized campaign to oppress women and, therefore, deserving of social condemnation and censure. A number of questionable and misguided men's movement initiatives and statements undoubtedly deserve being labelled a 'backlash' against women. But the term 'backlash' is frequently used as a catch-all for actions or statements by men about their concerns and roles in society, no matter how valid and well intentioned.

Susan Faludi brought the term into common usage with her best-selling *Backlash: The Undeclared War against Women*. She said: 'The truth is that the last decade has seen a powerful counter-assault on women's rights, a backlash, an attempt to retract the handful of small and hard-won victories that the feminist movement did manage to win for women' based on 'a bedrock of misogyny' (1992, pp. 12–13). Misogyny is another term thrown about regularly to cast aspersion on men who speak about gender issues in anything other than feminist terms. Referring to the 1980s and early 1990s, Faludi generalized: 'the backlash decade produced one long, painful and unremitting campaign to thwart women's progress' (1992, p. 492).

Backlash politics manifests itself in two ways. Academic research and scholarly investigation of men's issues have rarely seen the light of day other than as viewpoints through a feminist lens. Hearn (1993) says, 'there has been a major growth of clearly and explicitly focussed and clearly and explicitly critical studies of men', but adds, 'increasingly, men are being scrutinized in ways that attend to feminist scholarship'. Anything else is branded a backlash.

Even more so, in the mass media calls for attention to men's needs such as access to their children after separation are shouted down as a backlash. A number of instances are reported in the following chapters.

It is hoped that this text, by virtue of its detailed data and inclusive approach supporting the rights of women and men, will escape such labelling.

The changing roles and identities of men

The role of men in developed Western societies has changed markedly in the past few decades. From traditional roles as hunters and providers, protectors, breadwinners, father figures, heads of families and leaders – roles which were valued and celebrated in society, and on which men could base their identities – the roles and identities available to men today are either no longer unique to them or have been substantially diminished. Women can now be providers, protectors (such as serving in the military), breadwinners, leaders and heads of families, while still enjoying their traditional roles as nurturers and homemakers.

In the industrial era that spread from Europe and became the primary economic framework of the nineteenth and twentieth centuries, men went into waged work and men's identity was made in mines and on the factory floor (Connell, 1995, p. 36). This is confirmed in studies by West (1996), who reported that men who grew up in the 1930s and 1940s described their life and that of their fathers as centred on work. Work remained a dominant paradigm of men's lives in the corporate world of the 1980s and 1990s and, to a large extent, continues today despite talk of 'downshifting' and workplace flexibility. Such discussion has not yet been matched by any substantial social change, as evidenced by statistics on the working hours of men in the US, UK, Australia and other highly industrialized countries.

Seidler (1994, p. 116) says, 'men were supposed to be impersonal, career-orientated breadwinners providing support for their wives and families, a shoulder that others could depend on'. Industrial age men were raised to a 'utilitarian' versus 'ornamental existence', Faludi comments, work provided 'a truth on which a man's life could be securely founded. Out of that security grew authority – an authority based, as in the root meaning of the word, on having authored something productive' (2000, pp. 85–6). The historian John Morton Blum's description of the inherent virtue of 'husbandmen' further explains this role and source of identity for men during two centuries of industrialization (Faludi, 2000, p. 21).

As Western societies entered the post-industrial age (also referred to as the Information Age), major economic and structural change has occurred which has negatively affected men. Faludi points out that with a 'new economy', a new culture emerged in the late twentieth century (2000, p. 120). It was this period that saw 'the betrayal' of modern men (2000, pp. 21–30). Faludi reports that during the late twentieth century the major social forces affecting men were 'downward social mobility and unemployment'. With this came 'shame from the suspicion that the world discredits your claim to manhood, finds it useless, even risible' (2000, p. 144).

Faludi presents case studies including a group of men working in the Long Beach naval shipyard who devoted their lives to their work and took great pride in their achievements: 'The shipyard represented a particular vintage of American masculinity, monumental in its pooled effort, indefatigable in its industry, and built on a sense of useful productivity... the shipyard's men grounded their own worth and identity not in the masculine model of the warrior but in that of the builder' (2000, p. 55). Faludi documents how, when the shipyard closed, it left the men without work, the primary source of their worth and identity. That they were no longer 'breadwinners' and productive was a 'vast unspeakable shame' (2000, p. 65).

The US Bureau of Labor reported in 1996 that the fastest declining sectors in the world were leatherwork, shipbuilding and heavy industry – all men's jobs. In comparison, the fastest growing sectors were data processing, childminding and service industries – which mostly employ women (West, 1999).

More recently, a front-page report in *USA Today* (2002) cited research by the Institute for Women's Policy Research in Washington, DC which found men's jobs are more susceptible to economic downturns than women's. The report commented that in the last six economic downturns, factories have shed jobs, while the services sector has taken on workers, noting that seven out of ten workers in factories are men, while six out of ten workers in the services sector are women (Hagenbaugh, 2002). This is borne out by unemployment figures which show that men's rate of unemployment is higher than women's in many countries. Castells (1997) reports that the unemployment rate of men in the US in 1994 was 6.2 per cent, slightly higher than women at 6 per cent, while in Canada 10.7 per cent of men were unemployed compared with 9.8 per cent of women, and in the UK the difference in 1993 was more marked, with 12.4 per cent of men unemployed compared with 7.5 per cent of women seeking employment (1997, p. 168).

An Australian example of the precarious economic environment faced by many working-class men is Port Kembla, south of Sydney, once a leading steel-producing centre. At the beginning of the 1980s, Port Kembla employed 22,000 people, mostly men. In 2003, it employed 5,000. This parallels the experience of many miners in Britain during the economic rationalist years of the Thatcher administration.

When men are employed, statistics show that many work long hours, which inevitably affects their personal relationships and social involvement. Like men in many developed countries, in 2002 35 per cent of full-time Australian male workers were working 50 hours or more a week (Australian Bureau of Statistics, 2003, p. 120). This has increased from 23 per cent in 1982. Drago (2003) reports that Australian men, on average, work in paid employment 44 hours a week compared with women, who work 28 hours a week on average in paid employment, and the majority of women say they would prefer to reduce rather than increase their working hours.

In their findings of research among men published in 2005, Bob Connell and Julian Wood from the University of Sydney acknowledge that work in multinational and transnational corporations 'is not healthy, involving long hours, high stress, sedentary work, and frequent travel' (Connell and Wood, 2005, p. 355).

These statistics and research conclusions offer some explanation of why many men are absent from families so much and why they do not do more domestically. They also help explain why men, on average, earn more than women. Lower average pay for women in many cases is simply a question of maths – 44 hours a week usually earns more than 28 hours. It may be, as Summers (2003) suggests, that women are seeking and preferring part-time work because that is all they can manage given the shortage and high costs of child care. However, this does not support the argument that women are paid less – only that women work in paid employment less and occupy fewer high-paying positions which, at least to some extent, is explained by women's choice to have children (Belkin, 2003).

In her book based on extensive quantitative and qualitative research, *The Work/Life Collision*, Barbara Pocock (2003) identified that the 'work/life collision' has high social costs for mothers, fathers and families. She found that working lives are getting longer and private lives are shrinking – conditions that are particularly pertinent for men given their long average working hours and limited access to flexible work arrangements or leave for family or personal reasons such as paternity leave.

Bodies are a key part of identity, according to many gender researchers and writers, including de Beauvoir (1949), Greer (1999, originally published 1971) and, more recently, Grosz (1994), who focused specifically on this aspect of identity in *Volatile Bodies*. Nathanson and Young point out in relation to male bodies:

> In the remote past, men made distinctive and valuable contribu-
> tions to the community by virtue of their male bodies (apart from
> anything else)... their comparative advantages of size, strength and
> mobility... were important for hunting, pushing iron ploughs, or
> wielding weapons in battle... in the recent past, beginning with
> industrialisation, the importance of male bodies has declined steeply
> (2001, pp. 87–8)

While many of the roles once performed by men because of unique or special attributes of their bodies have become redundant, women retain their unique body roles such as giving birth. Nathanson and Young conclude that 'women as a class... retain both their biological identity and any cultural ones they choose'. But, they add, 'men as a class... have neither: biological identity is ruled out on the grounds that women can do everything men can do (although men cannot do at least one thing women can do), and cultural identity is being ruled out on the grounds that women should be encouraged to do everything men do' (2001, p. 88).

A key source of men's identity related to their bodies is fatherhood and a number of researchers have identified that this, in both its biological and social dimensions, is also problematic in modern societies. An Australian Institute of Family Studies conference in 2000 was told that 'boys and young men now live in complex cultural contexts where experiences of what it is to be a male and a father are rich and diverse, but also confusing and contradictory – even the definition of "father" is currently contested' (Sullivan, Graig and Howard, 2000).

Edgar (1997, p. 11) notes that men's biological repertoire in terms of reproduction is limited to insemination, whereas women's 'more complex range of capacities includes ovulation/menstruation, gestation (the growth of a child inside the womb) and lactation (breastfeeding)'. In contemporary societies, men's insemination role in fathering is being reduced to a sterile laboratory procedure of artificial insemination by sperm from anonymous donors in an increasing number of cases. Blakenhorn (1996) estimates that artificial insemination by anonymous donors accounts for around 30,000 births a year in the US. Further-more, recent medical experiments have reported that male sperm can now be grown artificially in a laboratory. As such technology continues to develop, men's biological role in fathering is being diminished and could become redundant.

As well as suffering a loss of identity as fathers because of artificial insemination and laboratory 'sperm banks', men have become objectified and marginalized as 'spunks' and sperm donors by some independent women who want to have children without attachment to a man. The high-profile businesswoman and environmentalist Anita Roddick, founder of *The Body Shop*, said of her one-time husband in an interview: 'I didn't particularly want a husband. All I really needed was some sympathetic sperm. Gordon obliged and Justine was born in 1969' (Langley, 2003). Roddick's comments are pertinent as she is widely seen as an exemplar and role model of a successful modern woman (she was made a Dame in 2003) and her comments were widely reported in major mass media.

Complicating fatherhood is that rising divorce rates in Western countries, together with child custody policies, have made separation from their children an increasingly common experience for men and is having a major impact on them. Research by Hawthorne (2002) among non-resident fathers involved in Family Court of Australia cases found that 56 per cent wanted more time with their children and that most were dissatisfied with their level of input into decisions concerning their children. He found 55 per cent had little or no say in decisions regarding their child(ren) and how their child support payments were spent.

In the UK, the Blair government published a Green Paper in 2004 outlining key proposed changes to post-separation child custody and father access, noting that 'with nine out of 10 parents with care being mothers, [post-separation parenting] is seriously gendered' (Burgess, 2004).

Family Court of Australia statistics show that in 2002–3 child custody was given to mothers in 69 per cent of contested custody cases that went to trial, compared with 22 per cent of custody awards to fathers. Uncontested custody arrangements under Consent Orders and settlements prior to Family Court trial saw children remain resident with mothers in 78 per cent and 76 per cent of cases respectively, compared with just 9 per cent and 13 per cent of custody orders to fathers. While custody to fathers has increased in the past decade, analysis of Family Court statistics shows custody is overwhelmingly granted in favour of mothers, even in cases where fathers go to court to seek custody of their children (Family Court of Australia, 2003).[1]

Hawthorne (2000) notes that a 'deficit paradigm of fathering' is promulgated in academic and popular discourse and argues that this deficit perspective underlies many studies of fathers. He supports Baker and McMurray (1998), who say non-resident fathers experience a system that they see as against them because so much of what is written about them is negative and implies that they are uncaring of children.

Men's concern with child custody laws and arrangements are surfacing publicly as well as in academic research. An historian from La Trobe University, John Hirst (2004), wrote a column in a national newspaper on the experience of Steve (a pseudonym) after his marriage broke up. Hirst reported:

> Without notice, his wife had left him and taken their two boys. She and the boys could not be found. Steve missed the boys terribly and was desperate to know that they were safe and to see them again. It seems it is not an offence in this country for a wife to secrete her children from their father – or at least not one that any authority takes seriously. In this case, the Commonwealth Government assisted the wife by paying her social security benefits and declining to tell Steve where she was. The wife proved elusive. She changed addresses and, when tracked down, refused to open the door to receive an order requiring her to attend court. Legal argument then ensued . . . By then six months had passed since she had left. Though she was evading the court, the Commonwealth continued to pay her benefits.

After reporting protracted hostile negotiations, Hirst continued:

> I went with Steve to collect his children for his first access visit, of which his wife had been given notice. No one was at home. Next day Steve learned from his lawyer that his wife had entered the legal arena with a claim that he was violent towards her and a danger to their children. Steve could contest these claims in court, but that would take time. Or, he could have very limited access immediately under supervision and accept the demands that his wife through her lawyer

---

[1] These figures may not add up to 100 per cent because of custody awards to non-parents and joint custody awards.

imposed on him. These were that he be psychiatrically assessed, that he take a course in anger management and that he be regularly tested for drug use. He still had not seen his boys. He would submit to anything to see them.

Hirst reported that, subsequently, the psychiatrist found Steve mentally sound and stable and said he should see his children. The anger counsellor reported positively. The drug tests were clean. After monitoring Steve with his children, the psychiatrist concluded he was a good father and no evidence of violence was found. Hirst concluded:

So the court finally awarded him the standard access – every other weekend. Nothing was said to the wife about her lies. Steve was simply meant to be pleased at getting this outcome which he had been awarded six months before and which his wife's accusations had taken from him. No citizen should have this power over another (2004, p. 13)

Another example of men's frustrations and concerns with fatherhood and what they see as a loss of status within families was published in the 'First Person' column of the London *Times*. The article by an anonymous man headed 'Only Losers Get Married' was written slightly tongue in cheek, but with serious undertones and telling points:

Marriage brings a man no more rights over the reproductive process than he had before. Zero. If a woman gets pregnant, she can abort the child as she wishes. The father-to-be doesn't have a right to be consulted, or even informed. At least two UK courts cases have confirmed this . . . But what if a woman lies that she is on the pill and gets pregnant? Presumably the man isn't expected to support that child, is he? Strangely enough, he is. The law does not recognize that mothers . . . can act fraudulently in conceiving this way; instead, it taxes the man. Even when it comes to children wanted by both partners, the law sides heavily with the wife, the ex-wife, the mother. Women win more than 90 per cent of custody cases. Men, for sure, are usually awarded access, but that means little – 50 per cent of the 50,000 contact orders made each year are broken – nearly always at the expense of the father. How can I pay lip service to a laughable institution such as modern marriage, an institution so obviously devalued, trashed and unbalanced, from the male point of view? (2004, p. 6)

Fathers-4-Justice staged a number of public protests in the UK to draw attention to the plight of separated fathers. David Chick climbed The London Eye on 11 September 2004 wearing a Spiderman mask (*The Sunday Times*, London, 12 September 2004, p. 2) and a few days later another member of the organization, Jason Hatch, climbed on to the balcony of Buckingham Palace wearing a Batman outfit. Hatch defied security to attach a large banner to the palace stating 'Super dads of Fathers-4-Justice – fighting for your right to see your kids' (*The Times*, London, 14 September 2004, p. 3).

Another important area where the identities of males is being affected and potentially shaped for life is in education. In the US, Christina Hoff Sommers (2000) claims that major failings and inaccuracies in research led to the high-profile feminist Carol Gilligan announcing in 1990 that American girls were in crisis, triggering a major shift in education focus to girls. Gilligan's reported findings prompted the American Association of University Women (AAUW) to commission a poll among girls. In 1991 the AAUW announced the results, claiming that most girls emerged from adolescence with a poor self-image. The AAUW then commissioned the Wellesley College Center for Research on Women to conduct a second study, which was published in 1992 in a report entitled 'How Schools Short-Change Girls'. The report claimed there was a direct causal relationship between girls' (alleged) second-class status in the nation's schools and deficiencies in their level of self-esteem and called for major change in the American education system (Hoff Sommers, 2000, pp. 21–2).

The relevance of this research to men becomes apparent in what followed. Hoff Sommers reports: 'In 1994, the allegedly low state of America's girls moved the US Congress to pass the Gender Equity in Education Act which categorized girls as an "under-served population"' and led to a major focus of resources and attention in education to the needs of girls. Boys were seen 'both as the unfairly privileged gender and as obstacles on the path to gender justice for girls' (2000, p. 23). This research shaped the landscape of education for the next decade in the US and influenced other countries including the UK and Australia.

However, Hoff Sommers claims there is evidence that the basis of Gilligan's claims and the US government's approach to education was wrong: 'The description of America's teenage girls as silenced, tortured, voiceless, and otherwise personally diminished is indeed dismaying. But there is surprisingly little evidence to support it.' She cites psychiatrists and paediatricians who reported research that found 80 per cent of adolescents of both sexes were normal and well adjusted, and a

University of Michigan and a US Department of Health and Human Services survey of 3,000 high school seniors around the same time which found 86 per cent of girls and 88 per cent of boys (highly consistent) said that they were 'pretty happy' or 'very happy' with school overall (2000, p. 19). Further, she cites extensive research which found girls outperforming boys, and boys suffering in the education system, evidenced by higher drop-out rates, lower academic performance and fewer progressing to university. Other research findings cited by Hoff Sommers (2000, pp. 25–30) and contradicting Gilligan's included:

- Girls read more books.
- Girls outperform males on tests of artistic and musical ability. '
- More girls are enrolled in university. The US Department of Education reported that in 1996 there were 8.4 million women enrolled in college, but only 6.7 million men. Furthermore, the US Department of Education estimates that, by 2007, there will be 9.2 million women in university in the US compared with 6.9 million men.

In relation to boys, Hoff Sommers (2000, pp. 25–6) reported:

- Boys are three times as likely as girls to be enrolled in special education programmes.
- Boys are four times as likely as girls to be diagnosed with attention deficit or hyperactivity disorders.
- More boys than girls are involved in crime, alcohol and drugs.
- More boys than girls commit suicide.

Hoff Sommers concludes: 'talk of girls drowning and disappearing in a society that favours boys... of "gender apartheid"... are outrageously and recklessly false' (2000, p. 93). 'Gilligan's central thesis – that boys are being imprisoned by their conventional masculinity – is not a scientific hypothesis. It is an extravagant piece of speculative psychology' (2000, p. 133).

   A number of education academics reject Hoff Sommers' views. Lingard (2003) says it is a matter of 'which boys' and 'which girls' are being talked about. The basis of Lingard's rejection of Hoff Sommers' views appears to be his opposition to essentializing or generalizing, and clearly there are differences between various schools, and the boys and girls who attend them, based on economics, class, ethnicity, and so on. But, interestingly, such differentiations were not made in arguments for increased attention to girls' needs in education. Gilligan's 1990 research, the 1992 research by Wellesley College, and similar education studies in Australia, did not identify 'which girls' were disadvantaged, but instead called for and gained affirmative action policies in favour of girls generally. Lingard describes calls for more attention to the needs of boys as 'a divisive political issue for policymakers and teachers' and rejects such recommendations in an Australian Federal Government report 'Boys – Getting it Right' which, he said, should be called 'Boys – Getting it Wrong' (House of Representatives Standing Committee on Education and Training, 2002).

However, in the US a number of research studies contradict Gilligan's claims and indicate that boys are not enjoying the advantages that have been alleged. In 1995, prompted by criticisms from scholars who questioned the research findings of Gilligan and the Wellesley College Center for Research on Women, the AAUW commissioned a further study of gender and academic achievement. This concluded that 'earlier reports of a tragic demoralization and short-changing of America's schoolgirls have been greatly exaggerated'. The more recent research found differences between boys and girls were 'small to moderate' (Lee, Chen and Smerdon, 1996, p. 1) and concluded that 'the public discourse around issues of gender in school needs some change . . . inequity can (and does) work in both directions' (Lee et al., 1996, p. 34).

Hoff Sommers also cites research by Hedges and Nowell, which found girls' deficits in maths were small but not insignificant, but went on to note of boys: 'the large sex differences in writing . . . are alarming. The data imply that males are, on average, at a rather profound disadvantage in the performance of this basic skill'. Hedges and Nowell (cited in Hoff Sommers, 2003, p. 33) warn: 'The generally larger numbers of males who perform near the bottom of the distribution in reading, comprehension and writing also have policy implications'.

In Australia, the education academic Peter West (1995) says there are gross inequities in the education of boys. He says, 'since the time of the Whitlam Government (1972–75), there has been discussion about programs to encourage girls. Much of the existing literature sees girls as victims, boys as villains'. A major study by Teese and Polesel (2003) found that, on average, 27–30 per cent of boys in the western and south-western suburbs of Melbourne do not finish secondary school and the drop-out rate rises to 40 per cent on the Mornington Peninsula south of Melbourne and to 46 per cent in north-west Melbourne. By comparison, the drop-out rate for girls peaked at 22.4 per cent.

As well as indicating that boys are at an institutionalized disadvantage in schools in terms of curricula and facilities, some research also indicates that boys may be actively discriminated against in school systems. A Macquarie University education publication reported:

> In Australian primary schools teachers typically nominate a boy as the most behaviourally troublesome student in the class and of the four students per class who are, on average, regarded as troublesome, three are typically boys. Our recent research on teacher attention to boys and girls in primary classrooms paints a grim picture of life in the classroom for many boys... Boys typically experience a very negative classroom environment... boys, on average, are told that their classroom behaviour is inappropriate 44 times per week (compared with girls 18 times). Praise for appropriate classroom behaviour is typically experienced about 12 times per week by both boys and girls... Many boys could be excused for the negative attitudes they hold about school and hence their poor reading levels. We are also left to wonder as to the effect that this barrage of disapproval might have on boys' self-esteem. (Wheldall, 2003)

West (1995) reports cases of prejudice against boys in school. He cites an incident in which a woman teacher reported difficulties with boys in her class. When the school principal went to talk to her, he found an 'All men are bastards' diary prominently displayed on her desk and numerous newspaper clippings on the walls documenting the evil men have done.

John Marsden (2002a) says of boys: 'theirs is an uneasy world. For 30 years now they've been getting the message that men are stupid, men are irresponsible, men can't handle commitments, men are at best bastards and at worst rapists'. Even some feminists have spoken out on negative portrayals of males that start with boys in the school system. Doris Lessing, interviewed by the *Guardian* newspaper, was reported saying:

> I find myself increasingly shocked at the unthinking and automatic rubbishing of men which is now so part of our culture that it is hardly even noticed... I was in a class of 9–10 year-olds, girls and boys, and this young woman was telling these kids that the reason for wars was the innately violent nature of men... you could see the little boys sat there crumpled, apologising for their existence, thinking this was going to be the pattern of their lives. (*The Guardian*, 14 August 2001)

A range of statistics and research findings point to significant problems faced by boys and men in contemporary societies.

- A 2001 Programme for International Student Assessment (PISA) study carried out by the OECD in 32 countries found that boys lag behind girls in every country studied (cited in West, 2002a). The 2002 Australian Federal Government report 'Boys: Getting it Right' reached the same conclusion, finding boys trail 19 per cent behind girls in final year examination results: 'The effects of educational under-achievement for the students themselves and for society generally are too profound to be ignored' (House of Representatives Standing Committee on Education and Training, 2002).
- More women are graduating from university in most Western countries. In the US, Hoff Sommers (2000) reports that 55 per cent of full-time university enrolments are females compared with 45 per cent males. A 2003 Organization of Economic Development (OECD) report shows that, in the 25–34 years age group, almost 42 per cent of women in the US have university degrees compared with 36 per cent of men. In Australia the gap is even wider, with 38 per cent of Australian women with university degrees compared with 29 per cent of men. The OECD reports that this trend is common across many Western societies except the UK where the rate is almost even (see Table 3.1) However, in the UK recent research reported by *The Economist* shows that, in key fields, female graduates are outstripping men. Data from the Higher Education Statistics Agency (HESA) and the Bar Council show that female medical students have outnumbered male students since the early 1990s and more women are now called to the bar than men (*The Economist*, 2005).

Table 3.1   Percentage of men and women attaining tertiary education

		1991	1995	2001
Australia	Men	22%	24%	29%
	Women	24%	25%	38%
New Zealand	Men	21%	23%	26%
	Women	25%	26%	31%
UK	Men	19%	24%	30%
	Women	18%	22%	29%
USA	Men	29%	33%	36%
	Women	31%	35%	42%

Source: OECD (2003), *Education at a Glance*.

- Between one in six and one in seven of all fathers do not live with their children, according to Clare (2000), and are forced by Family Courts to 'support their children and former wives at levels that leave them living in poverty' (Hawthorne, 2000). Even more significantly from a social perspective, researchers say non-resident fathers are 'victims of a system which neither acknowledges their deep sense of loss after separation nor legitimizes their grief' (Hawthorne, 2000), leaving them with 'a pervasive sense of loss' (Stewart, Schwebel and Fine, 1986, pp. 55–65).

Statistics also show that men have lower life expectancy than women in all major Western societies, higher injury rates at work, higher rates of alcoholism and alcohol-related problems, and suicide rates four to five times higher than women (Woods, 2001).

Citing problems experienced by men and boys should not be viewed as a 'competing victims syndrome' as Cox (1995) attempts dismissively to do. It should be possible to support feminist views such as those of Summers (2003) which hold that women face many inequities and still have a long way to go to gain equality, while at the same time recognizing that men and boys face inequities and unfairness which should be studied and addressed.

The spread of misandry

The difficult position of men and boys in modern and postmodern societies such as the US, UK and Australia is being exacerbated by a trend which is a primary focus of this book. Not only are the traditional foundations of male identity being eroded or taken away by economic, social and technological change, but the vacuum left is being filled with highly negative discourse on men and male identity. Nathanson and Young (2001, p. 295) conclude: 'The traditional universe on which men relied for self-esteem and self-confidence is crumbling. A suitable replacement has not yet emerged. And almost any attempt to create one is quickly denounced'.

Nathanson and Young found misandry widespread in popular culture in North America – specifically in the TV shows, movies, advertising and journalism they studied. They note that prior to the release of their book, *Spreading Misandry: The Teaching of Contempt for Men in Popular Culture*, few people, including those in academia, knew the word 'misandry', while the term for hatred and vilification of women, 'misogyny', is widely known and used. This may be, as some feminists claim, simply because misogyny is widespread and misandry is not. Or it may be, as evidence suggests, that hatred and vilification of men has simply been unrecognized – that it is a new 'problem with no name'.

Hoff Sommers (2000, p. 134) also identifies this trend in modern societies, referring to 'the tiresome misandry that infects so many gender theorists who never stop blaming the "male culture" for all social and psychological ills'. Similarly, Macdonald, McDermott and Di Campli (2000) identify and warn of the 'pathologizing' of men.

Research reported by Woods (1999) and West (1996; 2002b) specific-ally cites negative portrayals of men in the media. Woods says, 'When the word "men" appears in the media, it is often in relation to some negative attribute – men as rapists, sexual harassers and abusers, practi-tioners of violence, unfeeling (or at least out of touch with feelings) and concerned only with power and control'. West (1996; 2002b) conducted interviews with men of various ages on what it has been like to be a man from 1900 to the present. In relation to the past, West reports: 'We found that men were looked up to. To be a man was to have a job and a family. The men . . . were breadwinners, heads of families.' In his review of the way it is today, West reports from his interviews: 'Men are the butt of jokes on TV and radio. White males, perhaps heterosexual males, feel they are the only ones who can be ridiculed with impunity'.

Against this background of feminism and changing economic, indus-trial, technological and social conditions, there has been some growth in men's studies, as cited by Brod (1987), Kimmel (1987) and Newbold et al. (2002, p. 287) and an emerging men's movement. But men and male identity remain understudied and mass media treatment of men is largely undiscussed. Seidler (1994, p. 112) suggests that 'it might be that various studies will bring into question assumptions that both socialist and radical feminist theory make about men. I think this is something that should be welcomed'.

Germaine Greer observed in the conclusion of her widely acclaimed *The Female Eunuch*: 'The first significant discovery we shall make as we racket along our female road to freedom is that men are not free' (1999, p. 371).

4
The Role and Effects of Mass Media in Modern Societies

Mass media are a major focus of attention in modern societies, primarily because of their perceived *effects* on individuals and society – although this is not their only social significance, as we shall see later in this chapter. If mass media have significant effects, then analysis of how they represent subjects such as race, violence, women – and men – is of major social significance. If, on the other hand, mass media do not have any significant effect on society, then their content is much less relevant.

While mass media effects are taken as self-evident in much popular discourse, and even assumed in some academic studies, conclusions as to the effects and implications of mass media representations should not be based on assumptions, ideology or outdated theories. In examining the influences and effects of mass media, it is important to situate the examination within contemporary media theory, particularly in relation to media roles and effects.

Two failings that have undermined the value of a number of studies of mass media representations are: assuming media content leads to certain audience effects; and drawing conclusions based on small, unrepresentative samples of media content and poor research methodology. The first results from a lack of understanding of media theory and suggests an approach based on ideology rather than methodology. The second can lead to erroneous conclusions and, even where small samples of media content analysis produce qualitatively significant findings, these can be easily questioned or rejected on the grounds of not being true of media content broadly. The mass media themselves are quick to adopt a defensive position against any suggestion of influence one way or another and reject most or all allegations of bias.

'The conviction... that the media are important agencies of influence is broadly correct. However, the ways in which the media exert influence are complex and contingent,' Curran (2002, p. 158) concludes. Other researchers agree. Newbold et al. (2002, p. 310) say: 'although represent-ations most certainly do matter, their interaction with identity is very complex as indeed are all the relationships between media and reality'.

Early direct injection and transmissional views of mass media

Early media research assumed direct social effects, adopting a 'hypo-dermic' concept of mass media, also described as the 'transmissional' model, based on the well-known model of communication developed by Shannon and Weaver (1949), which described communication as transmitting a message to a receiver, with meaning being synonymous with content 'delivered like a parcel' (Reddy, 1979). In this view, power was thought to reside in texts and their producers; while audiences were perceived as passive receivers of information (Newbold et al., 2002, p. 25). Lull (2000, p. 98) summarizes: 'The first stage of media audi-ence research reflects... strong impressions of the... media as powerful, persuasive forces in society'.

The notion that mass media are powerful propaganda tools that are or can be unleashed on a hapless mass audience was central to the Mass Manipulative Model of the media and underpinned later cultural hege-mony and political economy models. Marxist and neo-Marxists theories attributed enormous power to mass media and claimed direct attitu-dinal and even behavioural effects (e.g. Adorno and Horkheimer, 1972; Marcuse, 1972; Habermas, 1989; Adorno, 1991; and McCombs, 1977, with his 'agenda-setting' theory). Marxists and neo-Marxists saw the media as 'managers of opinion at the behest of the powerful' (Curran, 2002, p. 45).

Humphrey McQueen is typical of Marxist and neo-Marxist theorists on mass media. In *Australia's Media Monopolies*, he states: 'The media try to divide and demoralize the working class because a confident, united working class is one of the last things the capitalists want to face' (1977, p. 43), and refers to mass media as 'capitalism's control of ideas' (1977, p. 6).

Theodor Adorno and Max Horkheimer, in 'The Culture Industry: Enlightenment as Mass Deception', in their *Dialectic of Enlightenment*, took a less political and more commercial view, describing media as part of the 'culture industry' which manufactures information products and imposes them on audiences. But, like Marx and others subscribing to the Mass Manipulative Model, Adorno and Horkheimer felt that the power of the mass media over audiences was enormous and potentially damaging (Gauntlett, 2002, pp. 19–20). For example, they blamed the media for the rise of fascism (Adorno and Horkheimer, 1972; Horkheimer, 1972; Adorno, 1991).

Minimal or limited effects thinking on the media

Landmark research in the late 1950s and 1960s refuted many claimed effects of the mass media and showed media power to be overestimated. Key studies were those of Katz and Lazarsfeld (1955) and Klapper (1960). Klapper concluded that 'mass communications ordinarily do not serve as a necessary and sufficient cause of audience effects'. He concluded that mass media were more likely to reinforce existing attitudes than change them or create new attitudes (Curran, 2002, pp. 132, 159; Newbold et al., 2002, p. 31). His findings became known as Klapper's law of minimal consequences and triggered a 'limited effects' view of mass media (Curran, 2002, pp. 132–3; Newbold et al., 2002, p. 31).

Klapper's views were supported by cognitive dissonance theory, as espoused by psychologist Leon Festinger, who found that people resist messages that are dissonant with their attitudes and accept information that is consonant with them (Grunig and Hunt, 1984, p. 123). However, even the 'minimal' view of media effects advanced by Katz and Lazarsfeld (1955) and Klapper (1960), which cites reinforcement of existing attitudes, opinions and behaviours rather than change or creation of new ones, is significant.

> [T]he media are powerful agencies of reinforcement. The effects tradition documents this extensively, yet makes little of it. This is because the absence of persuasion or change has been traditionally viewed as evidence of limited influence... The denial of reinforcement as a significant influence has persisted, despite some dissent, throughout the history of media effects research. (Curran, 2002, p. 159)

Curran cites and criticizes Perloff, who 'classifies any media effect that does not involve change consciously sought as a non-effect' (2002, p. 159), arguing that reinforcement is a key effect as it contributes to maintenance of political and social status quos.

Another approach which considers the influence of mass media to be limited is a pluralist view of society which emerged in the 1940s and was popular until the 1960s. Proponents of pluralism claim that there are many centres of power in society and that natural checks and balances are achieved through 'countervailing forces' which limit and mediate the power of the media (Newbold et al., 2002, p. 31).

Another line of media research that rejected the direct effects thinking of earlier research and first introduced the notion of audience interpretation became known as the 'uses and gratifications' model. Proponents claim that people use mass media to gratify their needs. Instead of asking what the media do to people, Katz (1977) turned the question round to ask, 'What do people do with the media?' (cited in Lull, 2000, p. 101).

Uses and gratifications thinking about mass media continues today, although it has lost some favour as it is linked to functionalist theory advanced by the American political scientist Harold Lasswell, which assumes people willingly engage with mass media and benefit from the experience – a notion that has been challenged by many later media theories (Lull, 2000, p. 111).

Political economy and cultural studies views of the media

Political economy thinking about mass media, rooted in structuralism, saw the dominant political, financial and industrial institutions of societies having a direct effect on the ideological forces maintaining control, including the mass media (Newbold, 2002, p. 219). Mosco (1995) defined political economy as the 'study of the social relations, particularly the power relations that influence the production, distribution, and consumption of resources, including communication resources' (cited in Newbold et al., 2002, p. 22).

Like Marxist thinkers, the radical political economy tradition continued to argue that the media are powerfully shaped by their political and economic organization (Curran, 2002, p. 113). This includes media ownership, cross-ownership, monopolies, competition, public service broadcasting and controls over quantity and content of advertising – what Gramsci calls 'society's superstructure' and which he describes as society's ideology-producing institutions (Lull, 2000, p. 49).

In this sense, political economy and later cultural studies views which came to dominate media theory from the 1970s reversed thinking that mass media had limited effects. However, they did not return to direct effects thinking. 'Rather, political economy and cultural studies started from the premise that reinforcement was not neutral.' Moreover, they took the concept of reinforcement further, arguing that 'reinforcement was the inevitable and contrived outcome of a system whose very purpose was to maintain order and to prevent change in societies that were riven by manifest inequalities' (Newbold et al., 2002, p. 34). Political economy theory saw mass media involved in 'manufacturing consent' – a concept made famous by Naom Chomsky (Herman and Chomsky, 1988).

Marshall McLuhan's famous adage 'The medium is the message' further focused attention on mass media and their role in society (Lull, 2000, p. 37). However, McLuhan's (1964) admonition pointed to the importance of the production and institutional processes of the mass media (e.g. their internal news selection criteria and production techniques) in shaping media messages. Previously, the focus had been on the suppliers of information and mass media had been viewed as a neutral channel.

'Agenda-setting theory' advanced by McCombs (1977), and later derivatives such as 'agenda-framing' (Gurevitch, Blumler and Weaver, 1986) and 'agenda-priming' (Blood, 1989, p. 12), shifted thinking further from viewing mass media as powerful propaganda instruments used by elites to manipulate public opinion and 'manufacture consent' towards a focus on mass media as the originators of messages. McCombs and others stopped short of seeing media power as absolute, but argued that while mass media may not tell people 'what to think', they set, framed or primed the agenda of 'what they think about' (Blood, 1989).

The Achilles' heel of political economy thinking about mass media was exposed by the emerging fields of content analysis and audience research (Newbold et al., 2002, p. 37). Whereas political economy theory focused only on quantitative (often crude) mass media content methodology, assuming quantitative repetition was equivalent to semiotic or affective significance, new methods of qualitative content analysis began to consider the subtleties of narrative structure, characterization and semiotics to determine likely meanings that audiences might take from texts. Cultural studies approaches to mass media borrowed from literary criticism and cinematic analysis and drew on linguistics and sociolinguistics. This approach shifted the focus away from the structuralist politics of Marx and Engels and the structuralist linguistic theories of Saussure to introduce qualitative methods which examined how different readers interpret texts differently. Even so, early neo-Marxist cultural studies saw mass media being used to influence or control audiences. However, they saw this as more subtle than direct control. Mass media, they argued, exerted influence through cultural hegemony.

Habermas (1989) proposed a variation on political economy thinking with his concept of mass media as a 'public sphere' of discussion which functions as a 'forum of public communication... in which individual citizens can come together as a public and confer freely about matters of general interest'. However, Habermas' concept of mass media as a public sphere of debate where reason and logic would prevail has been widely dismissed and seen as flawed because of its 'idealisation of public reason' (Curran, 2002, p. 45).

The 'ethnographic turn' – 'death of the author', birth of the reader

'The ethnographic turn' in social and cultural studies research brought a major change in thinking about mass media effects. Cultural studies approaches to mass media drew on literary analysis, linguistics and socio-linguistics (Newbold et al., 2002, p. 307). A key influence was Barthes' concept of the 'death of the author', which shifted emphasis from the author's intentions on to the reader (Barthes, 1977; Newbold et al., 2001, p. 37). This paradigm shift focused attention on 'human agency' in interpretation of texts (Lull, 2000, p. 9) and ushered in what Curran terms 'a reconceptualisation of the audience as an active producer of meaning' (2002, p. 115). In simple terms, texts could mean different things to different people in different situations.

Building on Stuart Hall's influential 'encoding-decoding' model (Hall, 1973, 1977, 1980; Hall et al., 1980), and his concept of the 'critical reader' (Hall et al., 1980), sociologists and modern media scholars point out that audiences actively construct the meanings of/decode media texts within a matrix of influences, rather than passively absorb predetermined meanings imposed on them (Mumford, 1998, p. 121; Newbold, et al., 2002, p. 307). Hall, supported by Morley and Chen (1996), suggested that a media producer may 'encode' a certain meaning into a text, which would be based on a certain social context and understandings, but when another person comes to consume that text, their reading ('decoding') of it, based on their own social context and assumptions, is likely to be somewhat different.

McQuail (1984), like 'uses and gratifications' theory proponents, reversed the classic question of media effects from 'what effect do the media have on people?' to 'how do people use the media?' and helped overturn previous simplistic assumptions about cause and effect between media and audiences.

In cultural studies approaches to mass media, texts are viewed as polysemic – that is, they offer the possibility of a diversity of reading, even if a preferred reading is intended by its producers (Newbold et al., 2002, p. 45). Curran (2002) and others agree. Curran says, 'the media have fractured meanings' (2002, p. 144), while Lull (2000, p. 162) uses the term 'multisemic'. The discovery, or rediscovery, of audience power in revisionist audience reception studies was an important development in media effects theory and debunked media ideology, leading to a 'more cautious assessment of media influence' (Curran, 2002, p. 115).

Fiske (1989, p. 127), one of the most strident cultural studies theorists, argues that it is the audience, not the media, which has the most power. More recently, scholars have proposed the view that Fiske 'hopelessly romanticizes the role of audience members' (Lull, 2000, p. 168). Tester (1994, p. 70) says that 'Fiske's work confuses the possibility that the audience might carry out oppositional readings of media texts with the claim that they actually do carry out such readings'.

Other scholars criticize cultural studies theory of mass media and its emphasis on the openness of texts, which Windschuttle (1998, p. 25) says leaves us 'adrift in a sea of linguistic relativism'. Windschuttle cites Cunningham and Turner (1993), who in their history of textual analysis in media theory, conclude:

> While textual analysis has had to relinquish any ambition to reveal the meaning through its consideration of media texts, it still insists that one cannot just wheel in any old meaning at all. Most agree that the text does have the power to limit the range of uses to which it is likely to be put. Exactly how much power, however, or how one might define the limits, is more difficult to decide. The balance of power between text and reader seems to vary from text to text, from reading to reading, from context to context, from audience member to audience member, and over time. (1993, p. 266)

Contemporary theory of media effects – a synthesis of views

Modern thinking on mass media recognizes that identities cannot be viewed as constructed by media representations alone (Newbold et al., 2002, p. 311). As discussed by Barthes (1972), Hall (1973), Cook (1980), Hall et al. (1980), Lovell (1980), Woodward (1997), Mumford (1998) and others, identity is influenced by a multiplicity of factors, such as race, nationality, ethnicity, social background, education, gender, sexuality, religion and interrelationships such as family, peers and occupation or work groups, as well as media content. Curran adds that first-hand knowledge, word-of-mouth relaying others' first-hand knowledge, sceptical dispositions towards the media, and internal processes of logic also influence audiences reading of media texts (2002, p. 121).

However, there are flaws in 'limited effects' or 'minimal impact' theories of mass media. Mass media *do* have significant effects for a number of reasons. Bardikian (1997) notes that throughout most of the twentieth century the trend in culture industry ownership was toward concentration in the hands of fewer and fewer multinational corporations (i.e. monopolies and oligopolies). Lull (2000, p. 191) says, 'the culture industries became part of a vast system of interrelated agencies'.

At the same time, globalization of mass media has led to this shrinking group of powerful, mainly Western publishers and broadcasters distributing homogenized media content worldwide. As Curran (2002, p. 158) points out, audiences' ability individually and collectively to make oppositional readings or interpretations of mass media content depends on their access to oppositional discourses. The growth of global monopolies and oligopolies in mass media has reduced diversity and audience access to alternative and oppositional discourses.

In addition, a number of studies suggest that the influence of traditional sources for interpretation and meaning such as the family, the Church and work have declined (Grossberg et al., 1998). For instance, a *Times Mirror* Center for the People and the Press (1994) survey reported that the Church has waned as a source of influence in the US, Canada, Britain, France and Germany, and in all countries except the US it was rated lower than television and newspapers as a source of guiding and influential information. Curran similarly notes: 'From the last quarter of the 19th century onwards, there was a cumulative process of de-Christianisation'. Also, he says, 'during the same period' there was 'decline of the factory, trade union, church, local neighbourhood and extended family' (2002, p. 23). These social changes leave many people more reliant on media representations for their view of the world and themselves.

Accompanying the decline in sources of alternative or oppositional discourse, modern mass media use increasingly sophisticated formats and genre including 'reality TV', 'docu-drama' and 'mockumentaries' (fiction made to look like documentary) in an attempt to increase their semiotic efficacy – i.e. make their mediated content appear as 'reality' to audiences. While reality TV is anything but reality, research shows that many media audiences have difficulty determining real life and events from mediated representations.

To some extent, the Internet, particularly the World Wide Web, has introduced an alternative source of information and discourse. On the surface, the Web appears to offer great potential and have few barriers to access. For instance, the cost of online publishing is low in comparison with the production of newspapers or operations of a TV network. Theoretically, anyone can say whatever they want and reach a global audience via the Internet with websites or 'blogs' (personal accounts, diaries or newsletters posted on websites).

However, a number of factors limit the power of the Internet as a significant source of alternative information and discourse. First, despite an estimated 300 million regular users in 2004 (Internet Industry Association), many of the world's 6.5 billion people do not have access to the Web. This is particularly the case in poor, remote and uneducated communities. Second, the best-funded, most promoted and most frequently visited sites are the online versions of leading newspapers, networks and news aggregators (e.g. CNN, MSN, etc.), which publish the same content as physical media and reports. Alternative sources on the Web, with some notable exceptions, are unreliable and have less credibility than official sites. This is exacerbated by the third factor: the main cost of reaching a wide audience through mass communication is not production or broadcasting/distribution costs, but audience reach through marketing. Consequently, only the best resourced (i.e. mainstream) media and media aggregators can effectively reach large audiences. As a result, while the Web is a highly effective channel for specialist groups such as academics, students, researchers and professionals, it is not yet an alternative to traditional mass media for information and discourse – although some blogs are challenging traditional media.

Most modern researchers accept that a synthesis of influences, comprising the content mediated by the producers, the semiotic complexity and efficacy of the medium, and interpretations by the reader collectively shape meaning from media texts. Newbold et al. summarize:

> [T]he tradition of media effects has undergone a number of transformations, above all in the past two decades. These transformations may be summarized as movements away from 'transmissional' models of effects towards a study of media within contexts of making of meaning, of culture, of texts and of literacy, in the interaction between media texts and media readers. Those who have asked how people make meaning from texts have had to look both at the ways in which texts are structured, and at the readers themselves. (Newbold et al., 2000, p. 46)

MEDIA EFFECTS THEORIES

Direct effects
Media assumed as all-powerful; audience as passive recipients

Minimal or limited effects theory
Joseph Klapper, Katz and Lazarsfeld found most common
impact of media communication was reinforcement, not change

Cultural studies – neo-Marxist
Media seen as powerful agents for ideological hegemony
by ruling elites and capitalism. Assumed major effects

Political economy
Media seen as part of political and economic structure; agents
of powerful institutions and capitalism. Assumed major effects

Political economy – 'Public Sphere' theory
Habermas proposed media were a public forum for all. This
view widely dismissed as 'romanticized' and naive

Cultural studies – 'New Audience Research'
'Ethnographic turn' introduced recognition of audiences as
active interpreters of texts and texts as polysemic. Shifted
focus to audiences and viewed media as less influential

Synthesis of views/integrated theory
Media are influential but through a matrix of factors including
audience education, race, sex, religion, etc, access to
alternative discourse (eg. family, peers) diversity of media, etc

Figure 4.1   Summary of evolution of media effects theory

Theory developed in public relations – a sector with a vested interest in understanding the power of the media – sheds light on the likely effects of mass communication. While studies by Stamm and Tichenor, Donohue, Olien and Bowers (cited in Pavlik, 1987, p. 77) refute the 'domino' view of mass communication, which suggests that messages lead to attitudes which, in turn, lead to behaviour, Grunig and Hunt (1984, pp. 147–58) propose what they call the 'situational theory' of communication effects. Grunig and Hunt found that mass communication can have significant effects on audiences contingent on a number of situational factors. They present four important factors that determine the likelihood of mass communication having effects: 1) the level of problem recognition (does the audience understand and perceive there is a problem to be addressed?); 2) the level of constraint recognition (does the audience feel empowered to do anything about it?); 3) the presence of a referent criterion (previous experience or knowledge of the subject); and 4) the level of involvement. If these situational factors are present, their research suggests that mass communication can have significant effects on audiences.

Figure 4.1 provides a summary of viewpoints and theories on the effects of mass media.

Mass media as reflectors of social and political opinion

Before leaving the subject of the significance of mass media content and examining mass media representations of men and male identity, it is important to recognize and note that a substantial body of research identifies that because mass media, particularly news media, report what individuals, groups and organizations are saying and doing, they *reflect* society. In other words, mass media may not be causing effects; instead they may be reflecting existing opinions and attitudes – or some combination of causing effects and reflecting the effects of other influences. The extent to which mass media *cause* effects and/or *reflect* existing conditions is a subject of considerable debate.

In listing ten problems with the media effects model, Gauntlett (2002, pp. 29–30) says, 'the effects model tackles social problems backwards'. He argues in relation to violence that 'to understand violent people, we should study violent people' as actual violence or a disposition to violence may be the cause of media representations of it, instead of concluding that media violence is the cause of actual violence. In the context of men and male identity, this raises questions such as 'are mass media representations of metrosexuals causing men to become or think they should be more feminine?', or 'are they reflecting that modern men are using beauty products and becoming more fashion-conscious?'

Mass media themselves are ambivalent on the point. In resisting regulation on issues such as violence, the media often advance the 'reflector' or 'mirror' model of media, decrying their purported role in influencing societies and causing various effects. On the other hand, in selling advertising, on which commercial mass media depend, they make strong claims to influence and *affect* audiences. Not to do so would be to deny any basis or effectiveness in advertising when there is considerable evidence to the contrary.

The answer to the age-old question of whether mass media create or reflect social reality is 'both' according to Lull (2000, p. 165) and Gauntlett (2002, p. 254). A number of factors determine which way influence flows. Two key determinants of whether and the extent to which mass media cause or reflect effects are: 1) the genre and type of content, and 2) the level of media access available to various viewpoints.

As well as arguing that entertainment media content such as drama and 'soap opera' reflect widespread audience attitudes in order to be popular (possibly a reasonable claim), media proprietors, producers and journalists claim that news reporting and news-related media content such as features, opinion columns, current affairs and talk shows reflect reality because they report what happens and what is said by various sources. 'We tell it as it is' is a common claim by reporters and editors. However, this ignores the fact that selection of subjects to report is, from the outset, an 'agenda-setting' or 'agenda-framing' function (Blood, 1989). No systematic method of sampling from all available topics and viewpoints is applied; news and news-related media select some issues and subjects to report and ignore others. Second, reporters and editors select sources to quote within articles while other potential sources of comment are ignored. Further, they select elements of what these sources are quoted saying, often editing statements to what broadcast media call 'ten-second grabs'. Thus, even news is a highly produced representation of reality and does not broadly reflect what happened on any given day – only small, highly selective parts of it.

Furthermore, the principal criterion for selection of news, current affairs and talk-show content which is the focus of this study is news value/newsworthiness, which further limits the ability of this type of mass media content to reflect social attitudes and viewpoints. While definition of news is complex, in general terms news articles, feature articles, opinion columns, current affairs reports and talk show segments must contribute something new or at least unknown to audiences to meet news media requirements. News and news-related media content by its very nature does not simply reflect social attitudes and viewpoints – it if did only this, it would not be news or newsworthy.

Externally contributed opinion columns and feature articles are arguably types of media content which reflect social attitudes and viewpoints because they are written by independent experts and authorities from various vantage points in society, not by media staff. However, even in these types of media content, the functions of reflecting and creating opinion overlap and fuse because of the selective nature of mass media content and the related issue of media access. Media content analysis shows that, along with a small group of journalists and programme presenters, media content is contributed by a relatively small number of politicians, heads of organizations, published authors, prominent academics (often those who actively promote their views) and 'celebrities' (loosely defined). Some mass media refer to these regular sources as 'talent', reflecting their preferred status as willing and skilled spokespersons and commentators.

Letters to the editor, theoretically mass media content broadly reflective of social views, are given very limited space – usually half a page or less. Those letters that are published are usually edited to a few paragraphs in most media. Similarly in radio 'talkback' programmes, callers are screened, with a limited number getting 'on air' and most are given a minute or even less to express their viewpoint. Dissenting views are often cut off abruptly by the producers or presenters.

These characteristics of mass media editorial content result in representations reflecting a narrow and limited range of attitudes and viewpoints. Often, these are vested interests and organized campaigners such as political leaders and apparatchiks, paid spokespersons of organizations, professional PR practitioners (Macnamara, 1993) and publicity-seeking commentators such as authors promoting new books and academics who use the media to promote their views.

Through their relatively narrow selection of sources to publish, broadcast or quote and their focus on news and newsworthiness, editorial mass media do not reflect widespread social attitudes, but particular viewpoints and attitudes. Further, mass media expose these selected attitudes and viewpoints to large audiences. In reflecting some views to large audiences, while not reflecting others, mass media combine a reflection of social attitudes and creation of social effects in a mixed model of communication.

The extent to which this occurs varies from medium to medium, issue to issue, and article to article, and can occur simultaneously even within the same article, such as a report or column reflecting views of one or more individuals or groups and communicating them persuasively to a larger audience previously unexposed to these views. Thus, reflecting societies and influencing societies are not discrete, alternative or separate functions, but interrelated and intertwined functions that often feed one off the other in a circle of influence. At the same time as they reflect attitudes and viewpoints from within society, by their selection and amplification of these viewpoints mass media are concurrently engaged in the creation and influencing of social attitudes.

Curran (2002, p. 165) says: 'the media are powerful ideological agencies, though not in the simplistic form of brainwashing proposed by members of the Frankfurt school'. Newbold et al. (2002, p. 16) concur: 'Today, it is commonly appreciated that the media do not simply mirror reality – even where that is their stated aim. Every form of representation involves selection, exclusion and inclusion'. Gauntlett (2002, p. 254) concludes on the media as 'mirror' or 'manufacturer' of effects debate: 'The power relationship between media and the audience involves a 'bit of both', or to be more precise, *a lot* of both'.

The dual multidirectional nature of mass media communication, *reflecting* audiences' views and causing *effects* in audiences, expands rather than limits the value of media research – albeit interpretation of findings of media research must take account of the complex interaction of both these potentials.

To the extent that mass media content reflects or mirrors social attitudes, it provides a database of recorded opinions and views which can be analysed to learn about a society – albeit with the important qualifications and limitations identified in this chapter. Sources analysis, a sub-element of content analysis, can identify groups or individuals that hold and propagate various opinions and attitudes, and issues and messages analysis can identify how prevalent certain views are. When mass media mirror social attitudes, media content provides a window to view and study society and media content analysis is a proxy of social research with the advantages that it provides a non-intrusive methodology and can analyse large volumes of data over extended periods. In this approach, mass media themselves are unimportant except as a portal or vantage point.

To the extent that mass media content is involved in the causation of social effects, media content analysis can draw inferences about media producers' intent and, with reasonable probability, make predictions about likely attitudes and sometimes even behaviours in audiences

(Neuendorf, 2002, p. 53). In this instance, the mass media are the focal point of study, with societies seen as consumers of mass media content.

Given the significant effects of mass media in certain circumstances, and their capacity to reflect societies in which they operate, it is doubly important to examine mass media representations of men and male identity.

5
Men in the Media – A Review: 1980–2001

As outlined in Chapter 1, feminists focused on mass media as one of the key battlegrounds in their struggle for independence, equality, rights and respect. A large body of research exists on the portrayal and treatment of women in mass media. This study cites only a few examples as the focus here is men and male identity. But it is useful to note women's concerns with mass media as they demonstrate that media representations of gender and gender identities are a long-standing and ongoing field of study and point to trends that inform investigation.

In the journal *Women and Film* launched in the early 1970s, Smith (1972, p. 13) declared: 'Women, in any fully human form, have almost completely been left out of film ... The role of a woman in a film almost always revolves around her physical attraction and the mating games she plays with the male characters'. Rosen (1973, p. 10) commented of movies: 'the cinema woman is a Popcorn Venus, a delectable but insubstantial hybrid of cultural distortions'. A decade later, Kaplan (1983, pp. 7–8) wrote: 'In Hollywood films ... women are ultimately refused a voice, a discourse, and their desire is subjected to male desire. They live out silently, frustrated lives, or, if they resist their placing, sacrifice their lives for their daring'.

Even in the 1990s, in the preface to a book of film reviews, Maio (1991, p. vii) refers to movie portrayals of women as 'often reprehensible'. She states further: 'Women are not only given less screen time, when we're up there on the screen we are likely to be portrayed as powerless and ineffectual ... where are the triumphant women heroes to match the winner roles men play constantly?' (p. 2)

Gunter (1995) reports content analysis of television advertising in the 1970s which found strong evidence of gender stereotyping in relation to women. For instance, 75 per cent of all advertisements featuring women were for kitchen and bathroom products. Coltrane and Messineo (2000) found that of almost 1,700 TV commercials broadcast between 1992 and 1994 characters in the ads 'enjoy more prominence and exercise more authority if they are white, or men'.

By the mid-1990s, a study of 500 prime-time TV commercials in the UK by Cumerbatch (cited in Strinati, 1995, p. 186) found that advertisers had become wary of showing women doing housework and, for the first time, men were shown cooking more often than women. But these, Cumberbatch says, were special occasions in contrast with the more routine cookery duties of women which traditionally had been shown.

Gunter (1995) provides a summary of findings from media studies of gender representations in television programmes such as drama and sit-coms and reports that media content studies in the 1970s consistently found that marriage, parenthood and domesticity were shown on television to be more important for women than men (1995, pp. 13–14). Citing Gunter, Gauntlett (2002, p. 43) adds: 'men were more likely to be assertive (or aggressive), whilst women were more likely to be passive'.

Newspapers have also been extensively studied in relation to how they represent gender. For instance, Stirling (1987, pp. 109–28), examining the treatment of women and men in Australian newspapers, explored a range of expressions and linguistic techniques and concluded that these served either to exclude women or to define them narrowly and negatively. Hawes and Thomas (1995) compared language bias against women in British and Malaysian newspapers and reported that sexist language in the Malaysian press was less explicit than in the British press, but even in Malaysia there was a bias towards males as a topic of serious news stories (1995, pp. 1–18).

Feminist studies of mass media have been particularly critical of portrayals of women as sexual objects such as 'page 3 girls' in popular newspapers and 'girlie' magazines, as well as in movies and advertising. However, even where feminist studies found no evidence of overt bias against or objectification of women in mass media, or media portrayals of women changing for the better, they allege that mass media reinforce male supremacy and subjugate women. Weatherall (1996, p. 77) examined the popular British soap opera *Coronation Street* and concluded: 'I found that scripts of . . . *Coronation Street* provided virtually no evidence of pervasive bias against women in language. Nevertheless, in particular scenes language was used in a way that assumed women's secondary status in society.

An extensive study of European TV soap operas by O'Donnell found that women were portrayed frequently and often in primary roles in 'soaps', but concluded:

> the matriarchal figures of so many soaps may be an expression of the structural weakness of women in contemporary European societies rather than of their personal strength. They are allowed to be strong when their strength has been depoliticized and others are struggling as they struggled before. The disappearance of men is irrelevant since the structures which gave them power as individuals remain in place. If soaps are a women's genre, their initial message may be flattering, but their ultimate message would appear to be survival in a battle where the other side's troops may disappear or retire but whose generals and heavy artillery remain primed for action off-screen. (1999, p. 224)

O'Donnell's explicit references to 'the other side's troops' and her military metaphors of 'troops', 'generals', 'heavy artillery' and 'battle' indicate a somewhat hostile position towards men and are suggestive of a gender war which is part of some feminist discourse, despite protestations to the contrary. Also, her conclusion that leading parts are given to women, but that is only because men are standing in the wings ready to take over if or when they choose, is a subjective deduction beyond the data.

Neuendorf (2002) cites a number of studies of gender role portrayals in mass media, including Greenberg (1980), Kalis and Neuendorf (1989), Weaver (1991), Drewniany (1996), Michelson (1996), Watkins (1996), Barner (1999), Lemish and Tidhar (1999) and Low and Sherrard (1999), and concludes that most gender-oriented studies of the media have found a 'message environment of androcentrism' (male domination), 'with males heavily overrepresented in sheer numbers and routinely given more important roles and sex stereotyping' (2002, p. 202).

Some feminists and women writers acknowledge that gender representations are changing. Caroline Regidor (2003b) writing on popular culture, particularly TV shows, states: 'Usually the camera, represents the male gaze, hence female figures are the subject of voyeurism in cinema history – think "Lolita".' However, in commenting on the popular TV series *Idol*, Regidor acknowledges that 'when the camera "pervs" on Millsy [a male contestant], the gaze is female' (2003b, p. 24).

Macdonald (1995, p. 90) cites major changes in mass media representations of women from the late 1980s through the 1990s: 'Believing both that feminism's battles had been won, and that its ideology was now harmless by virtue of being out of date, advertisers invented 'post-feminism' as a utopia where women could do whatever they pleased, provided they had sufficient will and enthusiasm'. It is questionable whether advertisers invented postfeminism and Macdonald's assertion that advertisers believe feminist ideology is out of date and harmless is not substantiated. However, Macdonald does identify a significant change in representations of women in mass media over the past decade or so.

A 1995–96 study by Lauzen and Dozier found 43 per cent of major characters in TV shows are women – up from 18 per cent in 1992–93 (Gauntlett, 2002, p. 58). The study examined the roles of women and men and found that, on a character-by-character basis, females and males were equal in all criteria studied (Gauntlett, 2002, p. 59). Gauntlett comments: 'the woman we expect to see in ads these days is the busy, confident, attractive success, in control of her professional and social life, and a kitchen slave to no one. Men do not tell her what to do; instead, she sometimes gets to have a laugh at the expense of men' (2002, p. 76).

Notwithstanding evidence of a significant change in mass media representations of women, feminist concern over portrayals of women in mass media continues, perhaps with good reason. But, to return to the objective of this study, in this period of change, what are the most prevalent representations of men in mass media? Are they as positive as many gender theorists have claimed? What do they say about men, to men and to societies?

What the past two decades of news, TV and movies have said about men

Busby (1975) conducted a comprehensive study of male images in mass media but, as Neuendorf (2002, p. 202) notes, the research is relatively dated. Other studies show that much has changed since 1975. In the late 1990s and early 2000s, some researchers began to look specifically at men and male identity and, notwithstanding limitations in relation to methodology and sample in some of these studies as noted in Chapter 1, their findings indicate an alarming trend and suggest the need for more study in this area.

Men in the press

Beynon (2002), a Welsh cultural studies academic, examined how masculinity was discursively constructed by the British quality press

(*The Times, Guardian, Sunday Times*) and in books such as Susan Faludi's *Stiffed: The Betrayal of Modern Man* and Anthony Clare's *Masculinity in Crisis* during 1999–2001. Beynon reported that four discursive themes were evident in media content of which the two key ones were:

1. 'Men running wild', such as bad fathers avoiding responsibility for their children or absentee fathers, men committing atrocities in places such as Rwanda and the former Yugoslavia; and
2. 'Emasculated men' such as portrayed on *Men Behaving Badly* and in TV commercials where men were depicted as 'utterly incompetent and infantile' (2002, p. 143).

Beynon concluded that representations of men are overwhelmingly negative in mass media, 'something dangerous to be contained, attacked, denigrated or ridiculed, little else' (2002, p. 143).

Men are also increasingly objectified and trivialized in women's magazines in the way that women were in men's magazines in the past. Gauntlett (2002) cites:

- *Cosmopolitan* magazine's 'Hunk of the Month' feature and naked male centrefolds published in the US edition in 2001.
- *Elle's* July 2001 US cover offering 'Hola boys: Eye candy for grown-up girls'.
- *B's* 'Lust' page showing male film and media stars.
- *New Woman's* 'Bloke' section.
- *More's* 'Men Unzipped' section and its male centrefold wearing only skimpy underwear.

Men on TV

A pioneering 1990 study of media representations of men by Askew and Ross (cited in West, 1995) reported that 'most of the male heroes in comics and on television, whether goodies or baddies, are violent'. Katz (cited in Newbold et al., 2002, p. 291) reports that 'violence on screen, like that in real life, is perpetrated overwhelmingly by males'.

One of the more contemporary and cogent analyses of mass media representations of men, already cited extensively, is provided by Nathanson and Young (2001) who used an art historical approach of formal analysis to examine mass media treatment of men and male identity, particularly on television and in movies. They state that, by the 1990s, misandry had become pervasive on American television (2001, p. 10). They point to TV programmes such as *The Simpsons* in which the father character, Homer, is lazy at work, chauvinistic, irresponsible and often stupid, and the son, Bart, is mischievous, rude, cruel to his sister, rebellious and naughty. By comparison, the mother and daughter are presented as thoughtful, considerate and mild-natured.

Another TV programme cited by Nathanson and Young as negatively portraying men is *Home Improvement*. They report an interview with star of the show, Tim Allen, by *TV Guide* critic Christopher Loudon who writes: 'Some would argue that *Home Improvement* is all about men being jerks' and 'how smart – and tolerant – women are'. Allen, who made his name in a stand-up comedy called *Men Are Pigs*, agrees that it is both. Just as some women perpetrate negative (mis)representations of women, some men contribute to and even exploit negative (mis)representations of men – in this case for a laugh and popular success. Nathanson and Young comment of *Home Improvement*: 'men in general are slobs and fools but can be trained or "housebroken" by women... without the civilising influence of Jill's feminist lessons, Tim would be just another male barbarian' (2001, p. 40). They add: 'Everything specifically identified as "masculine" on *Home Improvement* is overtly mocked, not celebrated... *Home Improvement* propagates exceptionally crude stereotypes of men' (2001, p. 41).

Men Behaving Badly, a British television programme broadcast in 1996–97, was a turning point in a trend of negative representations of men, according to Nathanson and Young. As the title suggests, it presents a litany of men's bad behaviour. Macdonald and Crawford (2002) agree, saying: 'TV shows as *The Simpsons*, *Home Improvement* and... *Men Behaving Badly* – which blatantly says it all – show negative images of men and boys – that men are incompetent'.

In his review of gender in contemporary TV programmes, Gauntlett (2002) points to three popular programmes as examples of a 'turning of the tide' that has occurred in relation to representations of women and men:

- *Ally McBeal* (1997–2002) who, Gauntlett notes, is a successful professional woman in a lead role focused on a quest for sex, pleasure and romantic love. 'Ally's colleagues, Ling and Nelle are tougher, and both have been out with men from the law firm who are typically portrayed as rather geeky and lacking self-assurance. The show sides with the women and often shows them making fun of the men' (2002, p. 60).
- *Sex and the City* (1998–2003) in which Gauntlett says female ridicule and objectification of men is taken further with 'male sexual

performance . . . subject to laughter and scathing review' (2002, p. 60). The four main women portrayed in *Sex and the City*, Carrie, Miranda, Samantha and Charlotte, regularly discuss men in disparaging tones, rating their sexual performance, objectifying them as 'studs' for women's pleasure and often deriding them as insensitive, shallow and stupid. Feminists argue that *Sex and the City* celebrates women's sexual liberation and that they only do what men did in the past. However, there is evidence of a reverse double standard in this. Women argued against such stereotyped and discriminatory portrayals, not on the basis that women should have equal access to such roles and forms of behaviour, but that such portrayals and behaviours were wrong – misrepresentations and sexist. As such, it should hold that they are equally wrong when applied to men.

- *NYPD Blue* (1993–2002) centred on the main detective character, Andy Sipowicz. When he was first introduced, Sipowicz was 'a stereotypical stout, sleazy, bigoted, divorced recovering alcoholic cop' (Gauntlett, 2002, p. 62). Even though the character has mellowed over the years – Sipowicz grieved over the death of his grownup son, he showed joy at the birth of his child, Theo, and a protective love and loyalty to his professional partners Kelly and Sorenson – men in the show are principally portrayed as tightly wound, angry, deficient humans exhibiting negative traits including alcoholism, gambling and violence.

Veronica's Closet is another TV show that, along with *Sex and the City* and *Grace Under Fire*, is largely about women's 'hunt for men' and in which men are objectified and trivialized, according to Newbold et al. (2002, p. 250). In these shows women discuss men as sex objects, often in crude and explicit terms in the fashion that women have long criticized men for doing in relation to women.

Nathanson and Young also identify television news magazines as sources of negative portrayals of men. They conclude from their analysis:

> The problem of journalistic bias – and, therefore, of manipulation – has been discussed many times from perspectives of both the right and the left. There is probably truth to complaints from both sides. When it comes to gender and relations between men and women, however, the bias usually favours women. It would be unthinkable for a journalist, except one willing to pay a high price in public hostility, to say anything that could be construed as unflattering or disadvantageous to women as a group . . . but things like that are routinely said about men. (2001, p. 69)

They instance the NBC *Today* show feature series 'He and She' in which people are interviewed about differences between men and women. Nathanson and Young (2002, p. 73) report: 'One woman, Marna LoCastro, has the nerve to go on national television and proclaim the superiority of women in blatantly stereotypical ways: "I think that we're more sensitive. I think we're more emotional. I think we're more, more caring. I think we're more dependable than males. I do"'. While this statement was made by a woman interviewee and not the programme's presenters, it is part of the content of news magazines, and Nathanson and Young comment that it is typical of statements made about men in popular discourse and an example of 'superiority feminism' that is prevalent in modern societies.

Men in the movies

A number of studies have reported on examinations of men in movies, including *Screening the Male* (Cohan and Hark, 1993), *You Tarzan: Masculinity, Movies and Men* (Kirkham and Thumim, 1993) and *Me Jane: Masculinity, Movies and Women* (Kirkham and Thumim, 1995). Also, some feminist studies of mass media portrayals of women have included an examination of men in movies including *Feminism and Film* (Humm, 1997) and *Working Girls: Gender and Sexuality in Popular Cinema* (Tasker, 1998).

A number of top-rating movies were analysed by Nathanson and Young (2001) and found to contain highly derogatory and negative representations of men and male identity. Their examples included:

- *The Color Purple* (1985), based on Alice Walker's best-selling novel, is a film in which 'every male character, without exception, is either a hopelessly stupid buffoon, a fiendishly evil tyrant or both. And every female character, without exception, is a purely innocent victim, a quietly enduring hero, or both' (Nathanson and Young, 2001, p. 13).
- *Thelma and Louise* (1991) presents overriding negative messages about men. Early in the movie, Thelma is the victim of an attempted rape by a man, whom Louise then shoots. During their drive to escape a murder charge, Thelma meets JD, a young man who asks for a lift but who, after seducing her, runs off with her money. On their journey, a truck driver makes lewd gestures at the two women. Feigning interest, they pull over then give him a lecture on sexist behaviour and, when he responds angrily, blow up his truck and drive off laughing. In the final scene, the two women commit suicide by driving over a cliff

rather than live in a world of men – Thelma with her boorish carpet salesman husband to whom she is unhappily married and Louise with her long-standing boyfriend Jim.

- *Silence of the Lambs* (1991) is 'a feminist discourse on male violence' which addresses gender in at least three way, Nathanson and Young say (2001, p. 158). It tells the story of two killers: Buffalo Bill, who kills only women, skins them and clothes himself in their skin, carrying a clear sub-text of violence by men against women and appropriation of women's identity' and Lecter, who kills both men and women and eats them. While the sub-text is less overtly sexist, it carries a clear message of male violence. The third gender dimension to the movie is portrayed in the relationship between the female lead and her male colleagues. Her male supervisor lacks confidence in her ability to do the job; and the official in charge of Lecter in the asylum to which he is confined, Dr Chilton, is 'openly lascivious', Nathanson and Young note. In short, all the men in the film are evil.

- In the contemporary version of *Beauty and the Beast* (1991), maleness is openly associated with beastliness. The movie was identified in *Premiere* magazine as one of the ten movies that defined gender in the 1990s. The original story of *Beauty and the Beast* is based on a translation of a 1756 text by Jeanne Marie (Madame le Prince) de Beaumont which, in turn, is believed to be based on earlier literary works and oral traditions (Nathanson and Young, 2001, p. 162). In the original version, the Beast is an educated and refined gentleman who gives Beauty every comfort she could want. However, in the 1991 Disney version, the prince is selfish and cruel and is punished by a good fairy. To make sure the message is clear, he is described explicitly in voice-over as 'spoiled, selfish and unkind'. Furthermore, the Disney version adds a character, Gaston, who is a village bully and braggart. 'Vain, ignorant, arrogant and preposterously macho, Gaston excels at hunting, brawling, drinking, and spitting', Nathanson and Young note. On the other hand, Beauty's evil sisters are eliminated from the story in the remake. So the story is one of two bad men and a flawless Beauty, Belle. She is compassionate towards the Beast despite his flaws, intelligent (a bookworm), ambitious and heroic in confronting the Beast. *Beauty and the Beast* informs study of representations of gender in modern mass media. Even though the Beast reforms at the end, the movie says positive things to girls and women and negative things to and about men – that maleness confers bestiality, inferiority and dependence (on a good woman to save him). All negativity in the film is projected on to men.

- *Sleeping with the Enemy* (1991) also contains overt gender discourse which is negative towards men, according to Nathanson and Young (2001). The male character, Martin, is shown searching for his wife, Laura, at a carnival wearing a black cape with an upturned collar, set against a hellish background of glowing, swirling, flame-coloured lights – a clear metaphor for Satan, the Devil. Cape Cod is shown as an alienating world representing patriarchy, while Cedar Falls to which Laura travels is a beautiful little town in Iowa of soft images and harmony representing matriarchy, where Laura meets two older women and forms an association. Nathanson and Young point out that sexual hierarchy is not eliminated, simply reversed. The movie demonizes Martin instead of presenting him as a psychopath in need of treatment and manipulates viewers towards revenge and anger so they want Laura to pull the trigger and kill him (2001, pp. 169–79).
- *Cape Fear* is another 1991 movie in which men are represented in highly negative ways. Of the two male characters, one is a convicted rapist who went to prison and the other is his lawyer who buried evidence that could have won his case. On his release, the former rapist sets out to take revenge on the lawyer and his family, killing his dog, raping his lover and pursuing his teenage daughter. 'All major female characters are good. They are victims . . . men have only one thing on their minds. The central theme of Cape Fear is that violence against women is caused by a cultural order created by men obsessed with women,' say Nathanson and Young (2001, pp. 186–7).
- *Little Women* in its 1994 remake by Gillian Armstrong substantially changed the character of the father from a wise, mature figure of moral integrity who left a deep and positive impression on the young women in the novel to a shadowy character who is incidental to the story. While the story is ostensibly about women, women's roles in the remake are enhanced, while men's roles are reduced and male characters demonized.
- *First Wives Club* (1996) is another film with clear anti-men overtones. In the story, three women who are allegedly treated badly by their respective husbands decide to get even. The movie is a humorous but vindictive story of how badly men act and how women are superior morally, politically and even professionally – as the women succeed in a matter of months in taking over and running their husbands' businesses in which they have no prior experience.

Nathanson and Young (2001) identify negative representations of men not only in fictional mass media, but also distorted and negative representations of men in allegedly factual media representations. They give as a cinematic example *The Long Walk Home* (1990). This tells of the early days of the civil rights struggle by and for black Americans. While sophisticated and meritorious in many of its aspects, the film represents the civil rights movement as 'initiated, led, and fought for by black women, not by black women and men' and portrays white women as supportive of black women, while 'every white man, without exception, is both evil and inadequate' (2001, p. 119). This is contrary to substantial documented history which reports that black men played leading roles in the US civil rights movement and that some white men as well as some white women supported their position. Also, some women, including feminists, did *not* support emancipation. Ann Douglas (1990) controversially points out that, while some white women did support civil rights for black women, white American suffragists of the late nineteenth and early twentieth centuries were anything but eager to secure the vote for black women. In fact, she says, 'white women won the vote by playing to the nation's anti-Negro sentiments' (1990, p. 254). The film rewrites history from a particular gender political perspective – and specifically writes men out of positive roles as protagonists and into negative roles as antagonists.

Nathanson and Young note that media representation, as well as allegedly reflecting and informing societies today, also 'projects the present – in this case, any notion of gender (or, even by implication, sex itself) that happens to be either fashionable or controversial right now – into the past as 'history' and [into] the future as 'science fiction' or "speculative fiction"' (2001, p. 108). An effect of popular culture not well understood is this long-term reshaping of reality through revisionist history and projected agendas. They cite *The Long Walk Home* as a case in point.

An example of negative representations of men projected into the future is the science fiction movie *Outer Limits*, set in the year 2055 when a goddess rules a paradise called Lithia (Earth in the future), assisted by her wise women. In fact, there are no men at all on Lithia; they have been wiped out in a 'great war'. Nathanson and Young note: 'Little girls are told explicitly, in a stereotypically hushed and soothing female voice, that the old order was destroyed because of men.' The narrative of the film states: 'And when the males of the earth had vanished, so, too, did wickedness and war and hatred' (2001, pp. 108–10). Never mind the contradiction that the goddess, a symbol of female empathy and compassion, consigned seven billion men to death.

Nathanson and Young point out that recent series of *Star Trek* have altered the famous signature slogan 'To boldly go where no man has gone before' to 'To go where no *one* has gone before'. Reasonable, it might be concluded. But, in comparison, they point out that *The Shadow* (1994) in its remake retained its slogan 'Who knows what evil lurks in the hearts of men' (2001, p. 234). The slogan could easily have been altered to 'Who knows what evil lurks in the hearts of people?' But it was not. Sexist language against women is removed or rewritten in the media. But sexist language denigrating or disparaging men remains, or is added, as evidenced by these analyses.

Craig (1993) observed that 'softer' male characters and so-called 'reconstructed males' began appearing in prime-time media in the 1990s and Newbold et al. (2002) note that 'media representations of men and masculinity(ies) have . . . changed over the years; they are more varied and include, for example, "softer" images of masculinity'. However, they add that 'particularly in relation to sport and situation comedies, the representation of hegemonic masculinity . . . still prevails in many media texts'. They also note that 'gay and lesbian media representations have, for a long while, been minimal and, in most cases, highly stereotypical' (2002, p. 294). Newbold et al. conclude that 'non-hegemonic forms of masculinity are being marginalized' and that 'many studies show that the media still tend to reinforce the dominant ideology of masculinity and fail to portray the changing cultural norms of masculinity' (2002, pp. 291, 289).

Where men are not being marginalized, demonized or trivialized, 'new age' representations of men suggest that they should become more feminine. As an example, Gauntlett cites the film *What Women Want* (2000) which shows a man (played by Mel Gibson) as insensitive and sexist before undergoing an epiphany and learning to think like a woman. While the film also contains stereotypical images of women, Gauntlett notes that it 'assumes that women are emotionally articulate, and asserts that men should be too' – implying that normally they are not (2002, p. 70).

Gauntlett also observes that analysis of men's magazines reveals that the publications are 'perpetually concerned with how to treat women, have a good relationship and live an enjoyable life'. But, rather than attempting to show men how to be men in this process, 'men's magazines have an almost obsessive relationship with the socially constructed nature of manhood'. They urge men to become more feminized – more like women – and more like what women want them to become (2002, p. 250). It is informative that mass media laud women to be women (be themselves), but advocate the reconstruction of men.

Other media analyses which have examined gender issues over the past few decades (in date order) include:

- Goffman (1976) – a study of gender in advertisements.
- Allen (1985) – a study of soap operas.
- Stirling (1987) – a study of language and gender in Australian newspapers.
- Lovdal (1989) – a study of sex role messages in television commercials.
- Geraghty (1991) – a study of women in prime-time soap operas.
- McKay and Huber (1992) – a study of media images of technology and sport.
- Gill (1993) – a study of broadcasters' accounts of inequality in radio.
- Messner, Duncan and Jensen (1993) – a study of gendered language in televised sports.
- Hawes and Thomas (1995) – a study of language bias against women in British and Malaysian newspapers.
- Elasmar, Hasegawa and Brain (1999) – a study of the portrayal of women in American prime-time television.

What is clear from studies of mass media representations of women and men in the past two decades that have been reviewed are:

1. While representations of women continue to remain a subject of debate, there has been a ground-shift during the second half of the 1990s and early 2000s from stereotyped, marginalized, trivialized and objectified representations of women to portrayal of women in increasingly positive, powerful, autonomous roles and identities and even as heroes and superheroes – although it is not disputed that portrayals of women should further improve.
2. A double standard is emerging: while it has become less acceptable or unacceptable to objectify, trivialize, marginalize or otherwise negatively represent women, it appears to be increasingly common and popular to portray men and male identity in highly negative ways.

Statements by prominent women about men further illustrate the open licence that appears to exist for denigrating men in public. Noteworthy examples are:

- 'Women have to learn how to kick men in the crotch' (Dr Martha Beck, life coach and author on *Oprah*, 25 September 2003).

- 'What's the point of a husband. I mean, who needs two babies?' (Julie in *Sex and the City*, the book).
- 'I totally agree. Except that now I want to have another baby. I was thinking of getting rid of my husband' (Janice's response in *Sex and the City*, the book).

Faludi (2000, p. 41) acknowledges: 'In the past half century, Madison Avenue, Hollywood and the mass media have operated relentlessly on men, too. The level of mockery, suspicion and animosity directed at men who step out of line is profound, and men respond profoundly . . . '.

As noted in Chapter 1 and shown by the research cited in this chapter, the majority of gender studies of media content have focused on entertainment media, particularly movies and television drama, as well as advertising. These findings are important as popular movies reach audiences of 100 million or more and top-rating TV programmes such as *Sex and the City*, *Ally McBeal*, *Home Improvement*, *The Simpsons*, and so on, also have massive reach, attracting audiences in the US alone of 20–30 million and many more worldwide. However, only one of the media programmes cited – the NBC *Today* show feature series 'He and She' reviewed by Nathanson and Young – was non-fiction allowing examination of how men are portrayed in allegedly factual media representations. Excuses that can be made, or latitude that can be claimed, for TV sit-coms, films and comedy shows – it's just entertainment, it's only done in jest, etc. – do not apply to news, current affairs and other non-fiction media. These genre allegedly tell 'the truth' about how the world is and what is happening in societies. In short, they represent 'reality' to millions of people every day. These important media genre are examined in detail in a major study reported in the next chapter.

6
Men in the Media Today – A Contemporary Study

Because of the lack of research examining mass media portrayals of men and male identity relative to studies of portrayals of women, the methodological limitations and weaknesses of some studies that have been conducted, and the paucity of analysis of news, current affairs, talk shows and lifestyle media as outlined in Chapter 2, a major analysis of the content of these mass media genre was conducted to examine representations of men and male identity as part of a doctoral thesis at the University of Western Sydney in 2003–4. The conduct of this research as part of an accepted PhD (Macnamara, 2005) attests to the rigour of the methodology and independent examiner review applied in this study.

While this study was conducted in Australia, the findings have international implications, particularly in major Western societies, for three reasons:

1. Several of the news, current affairs, talk and lifestyle TV programmes analysed are broadcast internationally with exactly or substantially the same content (eg. *60 Minutes*, *Oprah* and *Queer Eye for the Straight Guy*). The full media sample is listed in Table 6.1.
2. A number of magazines analysed are also international or contain substantial international content (eg. *FHM* and *Cosmopolitan*).
3. Many articles in Australian newspapers analysed were sourced from international services including Reuters, Associated Press and Agence France Pressé and many were syndicated from international newspapers including *The Times*, *Telegraph* and *Guardian* in the UK and the *New York Times* and other publications in the US.

Methodology and approach

Both quantitative and qualitative media content analysis were undertaken, based on the widely accepted guidelines of Kimberley Neuendorf (2002), Neuman (1997), Curran (2002), Gauntlett (2002), Newbold et al. (2002) and other media scholars who advocate the benefits of both types of content analysis. Silverman (2000) says, 'the days of the great divide between qualitative and quantitative research have now largely passed' and cites Bryman (1988) and Hammersley (1992), who also advocate that the two forms of analysis can be helpfully combined (2000, p. 157).

Quantitative content analysis was undertaken to bring a level of scientific reliability to the research which is not possible in small sample qualitative studies. As Hansen et al. (1998, p. 91) comment:

> rather than emphasising its alleged incompatibility with other more qualitative approaches (such as semiotics, structuralist analysis, discourse analysis) ... content analysis is and should be enriched by the theoretical framework offered by other more qualitative approaches, while bringing to these a methodological rigor, prescriptions for use, and systematicity rarely found in many of the more qualitative approaches.

Similarly, Jackson (1998) concludes: 'A beneficial synthesis of quantitative and qualitative methodologies ... allows a wide range and quantity of communications and their contexts to be analyzed and compared with rigor and structure'.

Shoemaker and Reese's (1996) categorization of a humanist approach which studies mass media content as a reflection of society and culture, and a behaviourist approach which analyses media content with a view to its likely effects, is also useful in understanding how media content analysis should be conducted and what conclusions and implications can be deduced. Whereas the behaviourist approach looks forwards from media content to try to identify future effects, the humanist approach looks backwards from media content to try to identify what is says about society and the culture producing it. Shoemaker and Reese say that social scientists taking a behaviourist approach to content analysis rely mostly on quantitative content analysis, while humanist approaches to media content tend towards qualitative analysis.

This study is interested in examining mass media representations of men and male identities both to identify possible effects on society and as a 'window' to view reflections of popular culture and contemporary

societies – i.e. it seeks to employ both behaviourist and humanist traditions identified by Shoemaker and Reese.

The methodology employed was extensively outlined in the PhD
thesis reporting the research (Macnamara, 2005). Key elements only are
summarized here to demonstrate the rigour of the research and under-
score the validity and reliability of findings.

Quantitative media content analysis was planned and conducted in
accordance with key steps essential in 'the scientific method' as outlined
by Neuendorf (2002). Reading and coding of articles was done by
humans, not computers. Even though computers enhance research in
many respects and advanced automated systems have been developed
as identified by Silverman (2000, p. 155), Neuendorf (2002, p. 40) notes
that 'the notion of the completely 'automatic' content analysis via
computer is a chimera . . . The human contribution to content analysis
is still paramount'.

Close attention was paid to objectivity, validity, generalizability and
replicability – key elements for reliable quantitative research. While true
objectivity may be impossible as Grbich (2004) and other poststructuralist researchers say, research should minimize subjectivity or achieve
intersubjectivity as discussed by Babbie (1986, p. 27) and Lindlof (cited in
Neuendorf, 2002, p. 11). This was done through three key steps:

- *A priori design* – A priori design of the research established the
  categories, issues and messages for analysis in a coding list (also called
  a coding book). This was done based on extensive preliminary reading
  of media content on the subject and review of literature in the field
  which Neuendorf (2002, pp. 102–3) says allows the researcher to
  'immerse himself or herself in the world of the message pool'. This
  grounded theory approach (Glaser and Strauss, 1967; Strauss and
  Corbin, 1990) focused the research on relevant variables, rather than
  issues selected ad hoc, and reduced subjectively during the research.
  The coding list used in this study is provided in Appendix A.
- *Use of multiple coders (readers)* – Two coders were used throughout the
  analysis and both male and female coders were used to offset gender
  bias. Following human coding, data were entered into a specialist
  media content analysis system, CARMA® (Computer Aided Research
  and Media Analysis) for quantitative analysis). Details of the CARMA
  system are provided in Appendix B.
- *Intercoder reliability assessment* – A number of articles were 'blind'-
  coded by both coders (i.e. without seeing the other's coding) and data
  compared to ensure that, in the words of Tinsley and Weiss (1975,

p. 359), 'obtained ratings are not the idiosyncratic results of one rater's subjective judgement'. The research employed a number of recommended measures of agreement and co-variance and high levels (0.8 and higher) of intercoder reliability were achieved. Where less than recommended levels of intercoder reliability were achieved, media content was recoded or the data excluded. The statistical formulae used to measure intercoder reliability for this study and statistical results of intercoder reliability assessment are reported in Appendix C.

Validity of this research was optimized by extensive literature review including reading the latest texts on content analysis methodology, reviewing gender studies and theory as outlined in Chapter 3, and a review of previous media analysis studies in relation to gender as outlined in Chapter 5.

Key steps to maximize generalizability were employed, including selecting a large representative sample, using rigorous coding methods, and conducting intercoder reliability assessment. This study is considered to have a high level of generalizabilty due to the large sample of national and international media and rigorous methodology employed.

Replicability mostly depends on open disclosure of information about research methodology and procedures and, for this purpose, the coding list, media sample and methodology were fully disclosed in Appendices to the doctoral thesis reporting the research. Summaries are provided in appendices to this text.

Sampling was informed by the work of Riffe, Lacy and Drager (1996) and Riffe et al. (1996), although the sample selected greatly exceeded most recommendations in order to maximize the reliability and generalizabilty of the study. News was defined, for the purposes of this study, as all general news in selected newspapers, including features, opinion columns, editorials and letters to the editor (but excluding specialist sections such as business, finance, sport and entertainment which have been studied elsewhere), as well as TV news bulletins and news-related media content, including current affairs TV programmes and magazines. Also, a selection of lifestyle media including men's and women's magazines was included because these media directly address gender and identity issues such as body image and sexuality. Several leading TV talk and lifestyle programmes were also selected because of their large audiences and relevant content. The sample of media studied is fully outlined and the basis of sampling explained in Appendix D.

Six leading newspapers, including their magazine inserts, six magazines and six TV programmes were monitored and analysed over a period of six months from 1 July to 24 December 2003. Table 6.1 provides a summary of the sample of national and international media studied. From this sample, a total of 650 newspapers (450 broadsheets and 200 tabloids), 130 magazines and 332.5 hours of television news, current affairs, talk shows and lifestyle programming were analysed.

Following the quantitative analysis of a broad sample of mass media, a sub-sample was selected for in-depth qualitative content analysis to gain

Table 6.1   Summary of media content collected for 2003–4 study (Macnamara, 2005)

Media	Frequency	1 July –24 December 2003
Newspapers:		Editions
The Australian	Daily Mon–Sat (6 per week)	150
Sydney Morning Herald	Daily Mon–Sat (6 per week)	150
The Age	Daily Mon–Sat (6 per week)	150
Daily Telegraph	Daily Mon–Sat (6 per week)	150
Sunday Telegraph	Sunday	25
Sunday Age	Sunday	25
Total Newspapers		**650**
Magazines:		Editions
The Bulletin	Weekly	25
Australian Women's Weekly	Monthly (*despite title*)	6
Cosmopolitan	Monthly	6
Ralph	Monthly	6
FHM	Monthly	6
Family Circle	Monthly	6
Good Weekend Magazine	In Sat *SM Herald* & *Age*	25
The Australian Magazine	In Sat *Australian*	25
Sunday Magazine	In *Sunday Telegraph*	25
Total Magazines		**130**
Television:		Hours
Nine News	Mon-Fri (5 x 30 mins pw)	62.5
A Current Affair	Mon-Fri (5 x 30 mins pw)	62.5
60 Minutes	Sunday (1 hour per week)	(*Off air 1st week Dec*) 22
Oprah	Mon-Fri (5 x 1 hour pw)	125
Frasier	Mon-Fri (5 x 30 mins pw)	(*Off air end Nov*) 52.5
Queer Eye . . . Straight Guy	Monday (1 hour per week)	(*29 Sep– 30 Nov*) 8
Total TV (hours)		**332.5**

a deeper insight into likely meanings and interpretations of the texts. McKee (2004) notes that the methodology of qualitative content and text analysis is poorly defined. He says: 'we have a very odd lacuna at the heart of cultural studies of the media. Textual analysis is the central methodology, and yet we do not have a straightforward published guide as to what it is and how we do it'.

Despite this lack of specific guidelines for qualitative text and content analysis, research procedures for qualitative text and message analysis are informed by the work of Denzin and Lincoln (1994), Hijams (1996), Mayring (2000; 2003), Patton (1990; 2002), Robson (1993) and Silverman (1993). Within the broad hermeneutic tradition concerned with text analysis, there are two main strands particularly relevant to qualitative content analysis. The first, narratology, focuses on the narrative or story-telling within a text with emphasis on the meaning that may be produced by its structure and choice of words. The second draws on semiotics and focuses attention on signs and sign systems in texts and how readers might interpret (decode) those signs and what they might say about the subjects (Newbold et al., 2002, p. 84).

Mayring (2003) notes that several computer programs have been developed for qualitative analysis, but stresses that these are to 'support (not to replace) steps of text interpretation'. In this study, manual (human) qualitative text analysis of a sample of texts was conducted, supported by additional analysis using MAXqda (MAX Qualitative Data Analysis for Windows) (dressing&pehl GbR & Verbi GmbH, 2004).

Sampling for qualitative analysis is not required to meet the statistically valid formulae of quantitative analysis. Nevertheless, sampling for in-depth qualitative study should not be simply drawn at the researcher's whim, and even random methods may not yield useful data, as the purpose of qualitative research is to investigate certain issues or themes in detail. Random or even representative methods of sampling may not capture the issues or themes which are the subject of qualitative analysis. Miles and Huberman (1994, p. 34) suggest three techniques which can be used together to yield rich results in qualitative analysis:

1. selecting apparently typical/representative examples;
2. selecting negative/disconfirming examples; and
3. selecting exceptional or discrepant examples.

By choosing a combination of typical, disconfirming and exceptional examples for study, qualitative analysis can explore the boundaries of the data field and identify the range of views, including discordant ones and extremes in various directions, as well as the typical. While quantitative research has the benefit of yielding empirical data that is generalizable and representative with a high probability, it reduces research findings to the average or median position on key questions. Qualitative analysis using the sampling approach identified by Miles and Huberman allows exploration of discourse at various points within the range.

Overall findings

A total of 1,799 articles and programme segments discussing men and male identity were found in the media sample during the sample period, comprised of 1,568 newspaper and magazine articles and 231 television reports or programme segments. As could be expected, the largest proportion of editorial media content was news articles (63 per cent). Significantly, this was followed by 232 opinion columns discussing men and male identity issues (13 per cent of total coverage) – a sign of substantial focus on men and men's issues in topical debate. TV news and feature articles each comprised 7 per cent of media content analysed; letters to the editor 4 per cent; TV current affairs reports 3 per cent, while 43 TV talk show and lifestyle programme segments comprised 2 per cent and editorials 1 per cent.

'All men are bastards', a popular desk calendar aphorism cited by West (1995), sums up the image of men portrayed in mass media studied. Analysis found that men are overwhelmingly represented negatively in mass media news, current affairs, talk shows and lifestyle media, with 69 per cent of mass media reporting and commentary on men unfavourable, compared with just 12 per cent favourable and 19 per cent neutral or balanced (see Figure 6.1).

Leading male profiles in the media

Media representations of men were categorized into profiles (overall themes) to gain an overview of the dominant images or portrayals of men and male identities. A total of 1,776 of the 1,799 media articles and program segments analysed contained an identifiable profile or theme. The leading profiles of men are shown in Figure 6.2.

Men are predominately portrayed in mass media as villains, aggressors, perverts and philanderers. More than 75 per cent of all mass media representations of men and male identity categorized into profiles

Media coverage overview

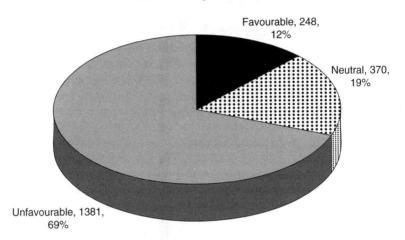

Figure 6.1   Overview of favourable, neutral and unfavourable media coverage of men and male identity. (*Note*: the chart shows 'mentions' which may total more than the number of articles analysed as some articles discuss men or male identity in relation to more than one subject.)

portrayed men in one of these four ways. In total, more than 80 per cent of media profiles of men were negative, compared with 18.4 per cent of content which showed positive profiles or themes. A full breakdown of the positive and negative profiles of men and male identities are shown in Tables 6.2 and 6.3.

The proportion of unfavourable reporting of men in most of the leading profiles was very high and the proportion of neutral/balanced reporting was low as shown in Figure 6.3 – i.e. media coverage is heavily polarized. There is little equivocation in relation to men in the media; they are predominantly evil. The main subject categories (topics) reported in relation to men that contributed to these profiles or themes are shown in Figure 6.3.

Men are mostly reported in mass media news, current affairs, talk shows and lifestyle media in relation to violence and aggression. A total of 1,178 articles out of 1,799 analysed (65 per cent) reported men as violent or aggressive. A breakdown of the types of violence and aggression reported in relation to men is provided in Figure 6.4.

Most subject categories (the main topics of coverage) identified in Figure 6.3 were reported unfavourably, as shown by the breakdown of volume of articles by favourable, neutral and unfavourable in columns

100

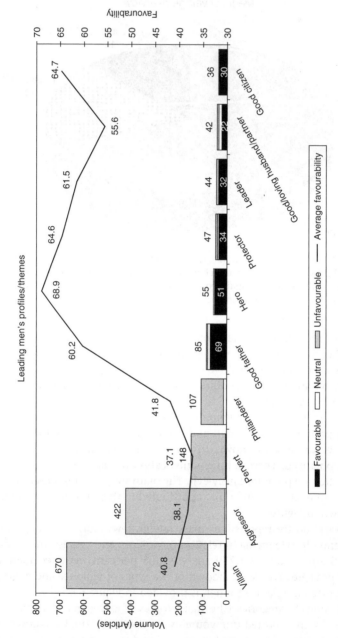

Figure 6.2 Leading profiles/themes in mass media representations of men

Table 6.2 Leading positive profiles/themes concerning men in mass media representations

Positive Profiles/Themes (+)	Number of Articles	% of Total Articles	Average Favourability
Good father	85	4.8%	60.2
Hero	55	3.1%	68.9
Protector	47	2.6%	64.6
Leader	44	2.5%	61.5
Good/loving husband/partner	42	2.4%	55.6
Good citizen	36	2.0%	64.7
Good provider	15	0.8%	53.3
Handyman	2	0.1%	47.5
Total	326	18.4%	59.5

Table 6.3 Leading negative profiles/themes concerning men in mass media representations

Negative Profiles/Themes (–)	Number of Articles	% of Total Articles	Average Favourability
Villain	670	37.7%	40.8
Aggressor	422	23.8%	38.1
Pervert	148	8.3%	37.1
Philanderer	107	6.0%	41.8
Power abuser	33	1.9%	37.9
Incompetent fool or lazy	25	1.4%	40.2
Deadbeat dad	24	1.4%	45.2
Workaholic	21	1.2%	46.4
Total	1,450	81.6%	40.9

and the average favourability rating for each subject category (see explanation of favourability and methodology used in Appendix B). Only 'commitment and responsibility' was reported slightly favourably overall. Second to 'violence and aggression', which was overwhelmingly unfavourable, 'fatherhood and family' was reported with a near equal mix of unfavourable and favourable content, while male 'sexuality', 'work and career', men's 'social behaviour' and men's 'physical and mental health' were all reported more unfavourably than favourably.

Figures 6.4–6.12 and associated discussion provide analysis of the various categories of media coverage overviewed in Figure 6.3.

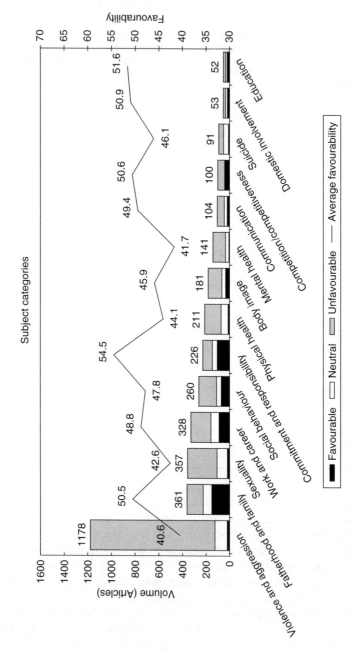

Figure 6.3 Leading issue categories of media reporting on men

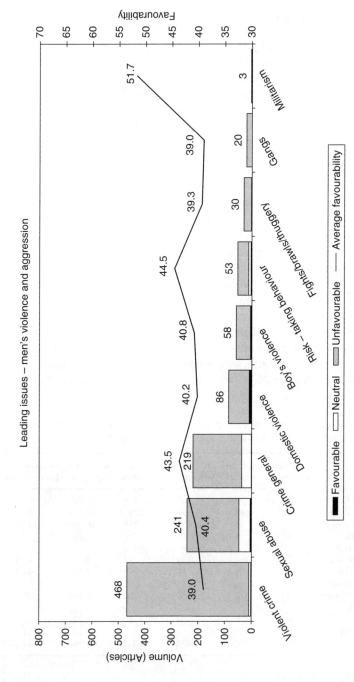

Figure 6.4 Leading issues in mass media reporting of violence and aggression by men

Men and violence

Violent crime, including murder, assault, armed robberies and attacks such as beatings, accounted for almost 40 per cent of all media reporting of male violence and aggression, as shown in Figure 6.4 and supporting Table 6.4. This was followed by sexual abuse (20.5 per cent), general crime (18.6 per cent) and domestic violence (7.3 per cent).

Crime statistics show that many incidents of violence are perpetrated by men and, with good reason, are reported by mass media. During the period of this study, a number of violent crimes drew international and national headlines including:

- The US sniper trial involving ten random murders in the Washington, DC area by two men was widely reported and the guilty verdict and death sentence for the main perpetrator, John Allen Muhammad, was accompanied by graphic reports of how he and his accomplice cold bloodedly shot their victims (National Nine News, 21 October 2003; *The Australian*, 19 November 2003, p. 11 and 26 November 2003, p. 9; *The Age*, 19 November 2003, p. 14).
- Reports of the discovery and release of home video footage of the Columbine school killers practising shooting at targets and boasting of the power of using automatic weapons were broadcast internationally and presented shocking images of male violence (National Nine News, 23 October 2003 and *The Australian*, 24 October 2003, p. 12).

Table 6.4 Leading issues in mass media reporting of violence and aggression by men broken down by favourable, unfavourable and neutral articles

Issues	Favourable Articles	Neutral Articles	Unfavourable Articles	Total Articles	% in This Category	Average Favourability
Violent Crime	2	8	458	468	39.7%	39
Sexual Abuse	5	42	194	241	20.5%	40.4
Crime General	1	36	182	219	18.6%	43.5
Domestic Violence	5	4	77	86	7.3%	40.2
Boy's Violence	1	4	53	58	4.9%	40.8
Risk-Taking Behaviour	3	9	41	53	4.5%	44.5
Fights/Brawls/ Thugs	0	2	28	30	2.5%	39.3
Gangs	0	0	20	20	1.7%	39
Militarism	2	0	1	3	0.3%	51.7
Total	19	105	1,054	1,178	100.0%	40.6

- The trial of 54-year-old Gary Leon Ridgway for the murder of 48 women between 1982 and 2003 in the Seattle area also drew worldwide headlines. Ridgway, who preyed mainly on prostitutes, confessed to the crimes. The case was widely reported and analysed in the media, including full-page features in the *Daily Telegraph* (7 November 2003, p. 31) and *The Australian* (7 November 2003, p. 11) and in major news stories (eg. *The Age*, 7 November 2003, p. 9).
- The disappearance and eventual discovery of the murdered British schoolgirls, Holly Wells and Jessica Chapman, brought wide publicity to another violent man, Ian Huntley. Photographs of the two girls in their red Vodafone-branded soccer shirts and reports of Huntley's cold-blooded murder of the girls appeared in all British media and many Australian media (eg. *The Australian*, 18 December 2003, p. 10).
- In Australia, Bradley John Murdoch, the man accused of murdering the British tourist Peter Falconio in the Northern Territory, was brought to trial in a blaze of headlines and photos of a grimacing and snarling Murdoch on front pages, including *The Age* (11 November 2003, p. 1) headlined 'Man Held over Falconio Case'. The case was also prominently reported in *The Weekend Australian* (15–16 November 2003, p. 3) and the *Daily Telegraph* (15 November 2003, p. 5). Murdoch was later found guilty of the killing.

Mass media also report violence by women. In this study, all media reports on violent crime were collected for analysis (i.e. by men and women perpetrators) to gain a comparison and identify any differences in treatment of men and women on this most prominent issue. This produced 112 additional media reports of female violence (bringing the total media articles analysed to 1,911). Examples of reports of female violence included:

- An elderly male shopkeeper was beaten and stabbed by a 21-year-old female ex-employee. The young woman alleged that the man had sexually harassed her, but the man was shown on television to be very elderly and frail, making the girl's claims seem unlikely (National Nine News, 22 August 2003).
- An American report of girls 'hazing' was broadcast on *Oprah* showing an incident of school girls beating and kicking juniors at Glenbrook North school at Northrock outside Chicago (*Oprah*, 30 July 2003).
- An even more serious case of sustained female violence was the subject of a lengthy *Oprah* interview. Dave Pelzer was reportedly described by US authorities as 'the third most abused child out of

38,000 cases in California'. For more than a decade, Pelzer's mother made him sit on the floor to eat, lie in a bath tub of ice cold water and be tied up for long periods without food. On several occasions, he almost died and was rescued only when his school teachers noted his emaciated condition and found him stealing food. His mother called him 'It' because she did not want to recognize him as human, Pelzer recounted on the show from his book, *A Child Called It* (*Oprah*, 18 November 2003).

Significant research by the child psychologist Peter Smith from the University of London reporting that bullies are just as likely to be girls as boys released at a Monash University forum in Australia was reported in only one Australian media outlet (*The Australian*, 21 November 2003, p. 5).

The most significant case of violent crime by a woman during the period of this study provides an important comparison with representations of male violence. Kathleen Folbigg was arrested, found guilty and sentenced for the murder of all four of her children. The children's deaths all occurred during infancy and Folbigg claimed all were victims of Sudden Infant Death Syndrome (SIDS). As incredulous as the claim was, a case was made that Folbigg should not stand trial for murder or go to prison. It was alleged during the trial she had been the victim of abuse by her father and that this had caused a mental disorder that rendered her not responsible for her actions (National Nine News, 29 August 2003 and numerous press reports). Folbigg was subsequently sentenced to 40 years' imprisonment with no parole, after much heated debate in the court and the media (National Nine News, 24 October 2003). But the case illustrates a significant difference in media treatment and discourse concerning male violence and crime and female violence and crime. The view was widely expressed that, as a mother, Folbigg could not be capable of killing her children unless she was deranged. In the hearing to determine her sentencing, calls for leniency were made on the grounds that her father had made her the way she was. In summary, it was argued that a woman was not capable of such a thing and, if she did it, it was indirectly caused by a man.

Conversely, the case of Stephen Pate, a former Olympian cyclist who was accused and charged for domestic violence, shows a different representation of male violence and crime. In a *60 Minutes* feature story, the reporter Tara Brown set the scene by stating that 'one in every four women are victims of domestic violence'. The programme then presented Pate's wife stating that he systematically 'pulled the curtains, making sure there was no witnesses' to the beatings. Notwithstanding major inconsistencies in the story such as a following statement by Pate's wife that 'he's grabbed me by the hair and I was screaming and he's pulled me to the ground and he's kneeling on me with his knee, hitting me, and I'm screaming in the middle of the front yard', the most contentious element of the *60 Minutes* story was an interview with Christine Nixon, Chief Commissioner of the Victorian Police. Speaking about men who commit domestic violence, Tara Brown asked: 'Do you see them as criminals, or someone who has a problem?' Chief Commissioner Nixon replied: 'No. I see them as criminals. What I think it's about is power' (*60 Minutes*, 31 August 2003). Nixon's statement is in conflict with international research on domestic violence such as that cited in the following media report from *Oprah* and reflects an alarming attitude in a State head of police. Her comment illustrates an attitude to male crime of 'lock them up and throw away the key'. This stands in marked contrast to the Folbigg case in which considerable attention was devoted to trying to understand why she committed the crimes and recognized extenuating circumstances.

Significantly, the same claims by Christine Nixon were repeated on *60 Minutes* in a follow-up report on 7 September 2003 – Fathers' Day. There was no mention of treatment or counselling aimed at prevention or rehabilitation.

While *Oprah* features many programmes reporting on women's fashion, shoes, food and other light topics and is part of the genre of daytime television, a major media report on the issue of domestic violence was presented by *Oprah* during the period of study. 'When families turn violent' and a follow-up one-hour special on the theme of 'Teach people how to treat you to break the cycle of violence' broadcast in October 2003 presented breakthrough research and thinking on this important issue and are worthy of special comment. In the first programme, Oprah Winfrey interviewed a spokesperson from the Tubman Family Alliance Center and Linda Mills, a professor from New York University. Mills is the author of *Insult to Injury: Rethinking Our Responses to Intimate Abuse* and a proponent of different approaches to domestic violence from the previously cited 'lock them up and throw away the key' method. The Tubman Center claims that the traditional way of dealing with domestic violence which 'tells the woman to leave and goes and arrests the abuser' is not working and advocates an approach to 'heal the whole problem'. Mills presented evidence including that around 1,000 women are killed or seriously injured by intimate partners each year in the US. While tragic, this is a relatively small number compared with other victims of crime and in proportion to total incidences of domestic violence. Significantly, she pointed out that 450 men are killed or seriously injured each year by intimate partners. 'Only one to three per cent of violent relationships end in injury', Mills reported, arguing that, based on the statistics, use of policing to address the problem is inappropriate. Mills argued strongly, based on research, that domestic violence is perpetrated by 'men with no ties to the community; men who are unemployed; men who are most likely to get arrested; men who are economically disadvantaged' and pointed out that 'these men, when they are arrested, it actually increases the incidence of violence'. Mandatory arrest does not reduce violence, she said, calling instead for a treatment approach to address the underlying causes of domestic violence (*Oprah*, 21 October 2003).

Oprah Winfrey initially expressed reluctance to accept this view, seeing it as a 'go soft' approach to combating domestic violence. But she visited the Tubman Center and interviewed men undergoing counselling and treatment. Her experiences led to the follow-up programme.

In the second *Oprah* programme, Winfrey broadcast extracts from her interviews with men who were abusers. In direct opposition to traditional feminist arguments that male violence against women is caused by a desire for power and control, abusive men and expert counsellors reported that abusers were driven to rage by fear of losing their relationship, insecurity and feelings of hopelessness. Unable to express these emotions appropriately, 'men often feel at a disadvantage verbally' and they succumb to anger, it was reported – what experts on the programme termed 'the anger blanket'.

Linda Mills and Tubman Center specialists argued strongly that it was necessary to 'help people heal'. 'After arrest, he's just madder,' Mills explained. She continued: 'It's not a he's to blame, she's the victim and if we do not get there [to a holistic treatment solution], we will not solve this problem.' Mills also attacked the notion that domestic violence is a 'man problem', pointing out that women are just as violent towards children as men are. This claim is supported by crime bodies such as the Australian Institute of Criminology.

Winfrey described her experience in producing the two in-depth reports as 'a big moment', openly admitting it had changed her mind on the issue (*Oprah*, 28 October 2003).

A constructive treatment and preventive approach to domestic violence addressing the causes, rather than a punitive approach to the manifested symptoms, is gaining ground among professionals, such as the work of the Tubman Family Alliance Center. In Australia, the first graduates of a tertiary course in running men's programmes for the prevention of family violence graduated from Swinburne University of Technology in Melbourne in late 2003 (*The Age*, 10 November 2003, p. 5). However, negative attitudes towards men dominate public discourse on domestic violence. As well as Police Commissioner Christine Nixon's comment ('I see them as criminals...I think what it's about is power', *60 Minutes*, 31 August 2003), the prominent health sciences lecturer and head of the Engaging Fathers project in Australia, Richard Fletcher, reported considerable resistance when he attempted to start a men's group in Newcastle to work with violent men. In an interview, he reported that female colleagues said, 'You're wasting your time. Men love bashing their wives' (Arndt, 2003).

Sexual abuse also figures prominently in portrayals of violence and aggression by men, with many allegations headlined in mass media. Noteworthy cases which made headlines during the six months period of this study included:

- Sensational claims, and subsequently charges, against the singer Michael Jackson for alleged sexual assault of and 'lewd acts' with boys.
- Allegations of 'groping' against the movie star and California Governor, Arnold Schwarzenegger.
- An alleged sexual assault of a teenage girl by the American basketball player Kobe Bryant, including allegations that a bodybuilder allegedly offered to kill the 19-year-old woman making the allegations to 'solve the problem' (*The Age*, 20 September 2003).
- Gang-rape allegations against eight English premiership soccer stars brought by a 17-year old girl (*Daily Telegraph*, 30 September 2003, p. 21 and 6 October 2003, p. 9; *Sydney Morning Herald*, 6 October 2003, p. 9).
- Allegations of 'text sex' against the high-profile Australian cricket star Shane Warne by a South African woman, Helen Cohen Alon, who alleged he sent a series of sexually explicit text messages. This case was interesting for a number of reasons including that it showed sexual assault could occur in cyberspace (*The Australian*, 11 August 2003, p. 1; *Daily Telegraph*, 11 August 2003, pp. 1 and 4).
- Shane Warne was also accused by a 16-year-old girl of 'tongue kissing' her during a night out on Australia's Gold Coast (*The Age*, 14 August 2003, p. 1).
- Stalking and harassment claims were made against the Australian Olympic swimming coach Greg Hodge by a former pupil, Emma Louise Fuller.

Also, allegations and charges against many less known men were widely reported in the mass media during the period of this study.

The claims and subsequent charges against Michael Jackson were reported worldwide, including in most of the media sampled in this study. While outside the sample of this study and therefore not included in the data, the international current affairs journal *Newsweek* devoted four pages to the Jackson case under the headline 'From Moonwalk to Perp Walk' (*Newsweek*, 2 December 2003, pp. 90–2). Despite his acquittal, the charges hang over Jackson.

A number of the claims against Shane Warne have been shown to lack substance. For instance, in December 2003, a Gold Coast man was charged with and pleaded guilty to blackmail over the alleged tongue kissing of a 16-year-old girl. The man admitted calling the Australian Cricket Board with an 'exaggerated version of the story and threatened to sell the story to media outlets' (*The Age*, 17 December 2003, p. 11). An appearance by Helen Cohen Alon on *A Current Affair* in return for payment (an insidious media practice referred to as 'cheque book journalism') stimulated speculation over her motives. But, as the TV programme reported in its headline: 'Shane Warne back in the headlines – for all the wrong reasons' and his reputation was further damaged irrespective of whether he was guilty or not (National Nine News, 11 August 2003; *A Current Affair*, 11 August 2003). Significantly, neither of these media reported the outcome, which was dismissal of the claims and police charges against Cohen Alon for extortion.

Claims of sexual assault by men extend across all levels of society. A series of allegations of sexual offences made against priests in the Catholic Church along with allegations of a cover-up of priest paedophilia made headlines during 2003 and 2004. Charges against two priests were widely reported during the period of this study. Also, in the period immediately preceding this study, the Governor General of Australia, Peter Hollingworth, was forced to resign over allegations that he covered up, or at least did not do enough about, sexual abuse by ministers of his Church while he was Anglican Archbishop of Brisbane. Other examples of media reports on alleged sexual abuse during the period of this study, implicating many fields and professions, included the following headlines:

- 'Five Men Appeal Rape Convictions' (*Daily Telegraph*, 21 October 2003, p. 9).
- 'No Bail for Paedophile' (*Weekend Australian*, 27–28 September 2003, p. 8).

- 'Child Porn Arrest' (*The Australian*, 22 October 2003, p. 5).
- 'Ex-Labor Identity in Court over Child Sex' (*Daily Telegraph*, 10 October 2003, p. 11).
- 'Ballet Teacher in Grope Claim' (*Daily Telegraph*, 1 November 2003, p. 15).
- 'Teacher Faces Sex Charges' (*Daily Telegraph*, 26 September 2003, p. 8).
- 'Ten Sacked over Abuse in Schools' (*Sydney Morning Herald*, 31 July 2003, p. 5).
- 'Army Rape Culture Denied' (*The Australian*, 16 October 2003, p. 11).
- 'Sex Case Magistrate Arraigned' (*Weekend Australian*, 15–16 November 2003, p. 10).
- 'Harassment at Work Rife' (*Daily Telegraph*, 13 November 2003, p. 26).
- 'Chatroom Groomer Preyed on 73 Girls' (*Sydney Morning Herald*, Weekend Edition, 11–12 October 2003, p. 37).

Reading mass media, any woman or girl could be excused for believing men are marauding monsters. Some media say as much, contributing to a highly negative and inflammatory discourse on men and supporting a generalization that male sexual aggression is pervasive. For instance, in an opinion column, the freelance journalist and columnist Sian Prior discussed crime statistics which show that, in reality, the incidence of many types of crime are falling or are stable. Under the sub-heading 'Crime statistics are cold comfort when one is confronted by male violence', Prior reported a man kicking her car door and shouting at her in traffic in the following terms:

Suddenly I was remembering all those other times I've been afraid. Fending off a gang of aggressive young men on a train station late at night. Walking home from a bus stop, being followed by a strange man in an overcoat. Backing away from a man who is smiling at me and masturbating in broad daylight in my local park. Locking my car doors while a man shakes his fist at me for taking the last parking spot outside the supermarket. This month the newspapers have been full of stories about men shooting their wives, murdering their fathers-in-law, men strangling prostitutes, men taking their own lives. I've been lucky. This kind of extreme violence has never touched me personally. Most of the men I know are gentle, talkative types. (And yes, I know women can be killers too.) But at the back of nearly every woman's mind lurks a fear of that naked masculine aggression . . . (*The Age*, 29 September 2003, A3, p. 2)

Sexual abuse and assault are sensitive issues. Clearly, from the statistics, these offences occur and all rational men and women equally abhor such behaviour. But abhorrence of offences that do occur should not incite generalizations or be used to shortcut the processes of justice, including the important presumption of innocence until proven guilty. It is not only men saying this. In a major feature article headed 'In the Name of Justice', the columnist Bettina Arndt noted: 'Seemingly every week some new accusation of sexual misconduct captures public attention' and reported that, when a man is accused of rape, 'even if he is innocent, his reputation is forever smeared'. The article quoted a Purdue University study which found that more than 40 per cent of rape cases were classified as false by police and FBI studies using DNA testing exonerated 30–35 per cent of 4,000 sexual assault cases examined over a four-year period (*Sydney Morning Herald*, 2 December 2003, p. 15).

A number of court cases have found that women do make false allegations against men. During the period of this research several prominent cases of alleged rape were found to be concocted. In Australia, a university lecturer falsely accused her husband of rape and coerced their two teenage children to lie that they had witnessed the assault. Testimony from a friend of the couple's daughter and surveillance tape revealed that the daughter was shopping at the time she allegedly witnessed the assault (*The Age*, 11 July 2003, p. 3; 4 September 2003, p. 8).

An internationally reported claim alleged that captured US Army private Jessica Lynch had been raped by her Iraqi captors. The allegations on this occasion were made by a man, Rick Bragg, a former *New York Times* reporter and author of a biography of Lynch, *I am a Soldier Too* (*Daily Telegraph*, 7 November 2003, p. 33). Lynch denied she had been raped and confirmed that the Iraqi doctors had cared for her and aided her rescue on 1 April 2003.

The woman who accused Shane Warne of harassment through explicit text messages was, following the period of this media content analysis, convicted of and jailed for extortion (*Sydney Morning Herald*, 9 September 2004, p. 3).

Men and fatherhood

The headline 'Fatherhood is in Fashion' was flashed around the world by the international news agency Reuters-Associated Press reporting on an international fashion show in Milan in January 2004 and published in leading national newspapers including *The Australian* (15 January 2004, p. 3). A photo showed a male model on the catwalk clutching the hand of a small boy.

113

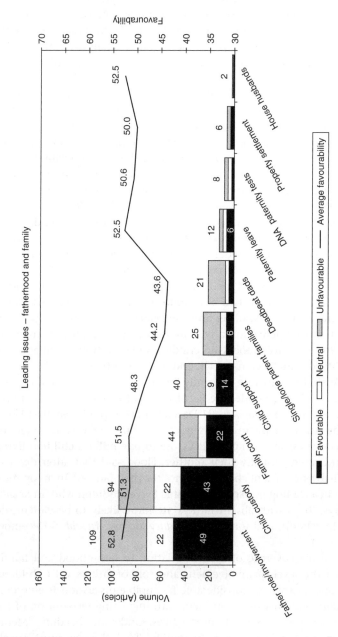

Figure 6.5 Leading issues in mass media reporting of men in relation to fatherhood and family

Analysis of mass media content undertaken in this study shows that, indeed, fatherhood is in fashion. The second leading category of media reporting on men was 'Fatherhood and family'. Some 361 media reports (20 per cent of the total sample of media articles analysed in this study) discussed men and fatherhood, including many opinion columns and feature articles.

Renewed focus on fatherhood is occurring internationally. In Britain, one so-called 'fatherhood expert' Adrienne Burgess has been a policy adviser to Prime Minister Tony Blair on family issues and claims that 'fathers are on the agenda'. Interviewed by Bettina Arndt, Burgess said, 'There has been a shift in public discourse'. She cited as examples Blair taking time off for the birth of his fourth child in 2000 and the Chancellor of the Exchequer, Gordon Brown, taking a month's paternity leave in 2003 (*Sydney Morning Herald*, 14 November 2003, p. 9).

In Australia, a sign of fatherhood reaching the political agenda was a National Strategic Conference on Fatherhood held in Canberra in August 2003. Speakers included Federal Sex Discrimination Commissioner Pru Goward and the 'fatherhood consultant' Adrienne Burgess. More will be said on these speakers and their views later. Also, a National Fatherhood Forum has been established and, following the period of this study, the Australian Prime Minister and the Leader of the Labor Opposition both announced policy initiatives directed at fostering involvement by fathers and male role models in children's lives, echoing similar social and political initiatives in the UK and other countries.

The Australian Institute of Family Studies was reported claiming that one in three children under the age of 18 has little or no contact with his or her father (*The Sunday Age*, 21 December 2003, p. 11). Michael Flood from the Australia Institute was quoted saying 'there is an epidemic of fatherlessness in Australia' with close to one million children living with one parent, usually their mother. Flood said that, after divorce, 'more than one third of children do not see their fathers'. In an opinion column in a leading newspaper, he cited Steve Biddulph who, in *Raising Boys*, says, 'boys with absent fathers are more likely to be violent, do poorly in schools, and join gangs (*Sydney Morning Herald*, 5 December 2003, p. 15).

Most media coverage of men in relation to fatherhood and family discussed the level of involvement and role of fathers with children. This is one area where considerable favourable discussion is emerging in contemporary discourse on men, with increasing recognition of the importance of fathers in children's lives. Under the headline 'Memo Feminists: Fathers Have a Role in Families Too', the columnist Angela

Shanahan wrote: 'During and after birth, in all the fuss over the mother, one sometimes forgets that babies belong as much to their fathers as to their mothers' (*The Age*, 27 August 2003, p. 13). Flood was reported saying: 'Fathers are important to the wellbeing of children and families, and supporting fathers positive involvement is a worthy goal' (*Sydney Morning Herald*, 5 December 2003, p. 15).

A number of celebrity fathers were profiled in mass media, including:

- A five-page feature on the actor Russell Crowe talking about the importance of his family and his newborn son (*Australian Women's Weekly*, December, 2003, pp. 49–54).
- A feature article on a group of musicians including Paul Kelly, Neil Murray and Colin George, who combined to produce a CD entitled 'Fatherhood' and talked about the importance of their children to them (*The Australian*, 20 November 2003, p. 12).
- A major feature in men's magazine *Ralph* entitled 'Sons of Guns' profiling three young sports stars talking about their famous fathers (*Ralph*, October, 2003, pp. 126–33).

Oprah broadcast a series of interviews with famous fathers including John Travolta, Will Smith and Arnold Schwarzenegger talking about their experiences of fatherhood. Of John Travolta, she commented: 'His eyes always light up when he talks about his children' (*Oprah*, 5 September 2003).

Also, in an in-depth special entitled 'Secret thoughts children have about their fathers', Oprah interviewed children about their relationship with their fathers and then interviewed the fathers to discuss their children's comments. The programme presented emotional scenes, with some men crying as they discussed their emotional connections to their children even though they admitted not communicating this adequately. One father reported 'a brick wall holding us back from communicating with each other', while another reported that when his ex-wife took his son away it 'crushed his heart' (*Oprah*, 2 July 2003).

In another programme Oprah interviewed Roland Warren of the National Fatherhood Initiative and a group of fathers who spoke of their innermost fears and desires, many of which revolved around their children. One of the fathers explained that 'every dad has a dream'. Oprah commented: 'I thought dads were just working all the time' (*Oprah*, 7 October 2003).

The relationship between fathers and their children was also positively portrayed in international media reporting of Iran's conjoined Bijani twins, who died during an operation to try to separate them. An interview with their adoptive father, Alireza Safaian, began: 'Alireza Safaian is filled with pain. For almost 27 years he cared for the Bijani twins . . . today they are gone and Mr Safaian wrestles with his emotions'. The headline of one media report read: 'A father feels the pain of separa-tion' and a sub-heading described how the twins' father was 'devastated by their deaths' (*The Sunday Age*, 13 July 2003, p. 6).

Australia's Federal Sex Discrimination Commissioner, Pru Goward, stated in a leading newspaper column: 'For too long, fatherhood has been ignored, taken for granted, seen as just about earning the money or laying down the law'. Goward acknowledged: 'Men, too, have been disadvantaged by the imposition of gender roles on their lives . . . for men, the onerous task of being the breadwinner, working in an often thankless job – perhaps ill-paid, long hours, bad conditions – have always been considered proof of their love for their family' (*The Age*, 26 August 2003, p. 11). Goward argued that more flexible work arrangements are necessary to allow fathers time off work to spend with their children.

However, along with recognition of the importance of fathers' involvement and the depth of many men's emotional connection with their children, discussion also contained an almost equal number of criticisms of men for lack of involvement with and commitment to their children. In a number of opinion columns and speeches, Goward blamed lack of father involvement with children on lack of family-friendly work-places. But she also said men have to be prepared to take time off and proposed the solution required changing work culture as much as chan-ging laws and providing paid paternity leave. In one opinion column, Goward said: 'Fathers will do their share of parenting when the mood at the office encourages them to' (*Sydney Morning Herald*, 12 August 2003, p. 11). Flood agreed, saying:

> Fathers' positive involvement in families after divorce is being hindered, but not by selfish mothers, nor by the Family Court. Fathers face the same obstacles to involvement they did before divorce: the excessive demands of family-hostile workplaces, the economic disad-vantages of involved parenting (which many mothers already suffer), and policy barriers to shared care. (*Sydney Morning Herald*, 5 December 2003, p. 15)

Under a headline 'Dads Who Care and Share are a Small Minority', a discussion paper titled 'Fatherhood and Fatherlessness' written by Michael Flood (2003) was reported by Farah Farouque and Adele Horin as saying that fathers are involved in the day-to-day care of their children in only

5–10 per cent of families and share the physical care of their children in only 1–2 per cent of families (*The Age*, 1 December 2003, p. 8).

An extreme example of public criticism of men over fatherhood and child access was an opinion article written by Trish Bolton, a tutor in media and communications at Swinburne and Monash Universities,[1] under the headline 'When it Comes to Child Access, Many Men Just Don't Want to Know'. Bolton recounted that, after she ended her marriage, the father of her two children kept in contact for 'a year or so', but continued:

> after less than three months, I knew it wouldn't last. Somehow, in that short time, his love for them just seemed to evaporate. I would watch helplessly as my little boy sat on top of his suitcase waiting for his daddy to arrive, legs kicking back and forth with anticipation, for a father who often did not keep his promise ... There's a backlash against single mothers. It is being fuelled by commentators such as Arndt who never miss an opportunity to portray single mothers as manipulative and self-serving, a men's movement that is deeply misogynous, and a Prime Minister who wants to drag women back into the kitchen where he thinks they belong. (*Sydney Morning Herald*, 4 September 2003, p. 15)

Bolton's tirade against fathers who do not maintain contact with children after separation drew letters to the editor from men, including one who wrote:

> It doesn't seem to have occurred to her that it is precisely these fathers and children who need the legislative back-up of a rebuttable presumption of joint custody, given that it is the present family law system that enables mothers who make access difficult to get away with their destructive and bitter combat by routinely awarding them sole custody. (*Sydney Morning Herald*, Letters, 5 September 2003, p. 10)

Bolton's claims are in conflict with research data such as Hawthorne's (2002), which shows that 56 per cent of non-resident fathers want *more* time with their children. Also research by Kruk (1993) in the US found

---

[1] This is cited to show that the author is an academic and was published with her academic position listed, not a reporter or a simply member of the public, which goes to the credibility and likely impact of the statements.

that father absence after separation is a case of 'defeated dads' rather than 'deadbeat dads', while Braver and O'Connell (1998) reported that the overriding reason that fathers disengage from their children is because they feel 'disenfranchised' by the court system or their former spouse or both (cited by Smyth, 2004).

Smyth, a research fellow at the Melbourne Institute of Family Studies, was reported in the media as saying the Institute's findings suggest 'three Rs – re-partnering, relocation, and residual bad feeling' – are responsible for lack of father involvement with their children. In other words, mothers remarrying or finding a boyfriend, moving away and tensions between the parents keep fathers from their children after divorce. Quoted by Muriel Reddy in a weekend opinion column, Smyth said further: 'You could add to this relative economic disadvantage and rotten behaviour in the form of abuse' (i.e. abuse of men as well as women) (*The Sunday Age*, 21 December 2003, p. 11).

Research investigating the difficulties faced by men in accessing family-friendly policies including paid paternity leave by the University of New South Wales sociologist Michael Bittman was also reported in the media sample studied. According to Bettina Arndt, Bittman found 'many men working in small teams felt they would be letting their workmates down if they took leave . . . but the crunch issue proved to be economic. Bittman found men don't take leave because it is not economically feasible'. Arndt cited research showing less than 5 per cent of Australian men take paid paternity leave when it is available (*Sydney Morning Herald*, 14 November 2003, p. 9).

An unsavoury portrayal of fatherhood involved the international tennis star Boris Becker who was forced to pay $48 million in a divorce settlement and child support after getting a young women pregnant in a 'five minute romp in a broom closet' of a London restaurant. One headline reported: 'Boom boom, 5 minutes, $48m' (*Daily Telegraph*, 5 November 2003, p. 36).

Another controversial element of fatherhood reported is the rising number of cases of men who find, through DNA testing, that they are raising or paying child support for children who are not theirs. In one case that made front-page news, a man was reported suing for the refund of $75,000 child support after learning that he was not the child's father. In another case, a man was awarded $70,000 damages after finding he had paid child support as a result of being misled by his former wife (*The Age*, 29 October 2003, p. 1).

DNA tests to prove paternity have emerged as a hotly debated topic. *A Current Affair* reported that 'secret DNA tests prove men are tricked into supporting children who are not theirs', citing research which allegedly shows that 20 per cent of men tested are not the biological fathers of their wives and partners' children. Basil Wainwright of the Men and Legal Equity Group was quoted saying that, in one study, 13 out of 35 men (40 per cent) obtaining paternity tests were not the biological father. Interviews with fathers who had found they were supporting children who were not theirs reported, 'men are being cheated and deceived by wives and partners for emotional and financial gain'. However, women's groups and mothers were reported to be strongly opposing paternity tests. Elspith McGinnis of the National Council for Single Mothers and their Children called for the banning of fathers secretly testing their children (*A Current Affair*, 18 August 2003).

An interesting conclusion from this analysis is that the most prolific and prominent editorial and opinion writers on fatherhood issues were:

- Bettina Arndt
- Pru Goward
- Michael Flood
- Adrienne Burgess
- Adele Horin
- Julie Szego
- Angela Shanahan
- Muriel Reddy
- Georgina Safe
- Christina Lamer
- Trish Bolton.

All but one of the most prominent commentators on fatherhood in the wide sample studied are women. Bittman and Smyth appeared in mass media only when quoted by the women columnists Bettina Arndt and Muriel Reddy. While not suggesting that women should not have views on fatherhood, Deleuze's warning that 'only those directly concerned can speak in a practical way on their own behalf' (Foucault, 1977, p. 209) and feminist claims to the superiority of 'self-validating' rather than 'other-validating' in objectivity/subjectivity debates (Hearn, 1993) are salutary. For whatever reason, men are largely absent in discourse on one of the topics which research suggests is most important to them.

Even more ironic and questionable on the grounds of subjectivity and experience is that Adrienne Burgess was quoted in several media articles as a 'fatherhood expert' and a 'fatherhood consultant'. She is the author of *Fatherhood Reclaimed: The Making of the Modern Father* (Burgess, 1997), a book that ironically was written before she and her husband, Martin

Cochrane, became parents. Following its publication, she became a policy adviser on fatherhood and child support issues to the Blair government before returning to her native Australia. Her gender (and childlessness at the time of writing the book) do not invalidate Burgess's views on fatherhood or her ability to contribute to the debate through research, but the dominance of female perspectives on key men's issues such as fatherhood, including describing men's feelings, concerns and level of interest, contributes a clear gender bias to discourse. A man writing in the same way on motherhood would be greeted with some incredulity.

Interrelated with child involvement by fathers, the next most discussed issues in connection with men and fatherhood, were child custody, the Family Court and child support. Discussion of single/lone parent families and 'deadbeat dads' (a term commonly used for non-resident dads and even enshrined in a 1998 US child support bill, as cited by Hawthorne 2000) also featured prominently in mass media reporting of men as fathers, some of which has already been cited.

A number of men and men's organizations are outspoken in their criticism of child custody laws, Family Court procedures and child support arrangements. However, despite men's complaints that child custody arrangements deny fathers adequate access to their children and strong criticisms by men of child support arrangements which, they say, cause them financial hardship and give them little say in how their payments are spent, the majority of mass media discussion of these issues comprised criticisms of men. Some media content – again mostly contributed by women writers – contained vitriolic attacks on men. Catharine Lumby, Associate Professor in the Media and Communications Department of Sydney University, in a full-page column in a national current affairs magazine wrote:

> Family law – or, more accurately, the law regulating marriage and divorce – is one of the most contentious areas of law on the books. But it's critical to remember that the intense controversy surrounding it is fuelled by the vocal criticisms of a tiny minority of the millions of Australians who've been through a relationship breakdown. And it's a tiny minority overwhelmingly made up of men . . . (*The Bulletin*, 8 July 2003, p. 31)

Lumby is contradicted by a report that a record 1,500 submissions were received by the Australian Federal Government Standing Committee on Family and Community Affairs which examined child custody issues (*The Weekend Australian*, 13–14 September 2003, p. 3). The media reported that, by April 2004, the inquiry had received almost 2,000 submissions and conducted 26 public hearings (*The Australian*, 27 April 2004, p. 1). That is hardly a 'tiny minority' fuelling the controversy. Notwithstanding, Lumby continued in her column to attack men's groups in the following terms:

> Fathers' rights groups... have been tremendously successful in gaining the ear of senior politicians. And yet their major claims have no empirical support... the real agenda is about reasserting a patriarchal model of the family... (*The Bulletin*, 8 July 2003, p. 31)

A number of writers are scathing of the Family Court in Australia, echoing similar criticisms to those made in other countries including the UK and US. Janet Albrechtsen described the court as 'a graveyard of reform' and pointed to a feminist bias in the court's approach. She said:

> The social experiment began with the best intention. The Family Court, established in 1976, promised a revolutionary system for dealing with family breakdown – one that sought outcomes in 'the best interests of the child'. But the 1970s were feminism's heyday. And so that message – the best interest of the child – was filtered through a feminist prism where the denigration of men refracted into the belittling of fathers. (*The Australian*, 24 December 2003, p. 11)

Federal MP Kay Hull, who was appointed chair of the Australian Standing Committee inquiry into child custody arrangements, interviewed by Diana Bagnall in a national current affairs magazine, said:

> There is not one person who has come in front of us, even those who have been successful in the Family Court, [or] who have shared-parenting arrangements, [who have not been] scathing and hateful about the processes that they went through... It's the cost and trauma of the adversarial process being fingered here, as well as a perceived bias against the parenting skills of breadwinners (usually male), but more and more working mothers find themselves fighting to prove their caring cred [sic]. (*The Bulletin*, 26 September 2003, p. 12)

Letters to the editor also showed major dissatisfaction, particularly among men, with their experiences of the Family Court:

> I can testify to the benefits of shared-care after divorce. But I can also confirm the horrific battle that men encounter in the Family Court

when they attempt to fight for their rights and the rights of their children to have equal access to their fathers. If [this proposal for shared access] is not supported, we will face a culture in which fatherhood is relegated to history, the epidemic of male suicide will continue to escalate, and men will face child rearing with fear rather than joy. (Name withheld, Queensland, *The Bulletin*, 15 July 2003, p. 8)

Spare a thought for those of us who have been, and are, in court fighting for the right to have our children on an equal basis. My ex-wife left me for another man, taking my children, and I have been fighting for them ever since. (Name withheld, ACT, *The Bulletin*, 15 July 2003, p. 8)

The same issue of *The Bulletin* reported that proposals for rebuttable joint custody that are opposed and described as 'unworkable' by a number of women's groups and agencies (e.g. The Sole Parents Union whose president, Kathleen Swinbourne, said overseas evidence showed the move was 'terrible for children, treating them as divisible pieces of property') were already law in eight US states (*The Bulletin*, 8 July 2003, p. 22).

Barry Williams, president of the Lone Fathers Association, was reported saying of existing child custody arrangements, 'the system is so stacked against men that it is fuelling a massive rise in the number of male suicides . . . we are dealing every night with people threatening suicide' (*Daily Telegraph*, 7 July 2003, p. 2).

While the Australian Federal Government's appointment of an inquiry into child custody arrangements gave men's groups and individual men, as well as women, a chance to communicate their concerns for and commitment to their children, negative stories of fathers not meeting their responsibilities were broadcast and published in mass media throughout the period of the inquiry. Under the headline 'Child Support Scandal', current affairs TV reported the case of a man who had not paid his former wife any child support over several years. The programme reported that there were 66,000 cases of fathers 'refusing' to pay child support, amounting to $617 million in unpaid child support (*A Current Affair*, 18 July 2003). The same programme followed up the issue the next week under the headline 'Sorry track record on child support', profiling the same man as a 'serial deadbeat dad' (*A Current Affair*, 23 July 2003). Then the programme followed up again on the issue a few months later, presenting more cases of fathers who had not paid child support. No fathers who paid child support were interviewed in any of the three nationally televised peak-viewing time programmes (*A Current Affair*, 1 September 2003).

A number of media articles reported fathers abusing and even killing their children, particularly following child custody disputes. For instance, a full-page feature in the *Daily Telegraph* examined male-perpetrated infanticide under the headline 'When a Father's Love Takes an Evil Turn' (17 September 2003, p. 27). The national daily *The Australian* also published a full-page feature the same day headlined 'When Dads get Deadly' (p. 13). It reported that 25 children are killed by their parents each year in Australia and fathers are responsible for 63 per cent of these. However, buried in the long article were statements by a research analyst from the Australian Institute of Criminology, Jenny Mouzos, that even though fathers were responsible for most such killings, 'the numbers are inflated by non-biological fathers (step-fathers) who kill children'. While not making these deaths any less tragic, Mouzos pointed out that figures on the distribution of parents who killed children by gender and biological ties shows 'mothers posed a more lethal risk to their own'. Biological mothers account for around 35 per cent of all cases, while biological fathers account for 29 per cent, Mouzos reported (*The Australian*, 17 September 2003, p. 13).

A difference in societal attitudes towards men and women committing filicide is evident in media discourse. Most filicides committed by mothers involves infants, and post-natal depression is commonly cited in such cases (e.g. Kathleen Fogbigg), leading to an increasing focus on a treatment approach rather than a punitive approach. However, despite reports and data showing that most men who kill their children do so in a state of severe depression (e.g. Australian Institute of Criminology statistics show most fathers killing their children also kill themselves), often following divorce and separation from their children, a punitive approach continues to be taken towards fathers who kill their children. Responses reported in mass media include calls for more Apprehended Violence Orders and refuges for women, with little discussion on help for men in distress. The two *Oprah* programmes previously cited were the only two examples of the latter.

A major front-page story in *The Age* headlined 'The Family Court: How it Can Push Men over the Edge' reported that the Court was investigating the extent to which its decisions contributed to male suicides. The article reported: 'Little research has been conducted in the area, but the most recent, published in the *Journal of Family Studies* seven years ago, found that separated men were six times more likely to commit suicide than married men' (*The Age*, 19 August 2003, p. 1).

Men and sexuality

As with most subject categories studied in relation to men and male identity, male sexuality was predominantly negatively portrayed. One third (33 per cent) of all discussion of male sexuality was in relation to paedophilia, as shown in Figure 6.6. Mass media salivated over the Michael Jackson case and numerous newspaper and magazines articles reported male sexual abuse, as cited under 'Men and violence'.

Homosexuality has become prominent in media representations of men, highlighted in TV shows such as *Queer Eye for the Straight Guy* and numerous media reviews that followed its international launch. Homosexuality is lightly and largely positively portrayed in *Queer Eye*. However, the programme and other mass media content studied continue to reflect gay stereotypes, and homosexuality is mostly negatively portrayed in media discourse in relation to gay marriages and social commentary reflecting homophobia.

Significantly, male heterosexuality was equally negatively portrayed in the media content sample studied. Male heterosexuality is mostly associated with traditional (hegemonic) masculinity and seen as violent, aggressive and dominating. Often homosexual men were portrayed as more sophisticated and sensitive than heterosexual men.

Male sexuality also faces what appears to be a growing trend of objectification, strikingly similar or parallel to the objectification of women which has been widely documented. The top-rating TV show *Sex and the City* is an exemplar in objectification of men as sex objects for the gratification of women. In a major feature published in the London *Observer* and reprinted in Australian media, *Sex and the City* scriptwriter Cindy Chupack advises women to pass on boyfriends after they have finished with them – which she terms 'man-me-downs' (*The Age*, 9 August 2003, A2, p. 2).

Women's magazines take objectification of men to extremes in much the same way as men's magazines have treated women in the past. Men in women's magazines are either young, virile, waxed 'hunks' with 'six-pack' stomach muscles and model looks, or figures of ridicule. For example, *Cosmopolitan* presents a 'Guy without a shirt' section featuring a young man in swimming trunks or underwear only. David Beckham was featured in the October 2003 issue with the sub-heading 'Want to see Becks take a free kick – naked?' Under the heading in the November 2003 issue the magazine unashamedly urged readers 'Check out this month's half-naked spunk'.

Mass media also portray men as sexually promiscuous and commitment-phobic. Feature articles in *Cosmopolitan* (November 2003) included

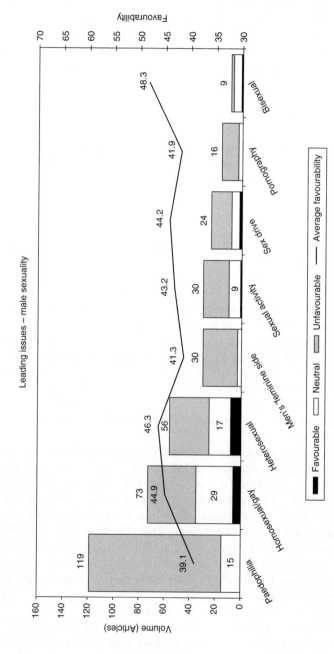

Figure 6.6 Leading issues in mass media reporting of male sexuality

'Cheatproof Your Relationship', 'Find out if Your Relationship Can Handle a Baby' and 'Remember that Idiot who Dumped You out of the Blue'.

Men's magazines such as *FHM* and *Ralph* also focus heavily on sexuality, particularly sexual activity and men's sex drive, mostly with a performative focus and often not in a way that reflects positively on men.

A notable feature of mass media portrayals of male sexuality is that when positive traits such as sensitivity and emotional depth are reported in relation to men, these are referred to frequently as men's 'feminine side', confirming a trend identified in Chapters 3 and 5. In Figure 6.6 this issue was categorized as unfavourable as it suggests that sensitivity and emotional depth are not male characteristics and that men can attain these positive characteristics only by becoming like women.

Men and work

Other prominent mass media representations of men are in relation to work and career. A number of researchers have noted the centrality of work in men's lives (e.g. O'Connor, 1983, p. 51; Segal, 1990, p. 297; Tacey, 1997, p. 124; Webb, 1998, p. 129). However, the leading issues discussed in mass media in relation to men's work and career indicate that a significant social shift is occurring. While career success was the most prominently reported issue, Figure 6.7 shows that career success received as much criticism as positive reporting in the sample studied and, overall, was seen as only slightly favourable. Work versus family and lifestyle balance is being extensively discussed in the media, particularly in opinion columns and feature articles, with increased recognition (or at least talk) of the importance of family and lifestyle outside of work and career success.

One media report headlined 'Working Yourself to Death' suggested that the Japanese phenomenon of *karoshi* (death from overwork) has arrived in Australia. The article reported that stress claims have increased, deaths at work have risen 30 per cent between 2001 and 2002 and the number of Australians working long hours (50 hours a week or more) has doubled in the past 20 years (*Daily Telegraph*, 21 August 2003, p. 22). Another media report cited a 2003 Relationships Australia survey which found that 90 per cent of couples believe that finding a balance between their work and lifestyle is straining their relationship (*Sunday Telegraph*, 14 December 2003, p. 51).

A number of books on work and its effects were reported and reviewed during the period of this study, including Barbara Pocock's *The Work/Life Collision* (2003) and a text written by four academics from the Royal

127

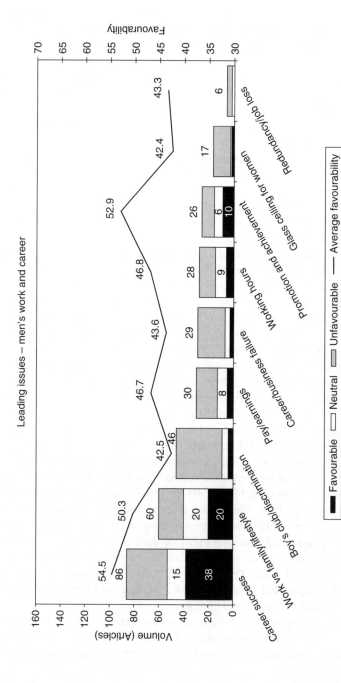

Figure 6.7 Leading issues in mass media reporting of men in relation to work and career

Melbourne Institute of Technology who traced workplace transformations over the past 20 years. The book, *Fragmented Futures – New Challenges in Work Life*, reported that workers are putting in more hours than ever before and since the late 1980s more than 1.2 million women have entered the workforce compared with 700,000 men – although it noted that around half of the new jobs for women were low-skilled (Watson et al., 2003).

A *Sydney Morning Herald* feature in its My Career section reported in relation to men and work: 'They also want to be part of their children's lives. Inside the office, however, it can be another story.' The article stated: 'There's a tension between what companies want productivity-wise and what an employee needs to do to be a good father, and they're often at odds with each other. The difficulty is that just as males are getting into their peak career mode, they're also getting into family mode' (*Sydney Morning Herald*, My Career, 4–5 May 2003, p. 1).

International trends in work and overwork were widely reported. For instance, the columnist Emma Tom cited research by a London-based market research company which found more than 40 per cent of men and 23 per cent of women said they would welcome spending evenings or the entire night at the office (*The Australian*, 22 October 2003, p. 15).

However, one positive example that things are changing, headlined 'New Generation of Men who Share the Load', noted that 'fewer and fewer modern young women are prepared to tolerate what their baby-boomer mothers took for granted – a bread-winning husband who kept his nose out of the child-rearing and home-making', and claimed that there has been 'a generational shift which is invisible to many commentators about the way child care and domestic duties are split'. The author James Woodford argued that 'many young couples are trying out new ways of sharing the work, simply because it makes more sense to do so, and are waiting for government and employer policies to catch up' (*Sydney Morning Herald*, 29 July 2003, p. 11). However, most men report that they do not have the flexibility or the financial capacity to cut back to part-time work or work from home and US research cited in the following pages has found that many of their wives either cannot earn enough to replace their husband's income or do not want to work. The high volume and conflicting nature of mass media messages on men and work suggest that today's men and women are living on the cusp of major social and industrial change.

Reports of discrimination against women and workplaces being a 'boys' club' continue to be reported frequently and unfavourably. The 'glass ceiling' was cited in 17 articles in the sample studied, particularly in relation to the legal profession and senior management positions in large corporations. For instance, in a major feature headed 'The Feminine Effect on the Law', then newly appointed Chief Justice of the State of Victoria Marilyn Warren argued that 'women who break through the glass ceiling have an obligation to help those below' and claimed that more women should be promoted to senior positions in the law because:

> women are adaptive and flexible... women bring to the law a strong sense of method... women bring a combination of typically feminine characteristics to the law: energy, patience, humour and insight... My list is not exhaustive. It is intended to highlight the difference that women bring to the law. (*Sydney Morning Herald*, 15 November 2003, p. 11)

Warren's comments are an example of what Nathanson and Young (2001) call superiority feminism, with the generalization that method, energy, patience, humour and insight are attributes which women are better able to provide than men.

A full-page feature headlined 'Engendering a Legal Minefield' reported 'the good news for women lawyers: more are getting plum jobs. The bad news: a male backlash'. There's that word again! The article claimed that 'women remain only a small fraction of those in senior positions in the law; women barristers continue to be denied an equal share of senior briefs; and female lawyers generally earn on average $20,000 a year less than men' (*The Age*, Insight, 6 December 2003, p. 8). British and Australian research confirms that even though more women than men are now called to the bar, their incomes are lower (*The Economist*, 2005). However, this may be nothing to do with a backlash and more to do with the more recent entry of large numbers of women to legal positions. It takes up to 20 years to rise to senior positions in professions such as the law and medicine.

Anne Summers' *The End of Equality*, which was widely reviewed and reported, identified the law as an example of a field in which women's advancement has 'ground to a halt in the face of male opposition' (another claim of a backlash) and attacked institutionalized forces in workplaces which she claimed can be addressed only by government regulation and support for women such as child care. In reviewing Summers' book, the columnist Emma-Kate Symons wrote: 'As Summers shows, some powerful men are trying to take back women's hard-earned gains of the 1970s and '80s through legal, political and social means' (*The Weekend Australian*, Books Extra, 29–30 November 2003, p. 6). Summers showed no such thing; she speculated that a 'backlash' by men was preventing women's advancement, with scant supporting evidence.

The conservative columnist Janet Albrechtsen has earned the ire of many feminists and has been branded a conservative by disagreeing with generalized claims of discrimination at work. Rejecting Summers' views, Albrechtsen said, 'nuance is still nowhere to be seen':

> Well-educated middle-class women like to tell us that women want a leg up, a short cut, and they want power. They want to run the show, sit in the nation's boardrooms, in its courtrooms and in parliament... Undoubtedly, discrimination may still be part of the answer. Yet there is also so much more to it than one-word slogans. Add some nuance and what looks like discrimination and regression starts to look a lot like a reflection of women's choices. Some women prefer the playground to the boardroom. Some women use the professions as a marriage market. Some women like to be kept. Nuance like this may be unpalatable, but that does not make it untruthful... feminism has some growing up to do. (*The Australian*, 3 December 2003, p. 15)

But Albrechtsen is one of very few voices raised in defence of men and, as noted in analysis of commentators quoted in mass media, it is interesting that this defence is mounted by a woman columnist and not a man.

American research showing that many educated women are choosing home and children instead of a career was reported, although it was not analysed in the context of claims of workplace discrimination. US Census Bureau data show the number of stay-at-home mothers has increased by 13 per cent in less than a decade. And it is not only women with limited or no opportunities who are staying at home, according to research. A report by Lisa Belkin (2003) titled 'The Opt-Out Revolution' published in *The New York Times Magazine* and syndicated internationally claimed that only 38 per cent of women graduates from Harvard Business School work full-time, and half of Princeton University graduates interviewed by Belkin had left their top-rating jobs (*Sydney Morning Herald*, 9 December 2003, p. 11). In another media feature it was reported: 'The stalwart feminists of the 1970s might be horrified, but it seems that their daughters – highly educated and driven since birth to be professional high achievers – are reaching their late 20s or early 30s and finding that a career is not all that it was cracked up to be' (*The Australian*, 15 September 2003, p. 10).

Some argue that women leaving the paid workforce is simply a sign of the workplace failing them through inflexibility and working to male rules. Belkin disagrees, saying that women are rejecting the workplace even when it is tailored to their needs: 'They are redefining the meaning of success in their lives' she was reported saying in a major feature entitled 'Reclaimed by Biology' (*The Weekend Australian*, 1–2 November 2003, p. 24).

Men bearing the brunt of industrial rationalization and corporate restructuring, suffering career burn-out and trapped in demanding jobs living alienated from their families may well feel that it was feminist generalizations about so-called male power and privilege that eulogized paid work over personal life and family and, in so doing, did a disservice to men and women.

One of Australia's leading daily newspapers, *The Age*, devoted a major series to 'Suicide: Men at Risk' and, as part of the series, interviewed seven prominent educated professional men on their experiences and the 'trials of manhood'. One of the recurrent themes in men's comments was the importance of work in providing their identities. A school teacher and former priest commented: 'We . . . define ourselves primarily through work. Once our work begins to take on a meaninglessness, everything else goes with that. We are Industrial Revolution people. We have been defined primarily by what we can output, not by what we can take in.' A school principal stated: 'I'm a school principal. If I'm not a school principal any more, what am I? (*The Age*, 20 August 2003, p. 13).

A headline 'Jobless, Single and Male: Society's Forgotten Outcasts' sounded a warning about the plight of men in post-industrial societies. Despite relative economic stability and low unemployment during the period of this study, Professor Sue Richardson from the National Institute of Labour Studies at Flinders University warned of a 'dangerous' under-class of young, unemployed, unmarried men. A prominent writer on social issues, Adele Horin, reported Richardson addressing a conference in Canberra where she said, '35 per cent of Australian men aged 35–44 in 2003 are not married and do not have a full-time job . . . compared with 20 per cent in 1978' (*The Sydney Morning Herald*, 2 October 2003, p. 11).

Significantly, as with fatherhood, the most prominent opinion writers and commentators on men in relation to work in the mass media studied were women, including:

- Pru Goward
- Bettina Arndt
- Angela Shanahan

- Susan Mitchell
- Emma Tom
- Barbara Pocock
- Adrienne Burgess
- Adele Horin
- Judy Adamson
- Julie-Anne O'Hagan
- Brigid Delaney
- Sherrill Nixon
- Melissa Marino.

Only four male commentators appeared frequently in media discussion of men and work and they were published less frequently than women writers. This gender imbalance in media voices talking about men and male identity raises important questions worthy of further investigation. Do media editorial policies in relation to social and gender issues favour women? Or are men unconcerned or disinterested? Or have men been silenced?

Men's social behaviour and body image – metrosexuals, SNAGS, lads and other stereotypes

Mass media representations of male social behaviour are widely varied, but again portrayals of men are predominantly negative, as shown in Figure 6.8. 'Metrosexuals' became the most prominent male identity portrayed in mass media in relation to men's social behaviour in 2003. Reportedly coined by the British author Mark Simpson in 1994 and made popular by New York trend-spotter Marian Salzman (Barker, 2004), the term is used to describe an alleged trend among men to be fashion-conscious and well-groomed to the point of feminization, such as wearing make-up and waxing to remove body hair.

Traditional physical aspects of masculinity such as strength, ruggedness and hirsute appearance are also represented in mass media, but much less so than metrosexual images and often in negative comparisons. Traditional masculine appearance is increasingly criticized in favour of David Beckham and Ian Thorpe-type images of hairless, coiffured gymnasium-sculpted male bodies and Botox-injecting metrosexuals.

The top-rating international current affairs show, *60 Minutes*, devoted a major segment to 'Metro Man'. Beckham was cited as the ideal metrosexual. Australian examples cited were the Olympic swimmers Ian Thorpe and Geoff Heugill, resplendent with their hairless bodies, along

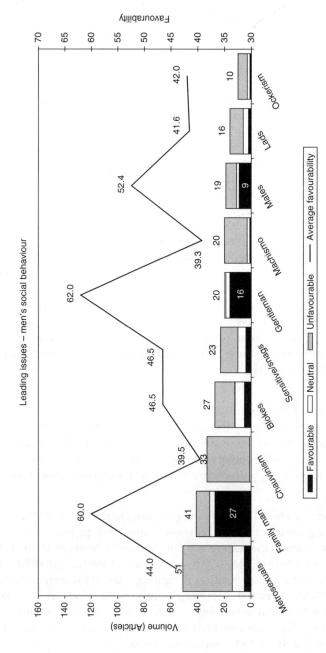

Figure 6.8 Leading issues in mass media reporting of men in relation to social behaviour

with the singer David Campbell. Charles Woolley reported: 'They're into makeovers, make-up and moisturizers, know everything there is to know about shirts and shoes and, for what it's worth, they're straight' (*60 Minutes*, 24 August 2003).

Australia's national current affairs TV show was not far behind in reporting on this 'news' about men. At least *A Current Affair* recognized the commercial motives behind the metrosexual trend with its report entitled 'The Boom Industry that Allows Men to Lie Back and Think of Make-up' (*A Current Affair*, 19 September 2003). Not to be outdone by *60 Minutes'* rhetoric, *A Current Affair* did a follow-up on Botox being used by men as well as women. The reporter Brady Hall matched Charles Woolley's alliteration describing 'the body beautiful Botox world' (*A Current Affair*, 2 December 2003).

Major features on 'Metro Man' also appeared in a number of leading newspapers (e.g. *Sunday Telegraph*, 20 July 2003, pp. 10–11) and men's magazines. *Ralph* (2 October, p. 125) published a quiz headed 'Are you a metrosexual?' in a tongue-in-cheek tone. But the underlying message was that, if a man is not a metrosexual, he is a sexist, football-loving, beer-drinking slob.

Despite the levity of some mass media coverage of the metrosexual phenomenon, there are signs that men are concerned and conflicted by the shifting kaleidoscope of identities paraded in mass media. A letter to the editor from a young man published under the headline 'Men in Need of Direction' stated:

> The increasing trend towards this portrayal of men in advertising is a representation of the indeterminate role of males in modern society . . . men are less secure in the part they have to play in the social structure . . . for the young male, there is a great deal of confusion about the contribution they have to make to society and in relationships . . .

The letter concluded by appealing against 'lauding one gender and denigrating the other' (*Daily Telegraph*, 7 July 2003, p. 10).

A Sunday magazine feature was sub-headlined 'Some modern males don't know whether they're Arthur or Martha (Stewart that is)' and commented that 'his generation is fighting a battle for masculinity on multiple fronts: personal grooming; housework, childcare, communication and general touch-feely-ness. It's no wonder many are floundering. Experts are calling this new male plight "Atlas syndrome"' (*Sunday Life* magazine, *The Age*, 9 November 2003, p. 12).

Janet Albrechtsen came out in strong opposition to the so-called metrosexual revolution. In a national column headed 'Stop Tampering with the Male' and with an overline stating 'Metrosexual man, representing the temporary triumph of androgyny over biology, is feminism's Frankenstein', she asked: 'What would liberated assertive, independent women find attractive about girly boys who hog the mirror?' Albrechtsen also questioned a study which defined a metrosexual as having 'little interest in military hardware or heroism, he prefers salmon pink shirts and loves to share his shopping with his friends. His most common vice is – brace yourself – being passive' (*The Australian*, 6 August 2003, p. 11).

Some commentators have cited mass media reporting of this alleged trend as nothing more than a cynical marketing ploy designed to sell products through exploiting men's ego and insecurity in the same way that women have been induced to buy make-up, hair care products and stay abreast of fashion. Miranda Devine, in a large opinion feature under the headline 'The Pain of the Modern Male Eunuch', commented: 'The new masculine metrosexual ideal seems to be imposing the same tyranny of lookism on men which women have long endured (*Sydney Morning Herald*, 18 September 2003, p. 17).

Muriel Reddy commented in a major Sunday opinion column: 'There is a whole rethink of just what it is . . . to be a man. The images include the "sensitive new age guy", the gay, the bisexual and the queer man, the 'new lad' and the metrosexual. It's a brave new world out there for men' (*The Sunday Age*, 21 December 2003, p. 11).

The traditional social role of 'family man', while favourably reported in mass media, appears less frequently than images of metrosexuals. 'Gentleman' remains the only other predominantly favourable image of men, but more often men are reported as chauvinists and as 'blokes' or 'blokey' – terms that are used almost universally as unfavourable descriptions. It is interesting that in the UK and Australia the term 'blokes', a common colloquial expression for men that was once positive (as in 'a good bloke'), has become a negative, while the equivalent American term 'guys' has largely become androgynous. For instance, Australian Sex Discrimination Commissioner Pru Goward blames 'the blokey culture' of certain industries for the absence of women in senior positions (*The Age*, 4 December 2003, pp. 1, 4).

Similarly, male mateship, which has been identified in much social literature as an important source of support and identity for men, has come in for attack. In Australia in particular, mateship has been celebrated in songs, poetry, films (e.g. *Gallipoli*) and novels. But mass media articles criticize male mateship as the root of many evils, including excessive drinking and drunkenness often leading to aggression, sexual abuse, domestic violence and risky behaviour such as dangerous driving. For instance, a summit on alcohol abuse in Sydney was reported under a page 1 headline 'Casting a Sober Eye on Grog and Mateship' and opened with the sentence: 'Australians' very notion of mateship may need to be rewritten' (*Sydney Morning Herald*, 27 August 2003, p. 1). 'Mates' and the term 'lads', which is commonly used in the UK for male friends, have become closely and unfavourably linked with machismo and boorish behaviour.

Men and commitment and responsibility

Analysis of discussion of men and male identity in contexts related to commitment and responsibility reveals an interesting contradiction and level of misrepresentation in discourse. Women's magazines and opinion columns frequently report that men lack commitment and even that they are 'commitment-phobic'. Yet, alongside criticism of men for lacking commitment is extensive reporting of men working long hours and even being workaholics, serving in the military, fire brigades and other national commitments, and regularly carrying out heroic rescues to save lives (community commitment). Considerable evidence shows men have consistently demonstrated commitment and responsibility in work, as protectors and as soldiers. Risking their lives as volunteers in war, as many men have done, is an evocative example of commitment and sense of responsibility (Figure 6.9).

What emerges from analysis of discourse reflected and propagated through mass media is that commitment and responsibility have been redefined selectively and narrowly. Commitment and responsibility to work has become a site of conflict and is mostly viewed as negative. Military commitment and responsibility are now shared with women – albeit these too have been denigrated at various times (such as during the Vietnam War) and claims are made that there would be no war if women were in charge. Commitment in sport (not analysed, but cited in some discussions of men) is mostly portrayed as immature or a refuge for hegemonic masculinity. In most cases, claims of lack of commitment by men relate to individual men postponing or avoiding marriage and having children. Such decisions are interpreted as a fault or 'problem'. Other possible reasons are rarely if ever considered. As identified in analysis of voices quoted in the media, discourse is being led by women and the only commitment and responsibility that seems to count is to the women themselves and their children.

137

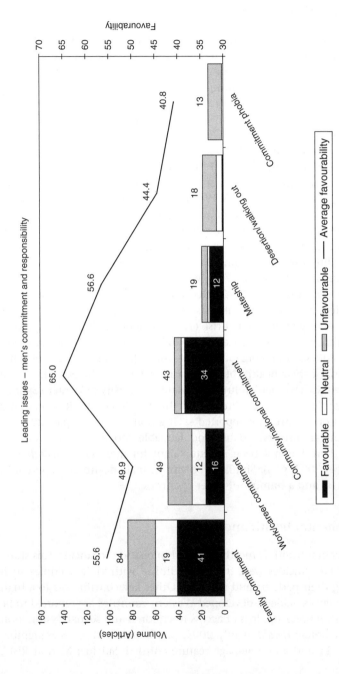

Figure 6.9 Leading issues in mass media reporting of men in relation to commitment and responsibility

Men's physical health

Men are portrayed as not taking care of their health, with the leading issues reported and portrayed in relation to men's health being alcohol and drug abuse. Disease among men is reported to be increasing and male health is cited as requiring attention – in itself a positive finding. However, preventive treatment and programmes to address men's health problems are little reported in mass media, with a few notable exceptions. For example, prostate cancer, a major killer of men, was discussed in just twelve of almost 2,000 articles studied in this media analysis – 0.67 per cent of content related to men.

Some media are calling for increased focus on prostate cancer. For instance, *Australian Women's Weekly* reported that 'every three hours an Australian man dies from prostate cancer' and urged women to help 'save your man's life' through testing (*Australian Women's Weekly*, November 2003, p. 183). Also, a major weekend newspaper feature headlined 'Killing me Softly' pointed out that 'prostate cancer is a threat to men, similar to breast cancer in women, but we're not doing enough about it' (*The Australian*, 20–21 December 2003, p. 20). Contributing to the neglect were reports that tests for diagnosing prostate cancer were flawed, leaving many men at risk (*The Australian*, 25 July 2003, p. 3).

A health conference in Cairns in 2003 called for a National Men's Health Policy, and concluded that Australian men 'are not only neglectful of their health, but are poorly served by the Federal system compared with women'. John Macdonald, University of Western Sydney health professor and co-director of the Men's Health Resource and Information Centre, was reported saying that, while the past 20 years had seen 'an understandable and laudable move towards women's health, there has not been an equivalent for men' (*The Australian*, 9 September 2003, p. 3). Similar problems in male health are reported in the UK, US and a number of other countries.

Men's mental health and suicide

Men's mental health is mostly reported in relation to suicide, this study found. Male suicides were frequently linked with violent crimes such as killing their partners and children. Other key contributors to a high rate of men's suicide in developed Western countries are reported to be relationship break-up, loss of access to children and sexual dysfunction (*Sydney Morning Herald*, 4 July 2003, p. 13; *Sunday Age*, 28 September 2003, p. 11 and a double-page feature entitled 'Suicide: Men at Risk',

The Age, 18 August 2003, pp. 13–15). *The Age* feature brought a reported 'flood of response' in letters to the editor (*The Age*, 23 August 2003, p. 12). One letter told of two parents' tragic experience of young male suicide. The parents wrote: 'It was Father's Day 2001 when our 19-year-old son Anthony, decided to leave and not return. We waited . . . hoping that he would call to ask to come home or to at least say that he was OK and didn't want to come home. A week later, on 8 September, the police came to tell us that our son was dead' (*The Age*, 15 October 2003, p. 10).

Men and communication

Men are widely reported to be unable to express their feelings and emotions and reluctant to talk. They are also reported to be poor at non-verbal communication and listening. The dominance of female writers on men's issues suggests that communication may be largely defined in female terms. As with commitment, the focus of communication discussed is mostly in relation to topics of interest to women.

There is also an interesting side-issue suggested in discourse on communication with 'communication' being widely discussed as synonymous with 'talking'. The two, of course, are quite different concepts. Male non-verbal communication, such as a nod, nudge, wink or slap on the back, is often not recognized in female-oriented discussion and traditional manly stoicism is frequently ridiculed and pathologized.

Male competitiveness

Other noteworthy findings of this study were that male competitiveness is frequently cited in mass media reporting and portrayals of men and male identities predominantly as causing harm rather than bringing benefits. Mass media references to male competitiveness causing harmful effects such as risk-taking and oppressive actions appeared more than twice as often as male competitiveness associated with benefits such as success in an endeavour or achievement. Male teamwork and cooperation were cited even less frequently.

Male competitiveness also was portrayed as leading to greed and was cited frequently in instances of men committing corporate fraud. While this study did not examine business media reporting, some notable corporate collapses were widely reported in general news, such as the disgraced Australian business tycoon Alan Bond being released from prison. *A Current Affair* raked over Bond's past, referring to him as perpetrating 'Australia's biggest ever corporate fraud' (*A Current Affair*, 4 November 2003).

The high-profile Australian multi-millionaire stockbroker Rene Rivkin also made it out of the business pages into mainstream news when he was convicted of insider trading and sentenced to prison (*The Australian*, 5 November 2003, p. 4; *Daily Telegraph*, 14 November 2004, p. 4; and a major Weekend Inquirer feature in *The Australian*, 1–2 November 2003, p. 17). Bond and Rivkin were two of a number of men in senior corporate positions who, like their counterparts in Enron, Worldcom and Tyco in the US and a number of other companies, were found to have succumbed to greed driven by aggressive competitiveness.

Men and domestic involvement

Men's role in child care was the most reported issue in terms of domestic involvement, followed by house cleaning, 'house husbands' (men involved full-time in family domestic duties) and cooking. Half of 28 articles discussing men and child care were positive, reporting men taking a major role in caring for their children. However, a significant number of articles criticized men for lack of involvement in child care. Media reporting on men in relation to house cleaning was almost all negative, citing men's lack of effort in the home as a common international problem.

An interesting observation is that domestic involvement (including terms such as child care and housework) is primarily defined as work inside the house. Only one article in this study reported or noted men's domestic work outside the house. Domestic involvement and 'housework' appear to be strictly defined as caring for children, cleaning the house and cooking. Attending to gardens, garages, paths, driveways, washing cars, cleaning out gutters, handyman repairs and maintenance are often not acknowledged. Definitional issues appear to be a significant factor in widespread claims that men do not do their share domestically and a broader definition of 'housework' may substantially alter the alleged inequity between men and women in this area.

Boys' education

Boys' education is a major and growing focus of mass media interest. Academic performance of boys was reported favourably in relation to some boys excelling in final year school results. However, the small number of reports of boys topping examinations belies the broader issue of boys falling behind girls on average and calls for a renewed focus on boys' needs. A major feature in *The Bulletin* entitled 'Through the Glass Ceiling' reported that 'men are the new second sex' when it comes to education. The three-page article reported that there were 75,000 more women than men enrolled at Australian universities in 2003 and 80,000 more women than men with degrees in the 25–34 age group. According to the report, female school teachers outnumber men four to one and women also outnumber men among university staff. As well as outnumbering males in education, females are also outperforming them. Boys fill detention rooms and remedial groups, *The Bulletin* reported. Meanwhile, women dominate six out of ten major tertiary fields of study and, of 145,000 students awarded degrees in 2002, almost 60 per cent were women (*The Bulletin*, 9 September, 2003, pp. 28–30).

The appointment by the Australian Federal Government Ministerial Council on Education of Richard Fletcher, a noted proponent of boys' educational needs, men's health and head of the Engaging Fathers Project, to a review of gender equity policies in education was not greeted enthusiastically by education authorities, despite Fletcher saying, 'I'm hoping that the new attention to boys will result in them achieving their potential but not at the expense of girls' (*Sydney Morning Herald*, 'Spectrum', 20–21 December 2003, p. 7).

Four controversial incidents that highlighted problems in school treatment of boys made national TV news and current affairs during the period of this study. In one, a six-year-old boy was suspended 30 times for behavioural problems. He was described as 'a runaway', 'a terror' and accused of 'abusing teachers'. However, the report investigated and found poor treatment by the teacher had substantially contributed to the problems. The teacher was disciplined (*A Current Affair*, 3 July 2003).

In another incident, a female primary school teacher was dismissed for her treatment of a young boy. The teacher allegedly stuck masking tape over the boy's mouth to stop him talking (National Nine News, 6 August 2003).

In an even more serious incident, four boys in Yarrawonga, Victoria were reportedly forced to lie on the floor of a classroom by a female teacher who then invited their classmates to walk over them, kick them and 'stomp on them'. Parents were outraged and called for an investigation (National Nine News, 30 October 2003). In a follow-up current affairs programme, one boy reported feeling bullied and humiliated. The 25-year-old teacher was disciplined (*A Current Affair*, 23 December

2003). However, the series of incidents raises wider questions about the approach of education authorities to managing boys in schools.

Eltham North Child Care in Melbourne was reported to have banned boys from wearing superhero costumes. The school claimed that wearing of superhero costumes such as Superman and Batman outfits made them boisterous and unruly and provoked violence. However, the decision was described by parents of the 3–5-year-old boys – mothers as well as fathers – as 'political correctness gone mad' (*A Current Affair*, 18 August 2003).

Leading messages about men

The predominantly negative portrayal of men in mass media is particularly demonstrated by the leading messages communicated about men in news, current affairs, talk shows and lifestyle media content. Figure 6.10 reports the top ten messages concerning men found in this study. This shows that men are mainly described as criminals, aggressive, violent, sexual abusers and predators. They are also represented and described frequently as chauvinists and misogynists, stupid or incompetent, insensitive, out of touch with their feelings and commitment-phobic.

Figure 6.11 further illustrates the overwhelmingly negative portrayals of men and male identities by contrasting positive and negative messages analysed. It shows negative iterations of most messages are far more frequent than positive iterations.

There *are* positive representations of men in mass media. Men are shown, albeit in a minority of cases, as commitment-oriented and responsible, protectors and carers, gentle and non-violent, and as law-abiding responsible citizens. These messages are reflected in mass media reporting of heroes such as firefighters and rescue workers, war heroes (particularly in news and feature articles around Armistice Day), Father of the Year awards, stories of police officers protecting communities, and profiles of respected male leaders.

A number of mass media honoured soldiers to mark the 50th anniversary of the end of the Korean War (27 July 2003) and on Armistice Day (11 November). For instance, following Remembrance Day 2003, the *Daily Telegraph* and *Sydney Morning Herald* published profiles honouring one of the world's oldest veterans, Marcel Caux, then aged 104.[2] After laying a wreath at the Sydney Cenotaph, Caux, who was wounded three

---

[2] Marcel Caux died in August 2004.

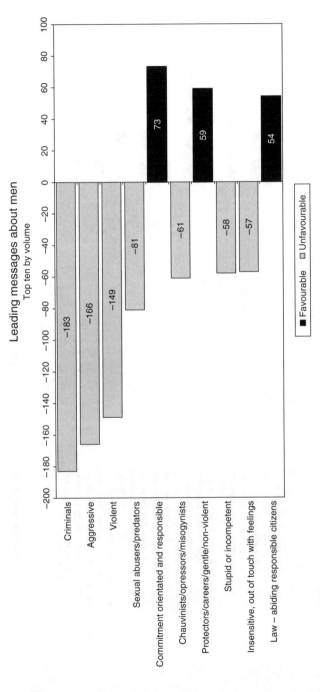

Leading messages about men
Top ten by volume

- Criminals: −183
- Aggressive: −166
- Violent: −149
- Sexual abusers/predators: −81
- Commitment orientated and responsible: 73
- Chauvinists/opressors/misogynists: −61
- Protectors/careers/gentle/non-violent: 59
- Stupid or incompetent: −58
- Insensitive, out of touch with feelings: −57
- Law – abiding responsible citizens: 54

■ Favourable □ Unfavourable

Figure 6.10 The 'top ten' messages about men in mass media

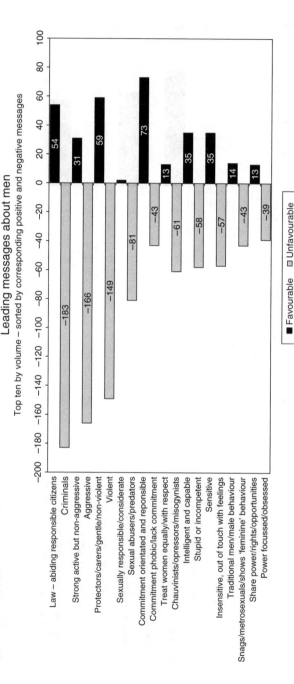

Figure 6.11 Comparison of leading positive and negative messages about men

times in the First World War and lived after the war as a declared pacifist, shook hands with children and said, 'Peace is so much better than war' (*Daily Telegraph*, 12 November 2003, p. 5; *Sydney Morning Herald*, 12 November 2003, p. 8). One leading magazine noted in a special report that 65,000 Australian men died during the First World War.

However, despite a number of noteworthy heroic profiles of men presented in mass media, Table 6.5 shows total unfavourable messages (1,082) outnumbered favourable messages (455) by almost two and a half to one. More than 70 per cent of all messages analysed were unfavourable, compared with just 29.5 per cent favourable.

Table 6.5 Detailed breakdown of leading messages in mass media representation of men by volume

Message	Favourable Mentions	Unfavourable Mentions
Criminals	0	183
Aggressive	0	166
Violent	0	149
Sexual abusers/predators	0	81
Commitment-oriented and responsible	73	0
Chauvinists/oppressors/misogynists	0	61
Protectors/carers/gentle/non-violent	59	0
Stupid or incompetent	0	58
Insensitive, out of touch with feelings	0	57
Law-abiding responsible citizens	54	0
Commitment phobic/lack commitment	0	43
Snags/metrosexuals/shows 'feminine' behaviour	0	43
Power-focused/obsessed	0	39
Not committed to children	0	36
Intelligent and capable	35	0
Sensitive	35	0
Groomed/waxed/feminine appearance	0	35
Paternal and care for children	34	0
Sex-, sports-, cars-, mates-focused	0	34
Strong active but non-aggressive	31	0
Don't do their share/lazy domestically	0	29
Strong, rugged, traditionally masculine appearance	23	0
Good communicators	21	0
Do not take care of their health/risk-taking	0	20
Work-focused	0	20
Poor communicators/women are better	0	19

Table 6.5   (Continued)

Message	Favourable Mentions	Unfavourable Mentions
Well rounded/balanced	16	0
Balance work/personal/family	15	0
Traditional men/male behaviour	14	0
Share power/rights/opportunities	13	0
Treat women equally/with respect	13	0
Do their share domestically	7	0
Fathers deserve equal child rights	7	0
Inconsiderate/Ineffective lovers	0	4
Don't deserve/can't be trusted with equal child rights	0	3
Care for their health	2	0
Sexually responsible/considerate	2	0
Boys do not/girls need more attention	0	2
Boys need special/more attention	1	0
Total	455	1,082

Gunmen, hitmen, conmen and man hunts – gender language continues (at least against men)

Noteworthy in this analysis was the number of times gendered language using 'man' as a suffix or prefix appeared in mass media headlines and stories – always in negative ways. Examples frequently cited include 'gunman', 'conman', 'hitman' and 'manhunt'. Headlined examples found during this study included:

- 'Chaos as West Gate Gunman Holds Police at Bay' (*The Age*, 17 September 2003, p. 1).
- 'A GUNMAN Fired up to Three Shots from a High-powered Weapon Yesterday' (*Daily Telegraph*, 10 December 2003, p. 1, capitalization in original).
- 'Gunmen Flee on Foot after Home Attacks' (*Sunday Telegraph*, 31 August 2003, p. 3).
- 'Ring of Steel to Shut down the Drive-by Gunmen' (*Sydney Morning Herald*, 23 October 2003, p. 4).
- 'Gunman in Court' (*Sunday Telegraph*, 2 November 2003, p. 20).
- 'Arrested Gunmen Linked to Gangsters' (*The Australian*, 23 December 2003, p. 3).
- 'Gunmen Ambush Iraq's Top Female' (*Daily Telegraph*, 22 September 2003, p. 18).

- 'Gunmen Kill Three Israelis in Gaza Raid' (*Sydney Morning Herald*, Weekend Edition, 25–26 October 2003, p. 20).
- 'Family Tears as Hitman Kills the Wrong Man' (*Daily Telegraph*, 9 December 2003, p. 1).
- 'Hitman Clue in Murders Investigation (*The Age*, 3 September 2003, p. 4).

When Australian-born Peter Finlay, writing under the pseudonym D. B. C. Pierre (with the initials standing for Dirty But Clean), won the Booker Prize for *Vernon God Little* in 2003, his gambling and criminal past were reported more than his literary achievements, with headlines including 'Conman's Booker Hopes' (*Daily Telegraph*, 14 October 2003, p. 6); 'Dirty but Clean Aussie Conman wins Booker' (*The Australian*, 16 October 2003, p. 7); and 'Australian Conman wins Booker Prize' (*Daily Telegraph*, 16 October 2003, p. 15).

Other male-gendered terms used in media reporting included 'wanted man' (e.g. 'Asia's most-wanted man lived the life of a dollar-a-day backpacker' in the *Sydney Morning Herald*, 27 August 2003, p. 8) and 'manmade'. Like all other uses, the latter was negatively presented in a major story on whale beaching headlined 'Man-made Hazards to Blame in Theory over Whale Strandings' (*Sydney Morning Herald*, Weekend Edition, 6–7 December 2003, p. 3).

Guidelines have been introduced in Australia as in many other developed countries to eliminate gendered language. The media regularly use the terms 'spokesperson' when speakers are male, with no uses of 'spokesman' or 'spokesmen' found in the extensive sample of coverage studied. Similarly 'chair' is used in place of the traditional 'chairman'. Men reading the media studied could only conclude that positive man words have been removed, while negative man words proliferate in media language.

Other noteworthy findings

Mass media studied also widely reported on Bryan Sykes' book *Adam's Curse* (2004), which claims that, ultimately, all men are facing extinction because the Y chromosome is deteriorating that men will die out within 150,000 years or so. More recent research reports that the Y chromosome may not be doomed as first thought, with the discovery of duplicate versions of the genetic code that can check the fidelity of male genes and repair any mutations (Broderick, 2003). However, the complexity of genetic studies makes them difficult to understand and mass media generally have promulgated the story that men are a dying breed. During the period of this study, headlines included:

- 'Y Men are on Their Way to Extinction' (*The Age*, 10 July 2003, p. 13).
- 'Y Men are Going to be Extinct' (Simon Benson column, *Daily Telegraph*, 25 August 2003, p. 19).
- 'Male Sex Hormones to Blame for Heart Disease' (*Daily Telegraph*, 17 September 2003, p. 3).
- 'Testosterone Makes the Heart Fail Faster' (*The Age*, 17 September 2003, p. 7).
- 'Cardiac Perils in the Genes for Men' (*Sydney Morning Herald*, 19 September 2003, p. 3).
- 'Y Factor Spells Doom for Men' (*Sydney Morning Herald*, 13 October 2003, p. 4).
- 'Degeneration Y: Adam is on the Eve of Extinction' (*The Age*, 13 October 2003, p. 3).
- 'XX-rated Negotiation Possible as the Y-front Faces Extinction' (Emma Tom column, *The Australian*, 15 October 2003, p. 11).

Such an onslaught of mass media messaging can do little for men's self-esteem and identities.

Cartoons also are a site of bias against men in mass media. No cartoons negatively portraying women were found in this study, but a number of cartoons depicted men negatively. For example:

- A large illustration by the well-known cartoonist Spooner showed a terrorist figure with the text: 'What a piece of work is man, how ignoble in passion, how limited in faculties, in form and moving how frenzied and degenerated, in action how like a fiend, in apprehension how like a man (with apologies to William Shakespeare)' (*The Age*, 16 October 2003).
- Another showed a figure attempting to sell Christian crosses to a customer saying, 'It's cheaper without the bloke' (*Sydney Morning Herald*, 13 November 2003, p. 14).
- A cartoon in a Health and Science supplement showed a confused-looking man sitting in front of a doctor who is peering into a microscope saying, 'I've just discovered your true manhood' (*Sydney Morning Herald*, Health and Science, 30 October 2003, p. 1).

This study focused on general news and current affairs, as well as talk shows and lifestyle media and did not analyse business reporting, entertainment or sport. Some researchers point out that men dominate senior positions in business and suggest that business media not included in this study represent men favourably. However, a study of business media coverage in Australia, Singapore, Hong Kong and Malaysia in 2003 found 'more than 70 per cent of reports on business related to corruption, fraud, poor corporate governance and ethics, insider trading, excessive executive payments, regulatory change to combat business fraud and malpractice, and poor customer service'. The ten-week study of 630 business media articles found 593 negative messages prominently reported compared with 385 positive messages in relation to business (CARMA International, 2003).

Other studies have shown that mass media reporting of sport principally portray traditional hegemonic masculinity which is increasingly criticized as too competitive, discriminatory and violent (e.g. Messner, 1988; 1992; Sabo and Curry Jansen, 1992; McKay and Middlemiss, 1995).

Therefore, it can be concluded that men are overwhelmingly represented negatively in mass media – not only in news, but in a wide range of representations and discourse reflected in and propagated through mass media.

Leading voices – who's talking about men?

Discourse on men and male identity reflected in and propagated through mass media editorials, opinion columns, features and letters, as well as comments quoted in news media articles, is largely contributed by women writers, academics and researchers. Furthermore, male voices given resonance in mass media discourse are, in most cases, pro-feminist men. Analysis of the sources of statements and quoted comments shows that, of the total sample, 21 per cent of mass media reports and comments on men were attributed to men generally, with a further 7 per cent sourced from male authors and columnists and 5 per cent from male academics and researchers. Reports and comments on the same subjects were almost equally contributed by women – 16 per cent from women generally; 10 per cent from female authors and columnists and 2 per cent from female academics and researchers. Overall, 33 per cent of mass media content relating to men was based on quotes from men, with 28 per cent contributed by women.

The most significant finding in relation to voices in mass media discourse on men is that opinion columns discussing men are mostly authored by women (10 per cent) compared with 5 per cent from male authors and columnists. Opinion columns are noteworthy because they are featured sections contributed by alleged experts and authoritative

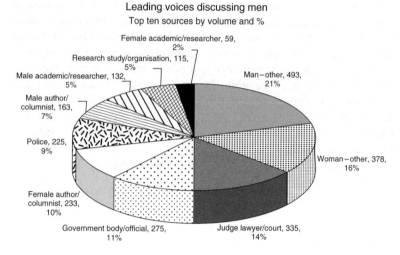

Figure 6.12 Breakdown of media content analysed by sources of comment

commentators dealing with major social, political and economic issues.

Sources analysed and reported in Figure 6.12 are not to be confused with by-lines (the writers) of news reports, which were excluded from this analysis. While a case can be made that the gender of writers is irrelevant in the case of news (which is third person reporting), sources of comment in this sample – the experts, authorities or subject experiences quoted – could be expected to be dominated by men. As men hold most positions of authority in politics, business, the police and the military, statistical probability suggests that men should comprise the majority of sources quoted on issues such as crime, work, and so on. In particular, when the subject of discussion includes specific male subjective experiences such as fatherhood, male sexuality, body image and male identity, it could be argued that men's experiences, feelings and viewpoints on these issues are the most relevant.

Certainly women are entitled to hold and express opinions on men. As close observers and partners of men in relationships, families and businesses, women have a vantage-point from which to contribute useful insights. But, the finding that women dominate opinion columns commenting on all men's issues studied reveals a disturbing reverse discrimination and inequity. Men's subjectivities, recognized as key components of knowledge in poststructuralist theory, are under-represented in discourse.

While the majority of media columnists writing on gender issues are women, in the interests of balance it is noted that not all write negatively about men. Bettina Arndt, writing in *The Age* under the headline 'Stop Sneering at Men. They Need Our Help', strongly attacked feminist and women's group criticisms of Australian Federal Government proposals to reform child custody laws to give men increased rights and access including possible joint custody. Responding to Labor MP Nicola Roxon, who labelled the Prime Minister's announcement as 'playing dog-whistle politics to men's groups aggrieved by the Family Court', Arndt observed: 'She used the phrase "men's groups" as if she was talking about something that had crawled out from under a rock.' Arndt pointed out that the Prime Minister's move for reform was triggered by alarming statistics from the Australian Institute of Suicide Research and Prevention at Griffith University which show that relationship breakdown and resulting loss of access to children are the major cause of male suicide, now four times the rate of female suicide. Arndt continued: 'It remains a mystery why so many men's issues, including male suicide, attract blatant sneers. Perhaps women like Nicola Roxon, with strong feminist histories, are still in the grip of the anti-male fervour that poisoned sectors of the women's movement 30 years ago' (*The Age*, 4 July 2003, pp. 4–6).

Women writers such as Bettina Arndt and Janet Albrechtsen who have defended men or criticized feminist approaches frequently incur the wrath of other women writers in the mass media. In a column headed 'Women Behaving Badly', Stephanie Dowrick took issue with female journalists who, she said, 'seem to have it in for other women'. Dowrick asked, 'What drives a woman to write so negatively and obsessively about other women?' The clear implication of Dowrick's polemic seems to be that women should not criticize other women in any circumstances. She continued her attack on male sympathetic women in the following terms:

> Consciously or unconsciously, penis-envying women have tended either to align themselves with men (becoming 'one of the boys') or to live out the worst conventionally male attributes such as competitiveness, aggressiveness, vengefulness and misogyny. (Good Weekend magazine, 'Inner life' column, *Sydney Morning Herald*, 1 November 2003)

Dowrick's statement is open to criticism on three grounds: 1) it contains dubious logic with its implication that women should always support women irrespective of the merits of their case in a lemming-like loyalty on the grounds of gender; 2) it generalizes that aggression, vengefulness and misogyny are male attributes; and 3) it contains a derogatory description of women who are sympathetic to men as 'penis envying'. The phrase 'the worst conventionally male attributes such as competitiveness, aggressiveness, vengefulness and misogyny' resonates with the misandric rhetoric of radical feminist discourse continuing to be propagated through major mass media.

An even more polemic diatribe against men was written by Julie Doohan in a column in the *Sydney Morning Herald*. She describes the process of dating and marrying a man in the following terms:

> You take him out of the pub when he can no longer stand and pour him into the hatchback he has designated you to drive... Suddenly your weekends are taken up with your undivided attention and moral support for him while he is playing soccer, cricket, pool, football, riding dirt bikes, karate. You wait patiently for the final whistle and drive him to the pub for drinks with the boys... He has coffee while you do the dishes, he watches the evening news while you prepare dinner... You put a mirror in the bedroom that he stops in front of every time he walks past... You prefer the fragrance of the air freshener, he prefers the smell of his own gases... Suddenly all your friends have kids. Getting together becomes an opportunity for the female to have some kind of adult conversation, the male to drink and make himself look ridiculous... (Heckler column, *Sydney Morning Herald*, 23 September 2003, p. 18)

While the title of this column suggests it is satire (see reference above), the content represents men as lazy, egocentric, uncouth drunkards and fools. Its tone is one of sarcasm and patronization and it uses sharply critical language such as 'make himself look ridiculous', suggestive of disgust and dislike. (This text is further discussed under 'Findings of in-depth qualitative media content analysis' later in this chapter.)

Differences between media

As could be expected, daily newspapers contained the most representations of men and male identities, as shown in Table 6.6. Interestingly, the average favourability of tabloids (*Daily Telegraph* and *Sunday Telegraph*) and broadsheet dailies often referred to as the 'quality' press (*The Age*,

Sydney Morning Herald and *The Australian*) was similar and newspapers were reasonably consistent overall. All were unfavourable on average in their portrayals of men, with heavy emphasis on news reporting of crime, corruption, sexual abuse and assault and other offences.

Table 6.6 Volume and favourability of media reporting on men and male identity listed by volume

Media	Favourable	Neutral	Unfavourable	Volume	Average Favourability
The Daily Telegraph	47	63	390	500	43.9
The Age	45	92	280	417	44.9
The Sydney Morning Herald	34	80	171	285	45.3
The Australian	23	50	181	254	44.1
National Nine TV News	10	8	127	145	39.1
The Sunday Telegraph	13	11	56	80	45.8
A Current Affair	10	1	41	52	42.5
The Bulletin	11	8	10	29	50.9
The Sunday Age	9	7	13	29	49.5
The Weekend Australian	5	11	13	29	48.1
Oprah	10	3	11	24	53.3
'Good Weekend', Sydney Morning Herald	2	6	12	20	46.0
Cosmopolitan	4	1	14	19	46.1
Frasier	0	1	15	16	41.9
Australian Women's Weekly	5	2	9	16	47.2
Weekend Australian Magazine	3	8	2	13	51.9
Sunday Magazine – in The Age	2	6	6	14	47.9
60 Minutes	2	0	5	7	46.4
Family Circle	5	0	2	7	62.9
The Sun-Herald	1	2	4	7	45.7
Queer Eye For The Straight Guy	0	0	6	6	40.0
FHM	2	1	2	5	50.0
Ralph	2	0	2	4	50.0
Total	**245**	**361**	**1,372**	**1,978**	**44.6**

(*Note:* Total volume exceeds the number of articles analysed as some articles were coded as both favourable and unfavourable due to mixed content.)

Weekend newspapers were slightly more favourable than dailies, with a number of lifestyle features and profiles on male leaders, personalities and stars, although they also contained more unfavourable coverage than favourable representations.

Family Circle was the most positive towards men of all media analysed, but published a low volume of articles on men and men's issues, with its content predominantly focused on women's issues and concerns in relation to family, children and relationships.

Television news contained the most unfavourable reporting and portrayals of men and male identities – 39.1 average on the favourability scale used where 50 is neutral and the average for all press and TV coverage analysed was 44.6. TV news predominantly focused on crime, including murders, beatings, rapes, gangland killings, sexual assaults and armed robberies. TV news also reported male hero stories, such as rescues and tributes to servicemen and women on occasions such as Armistice Day and the 50th anniversary of the end of the Korean War which occurred during the period of this study. But these positive stories were a small proportion of the coverage related to men. Given its large audience and the widely reported impact of television, TV news is a major source of negative representations of men.

The next most unfavourable media were *Queer Eye for the Straight Guy*, *Frasier* and *A Current Affair*. *Queer Eye for the Straight Guy* became one of the most watched cable TV programmes in the US in 2002 and launched to ratings success in Australia in September 2003. It was an obvious choice for analysis given its overt gender themes. *Queer Eye*, as it is commonly abbreviated, represents gay men in a largely favourable context. The 'Fab Five' are talented presenters with a flair for fashion and interior design and are sympathetic and empathetic to the heterosexual men whom they 'make over' in the show. However, the programme depicts heterosexual men before their makeover as being poorly dressed and groomed, domestically incompetent, unsophisticated, untidy and often unclean. Heterosexual men need to be reconstructed by the 'Fab Five' to the knowing smiles and gratitude of their long-suffering wives and girlfriends. Also, despite its casting of gay male characters in positive mainstream roles, gay men are portrayed in highly stereotypical ways.

Frasier was chosen as representative of TV programmes in the general lifestyle category. While within the genre of comedy, Frasier is a psychologist who gratuitously dispenses advice on his radio show and the programme deals with themes including love, dating, sex, marriage, family relationships, fatherhood and men. The programme does not provide substantial representations on men given its humorous and satirical format which cannot be taken too seriously. However, both Frasier and Niles are presented as boorish and arrogant snobs and Frasier is shown as patronizing of his long suffering producer, Ros.

The TV current affairs show *A Current Affair* broadcast a number of high-profile reports on men, particularly sensational stories such as claims of sexual assault by prominent men, domestic violence and 'dead-beat dads', as instanced in this study. The international current affairs programme *60 Minutes* was more favourable overall, broadcasting a mix of favourable and unfavourable reports. One noteworthy segment broadcast internationally titled 'Band of Brothers' filed by the US reporter and former soldier Mike Cerré gave a moving and positive account of several days with Fox 2/5 Company, a US Marines unit which spent 189 days on active duty in Iraq in 2003. Cerré took a neutral position on the merits of the war and did not sensationalize or eulogize the exploits of the soldiers. He even stated that there was nothing special about Fox 2/5: 'They were ordinary soldiers sent to do a job', he said. The report showed a group of frightened young men, coming to grips with the stresses and confusion of battle, coping with the harsh elements of the desert and facing imminent injury or death. During the filming of the report, First Sergeant Smith, the unit's mentor and senior non-commissioned officer, was killed by enemy fire. Cerré traced the effects on the men as they saw death first hand, their triumphant entry to Baghdad, and their return home and thoughts of what they would say to Smith's wife. He reported with a tone of both respect and tragedy: 'I went to war with Fox 2/5 Company and watched them become men' (*60 Minutes*, 28 September 2003).

Oprah, presented by Oprah Winfrey, an international daytime television talk show with a very large global audience, deals with a wide range of issues, including health, beauty, self-fulfilment, fashion, personal success, personal crises and social issues. While commonly seen as a women's programme, *Oprah* presents substantial content on men and men's issues, several examples of which have been cited and which were some of the most positive and sympathetic portrayals of men and male identity analysed in this study. One programme in particular involved six men talking about their concerns as fathers. They were given a significant amount of time to speak in their own words. Then their views were presented on video to their wives and the audience, after which open discussion was invited. Another significant *Oprah* special cited in this study involved a two-episode discussion of domestic violence which presented a range of views including men's perspectives and considerable research on the issue.

As a current affairs magazine, *The Bulletin* has little interest in crime stories – a major source of unfavourable representation of men. Instead, it published feature articles reporting research into education, politics, science and topical issues such as the 50th anniversary of the end of the Korean War and achievement awards. *The Bulletin* averaged 50.9 on the favourability scale used, slightly above neutral (50.0) and was one of only three media in the sample to average above 50 (neutral).

Among women's magazines, *Cosmopolitan* contained extensive comment on and portrayals of men, mainly in the context of objectification (e.g. the 'Guy without his shirt' section and features advising women on how to tell if a man is committed and how to keep a guy). *Cosmopolitan* also reinforces stereotypes of men as sex-obsessed (eg. a lift-out section titled 'The Penis Monologues' published November 2003).

Men's magazines such as *Ralph* and *FHM* do not present men with much to be proud of, containing a raunchy cocktail of machismo, sexism, chauvinism and what can only be described as smut. Rather than being at the cutting edge of representing men in positive and progressive ways, so-called new age men's magazines represent reactionary, stereotyped images of men. Significantly, men's magazines contributed many of the unfavourable articles about men analysed in this study, albeit balanced with some sympathetic reporting on men and men's issues such as male health.

Findings of in-depth qualitative media content analysis

A number of significant mass media portrayals of men and male identities were further analysed qualitatively and in depth to identify the underlying attitudes towards men and the male identities that they reveal and the meanings that they might convey to men, boys, women, girls and society about men and male identity. In the doctoral research study from which these data are drawn, in-depth qualitative analysis included positive as well as negative portrayals of men and male identity, based on Huberman's (1994) recommendation for qualitative sampling in three stages:

- typical or representative examples;
- negative or disconfirming examples; and
- exceptional or discrepant examples.

Here, just three examples of mass media articles about men are cited from the most common and typical representations found – i.e. negative portrayals.

Example 1

> Suddenly I was remembering all those other times I've been afraid. Fending off a gang of aggressive young men on a train station late at night. Walking home from a bus stop, being followed by a strange man in an overcoat. Backing away from a man who is smiling at me and masturbating in broad daylight in my local park. Locking my car doors while a man shakes his fist at me for taking the last parking spot outside the supermarket. This month the newspapers have been full of stories about men shooting their wives, murdering their fathers-in-law, men strangling prostitutes, men taking their own lives. I've been lucky. This kind of extreme violence has never touched me personally. Most of the men I know are gentle, talkative types. (And yes, I know women can be killers too.) But at the back of nearly every woman's mind lurks a fear of that naked masculine aggression... (Sian Prior, 'Figures and Front Mask the Fear Within', opinion column, *The Age*, 29 September 2003, A3, p. 2)

The context of this paragraph is a simple, albeit unpleasant, incident reported in preceding paragraphs of the newspaper article – a man kicks Prior's car door and shouts at her while she is waiting to turn at an intersection. There is no evidence to show whether the man is unjustifiably aggressive or whether, for instance, Prior had not seen him and almost run him over causing him to react. However, even giving the author the benefit of the doubt, the text traverses from this simple, inconclusive incident to a series of recollections of past events and then, at the end, attempts to link these to make a generalization about men – that they exhibit 'naked masculine aggression'.

The grammatical construction of the text uses a series of incomplete sentences each beginning with a participle – 'Fending off a gang... Walking home... being followed... Backing away from a man... Locking my car doors...'. Use of participles, rather than past tense verbs, brings these unrelated events into closer proximity and suggests they are ongoing, even though they occurred some time in the past. The close grammatical linking of these events also suggests an interrelationship and creates unification of what, in reality, are almost certainly totally unrelated events occurring at different times and in different places. Linking these events in a series of run-on sentences achieves the effect of the whole being greater than the sum of the parts. To the reader coming across these incidents presented as a list in this way, the likely impression is that there is a lot of male aggression and violence about. Use of the words 'all those other times' in the opening sentence primes the audience to believe that there have been many instances of male violence observed by Prior.

It is also significant that the author writes in the first person, sending a signal to the reader that she is an eye-witness to the events (and the victim), giving her voice credibility and enlisting sympathy from the audience – two powerful factors in creating meaning.

On close examination, it is doubtful whether some parts of the text are truthful or reliable. For instance, the second sentence refers to 'fending off a gang of aggressive young men'. How could one woman fend off a *gang* of young men? The third sentence talks about 'being followed by a strange man in an overcoat'. Breaking down this phrase reveals further questions about the authenticity of the text. The word 'strange' is used, even though, presumably, the author could not observe the man clearly as he was behind her, and the basis for her description of him as 'strange' is unclear. Furthermore, the phrase 'in an overcoat' employs clichéd imagery – a man in an overcoat being a hackneyed shorthand image for a sexual pervert. Was the (strange) man following her really wearing an overcoat (not many men in Australia do), or is this a literary device – a fiction?

Then Prior employs a somewhat ironic twist and a circular argument in an attempt to present third party endorsement to support her claims of pervasive male violence. She mourns that 'this month the newspapers have been full of stories about men shooting their wives' when, in fact, Prior herself is contributing to the filling of newspapers reporting on men allegedly committing various offences – even though nothing has actually happened to her. This statement is a case of the media reporting the media.

What she reports the media reporting is also significant. In the space of a few lines, the author moves from a man kicking her car door and shouting to men 'shooting their wives', 'strangling prostitutes' and 'taking their own lives'. The text implies that this is a logical progression of male aggression.

The phrase 'I've been lucky' preceding the admission that 'this kind of extreme violence' had never touched her personally shifts the perspective from violence being deviant behaviour to male violence being the norm – she has been lucky *not* to have been killed by a man. Statistically, her safety was not luck. In reality, a very small number of people are attacked or killed in Australia each year. But Prior makes it sound like a common occurrence from which she has narrowly escaped by sheer good fortune.

The acknowledgement that she has not personally experienced extreme male violence, that most of the men she knows 'are gentle talkative types' and that women can be killers too suggests that Prior is finally going to withdraw from her negative rhetoric and represent a balanced view of men. But she immediately follows this with 'But' – a conjunction to indicate opposition and exception – and continues, 'at the back of nearly every woman's mind lurks a fear of that naked masculine aggression'. The phrase 'every woman's mind' explicitly suggests that all women live in fear of men – a generalization without foundation. And use of the word 'naked' to qualify masculine aggression is suggestive (symbolic) of primeval, primitive male behaviour.

From both a narratology and semiotic perspective, this text contains signs indicating that all or most men are extremely aggressive and violent and that they engage in threats, assault, sexual perversion and murder on a regular basis. Its use of voice (first person eye-witness subject), tense (frequent use of participles instead of verbs), poetic imagery, clichés and adjectives ('naked') are selected and combined to create meaning beyond the facts. In reality, little or nothing has happened – no damage to the car was reported and the violence was a man 'shouting'. In media terms, it is a non-story. But, Prior manages to present images of male gangs, stalkers, sexual perverts, harassers, shooters, stranglers, murderers and suicides in the space of one paragraph.

Only close examination reveals the inconsistencies in the text. Most readers scanning the text are likely to come away with an impression of pervasive male violence and aggression based on claimed first hand experience by the author.

Example 2

> You take him out of the pub when he can no longer stand and pour him into the hatchback he has designated you to drive... Suddenly your weekends are taken up with your undivided attention and moral support for him while he is playing soccer, cricket, pool, football, riding dirt bikes, karate. You wait patiently for the final whistle and drive him to the pub for drinks with the boys... He has coffee while you do the dishes, he watches the evening news while you prepare dinner... You put a mirror in the bedroom that he stops in front of every time he walks past... You prefer the fragrance of the air

freshener, he prefers the smell of his own gases... Suddenly all your friends have kids. Getting together becomes an opportunity for the female to have some kind of adult conversation, the male to drink and make himself look ridiculous... (Julie Doohan, Heckler column, *Sydney Morning Herald*, 23 September 2003, p. 18)

The first characteristic of this text that stands out is the use of second person voice. This writing technique is not uncommon in highly personalized writing which seeks to create an intimacy with the reader by moving the reader into the frame of the subject and, by implication, excluding 'third' persons. But immediately the text indicates that it is not simply a discourse between subjects sharing a common experience. The opening words 'You take him' show a mix of second person for women and third person for men to set up an oppositional binary and a conflict that runs throughout the text – 'us and them'. This framing of the narrative positions the reader with the author as subject (you) and men as objects (him).

The next phrase 'out of the pub when he can no longer stand up' sets the scene. She has to take him home because he is 'unable to stand up let alone walk'. The phrase 'pour him into the hatchback' employs a clichéd verb used for drunks which emphasizes the excess of the man's drinking and his helplessness – he is 'poured' like liquid or jelly, lacking shape, strength and substance. The final phrase of the first sentence referring to the hatchback 'he has designated you to drive' positions the man as dominating, patronizing (the hatchback is presumably not the principal family car), as well being a drunken, selfish, boorish fool.

While the text mainly uses active verbs in association with the second person to denote the active forthright female subject – e.g. 'You take him out of the pub' and '[you] pour him into the hatchback' – passive verbs are employed in connection with negatives to emphasize loss and a sense of victimization – 'your weekends are *taken up*'. 'Taken up' suggests theft and invasion of the woman's free time and freedom by this demanding, selfish man. In other words, positive things are done by the author; negative things are done to the author by a man.

The pronouns you and your are used ten times, on each occasion doing something for *him* directly or indirectly – taking him home, driving him, giving him attention, waiting for him, driving him again, doing the dishes, preparing dinner, decorating the house, freshening up the house. Meanwhile, *he* is falling down drunk, poured into the hatchback, showing off at soccer and other sports, going to the pub, sitting having coffee while she works, admiring himself Narcissus-like in the mirror that she hung, smelling up the house, drinking and making a fool of himself.

Phrases such as 'he prefers the smell of his own gases' venture into sarcasm and a patronizing tone, as well as shifting voice to third person omniscient – a technique of fiction writers. The author could objectively observe that her husband farts if he does so, but she is unlikely to know that he prefers this smell. Even if it is true that he is flatulent, he is not likely to have stated that he prefers passed wind to fresh air. In this phrase, the author is venturing beyond reporting of events and facts into subjective comments and the techniques of the all-knowing omniscient narrator of fiction. She is describing his thoughts and mental state, making them (or at least her derogatory representation of them) visible to the audience. This is a clear sign embedded in the text to incite disdain for the man.

The paragraph concludes with an even more telling sign of what the text is about. The final lines describe 'get-togethers' with friends as 'an opportunity for the female to have some adult conversation', clearly implying that she does not have adult conversation at home. But, most significantly, use of the article – '*the* female' and '*the* male' – turns her personal anecdote into a generalization about women's and men's social habits. 'The male' signifies that not only the man who is the subject of her narrative but men generally drink and make themselves look ridiculous. Doohan's text is a diatribe against men given vent in the news and editorial pages of a high-circulation mass newspaper.

Example 3

> My children were three and seven when I ended my marriage. Their father kept in contact with them for a year or so, but after three less than three months, I knew it wouldn't last. Somehow, in that short time, his love for them just seemed to evaporate. I would watch helplessly as my little boy sat on top of his suitcase waiting for his daddy to arrive, legs kicking back and forth with anticipation, for a father who often did not keep his promise... There's a backlash against single mothers. It is being fuelled by commentators such as Arndt who never miss an opportunity to portray single mothers as manipulative and self-serving, a men's movement that is deeply misogynous, and a Prime Minister who wants to drag women back into the kitchen where he thinks they belong. (Trish Bolton, 'When it Comes to Child Access, Many Men Just Don't Want to Know', *Sydney Morning Herald*, 4 September 2003. p. 11)

The very first word of this text, a pronoun (which text and discourse analysts study assiduously), sets the tone. '*My* children' contrasts with the second sentence that also begins with a pronoun '*Their* father . . .'. Pronoun use reveals that the author believes that the children are hers rather than theirs – although the main point of the text is that he has obligations and responsibilities to them. The first sentence also makes it clear that she ended the marriage. (She may have had good cause, although the reasons are not stated.)

The second sentence indicates that the father kept in contact for 'a year or so' – a not inconsiderable amount of time if he was really intent on leaving his children's lives as she alleges – but adds that 'after less than three months, I knew it wouldn't last'. The latter statement is interesting for its use of the first person pronoun 'I' and the definitive verb 'knew'. She does not say she 'suspected' or 'was concerned' that it wouldn't last. She 'knew'. Such a statement indicates either fortune-teller powers – or an arrogant and self-important viewpoint.

The author goes on to state 'his love for them just seemed to evaporate'. Again, this goes beyond reported conversation or observation and imputes reasons and intent. In reality, she is unlikely to know how he felt about his children and her claims contradict extensive research. Surveys and interview data suggest that separated fathers fret for their children – some even commit suicide. This sentence illustrates a characteristic common in many discussions by women of men – a tendency to speak not only for themselves but for men as well. And not only for men's actions which women could observe, but men's thoughts, feelings and even the extent of their love for their children which, particularly when living separately, they have little if any capacity to know.

The sentence 'I would watch helplessly as my little boy sat on top of his suitcase waiting for his daddy to arrive, legs kicking back and forth with anticipation' contains a number of signs which seek to play on the emotions of the reader. The verb 'watched' suggests the author is simply an observer with no part in the scene and the adverb 'helplessly' to describe her position evokes pathos and sympathy, when in reality the text reveals that she chose to end the marriage. Even though he may have been an undesirable husband, she was clearly not helpless. And the negative and judgemental tone of the author's statements about her ex-husband suggests that she may not be merely a helpless bystander; her attitude towards him and stated views evident in the text may be a contributing factor to his absence. This is not argumentative to suggest that she is to blame for her son's fatherlessness; it is presented simply as a possibility. But it is a possibility to which the reader has little if any access. The man's perspective is beyond the text and the reader is left with an image of a helpless woman and a little boy kicking his legs waiting for his daddy who never comes.

Use of the term 'his daddy' stands out as an intentional linguistic device. Earlier, the author describes the man as 'their father'. But when he does not visit his son, the language switches to the more emotive 'his daddy'. The man is described with the more distant term when he is close up; then with the more emotionally close term when he is absent. The phrase 'legs kicking back and forth in anticipation' also is symbolic of the child kicked back and forth physically and emotionally between the mother and the father and presents a visual image of a sad, lonely boy – sadness and loneliness caused by his father. The child may have been kicking his legs back and forth in boredom – many boys do. The author ascribes intention to the father and the son, which are signs to the reader on how to interpret the narrative.

Then the subject broadens to writers, the men's movement and the Prime Minister where further manifest signs are presented on how this text is to be interpreted. The term 'backlash', a feminist hallmark cited several times in this book, is used. Also, a number of generalizations are made – commentators such as Bettina Arndt 'never miss an opportunity' to denigrate single mothers; the men's movement is not only women-hating but 'deeply misogynous'; and the Prime Minister 'wants to drag women back into the kitchen'. The terms 'backlash', 'misogynous', 'drag' in relation to women, and reference to the 'kitchen', are symbols of male violence, chauvinism and subjugation. This narrative is not about one mother's experiences of child custody and visitation. It presents signs suggesting that a more pervasive and sinister movement (or even conspiracy) by men generally is afoot and acting against women.

The concluding words that provided the headline of the article, 'When it comes to child access, many men just don't want to know' confirms this polemical objective and provides yet another example of women generalizing men's intentions and feelings as well as their behaviour. From her experience as narrated, the first person author could observe that when it comes to child access, *some* men don't *turn up*. But whether *many* men 'don't want to *know*' can be revealed only through interviews, discussions or surveys among separated fathers. Such research has been conducted (e.g. Hawthorne, 2002) and this suggests that the majority of separated fathers *do* want to know and want increased access to their children.

From a narratology perspective, the story suggests this woman's ex-husband is a 'deadbeat dad' and, most significantly, that he is typical of many separated fathers.

Semiotic and semiological analysis which focuses on the meanings interpreted by the audience is problematic in this and the other texts cited because it is not clear without audience research whether, or to what extent, readers 'see through' such polemic. One interpretation is that the preceding text is about the understandable frustration and anger of a single mother whose ex-husband shirked his responsibilities to their son. Alternatively, in the mind of a reader armed with more favourable experiences or statistics on the relatively small number of fathers who are 'deadbeat dads', the meaning could be that Bolton is presenting an extreme example non-typical of fathers and, therefore, while she deserves sympathy, her argument against increased father access should be rejected. A more extreme reading could be that Bolton is a whingeing single mother who threw her husband out, is bitter and hostile towards him, which possibly accounts for his absence, and is now angry at the world for her predicament. In a structuralist view, there is one meaning coded in the text, but it is a matter of some contention how this is identified and what validity such a reading has. In a poststructuralist view, any one of these readings, or others, may be equally valid.

What is known about the audience of these three samples is that they are readers of the *Sydney Morning Herald* and *The Age* respectively. Demographic data indicate that, conservatively, 879,000 people potentially read the two articles that appeared in the *Sydney Morning Herald* (its audited circulation at the time) – 1.76 million readers in total. A further 689,000 people potentially read *The Age* column (its audited circulated at the time), giving a total readership of almost 2.5 million. Demographic data also show that these newspapers are read by a mass audience spread across a wide socio-economic spectrum, although most are better educated than average. The audience is approximately 50 per cent men who are likely to read these texts quite differently from women. This suggests that many readers are likely to interpret the texts differently from the authors' intended meanings. But others may not be equipped to make oppositional or alternative interpretations of the signs presented and are likely to draw meanings from the signs which speak their language (e.g. 'you pour him into the hatchback', 'you take him home', 'waiting for a father who often did not keep his promise', etc.).

The semiologist or semiotician can, at best, make an educated guess as to readers' interpretations without conducting audience research. What can be concluded is that qualitative analysis of the texts shows the highly negative and at times vitriolic nature of representations of men and male identity in mass media today, despite introduction of anti-discrimination and anti-sexism policies. Men could conclude that these policies work one-way to protect women, but offer no protection to men from highly discriminatory and sexist discourse. And the frequency of negative representations of men and male identities as shown in this study suggest that at least some, if not many, get through and impact on readers – men, boys, women and girls.

In a second verifying phase of qualitative media content analysis, six media articles were selected for in-depth qualitative study using MAXqda, a specialist software program for qualitative data analysis (Dressing&pehl GbR & Verbi GmbH, 2004). These texts were imported into MAXqda and analysed against a set of text categories and codes. The preceding manual (human) analysis of the texts by the author focused attention on signs such as pronouns, voice, tonal qualities and other qualitative criteria, but did not fully adhere to Mayring's (2003) suggested approach of inductive category development and deductive category application. Use of MAXqda allowed text categories to be set up based on the research questions posed, the theoretical framework of this study, and understanding of the texts studied, and for codes to be applied in a systematic way to the selected texts. Like a number of qualitative text analysis programs, MAXqda allows dictionary-supplied categories to be applied to texts, or categories to be created by the researcher. Given the specialized nature of this study, categories were created in the program for:

- overall focus of texts;
- tone;
- messages;
- key words.

Specialized codes were created in each category reflecting the issues and messages, both positive and negative, identified in this study during quantitative analysis. Overall focus of text codes were created based on Nathanson and Young's categories of male representations identified in the chapters of their 2001 study – blaming men; laughing at men (i.e. to ridicule or trivialize); looking down on men; bypassing men; dehumanizing men; and demonizing men. The negative category of 'marginalize' was added, reflecting findings of quantitative analysis in this study, and positive categories correlating to each negative category were created to allow analysis to be balanced. For instance, 'blaming men' was matched by 'supporting men'; 'demonizing men' was matched by 'eulogizing or praising men', etc. In addition to ten codes for overall focus, eight codes were established to identify tone (respect, friendship, love, partnership, anger, ridicule, sarcasm and fear) and 20 messages were tracked (ten positive and ten negative) as identified in quantitative analysis and listed in the coding list in Appendix A.

This analysis further confirmed the predominant focus on male aggression and violence and overwhelmingly negative representations of men and male identities. Qualitative text analysis using MAXqda found:

- The predominant overall focus was demonizing men, followed by trivializing men.
- The most common tones evident in the texts were fear, ridicule and anger. Respect, friendship, love and partnership did not appear in the texts selected.
- The leading messages were that men are aggressors and violent and that they are criminals. Work and responsibility also featured in the texts, but not as frequently as violence and crime, and irre-sponsibility was cited equally with responsibility. Hero, protector and committed/commitment each appeared only once, as did sexual abuser and 'deadbeat dad';
- The leading key words found were 'murder/murdering', 'killing/killers', 'drinking/drunk' and 'misogynous' – all on more than one occasion in just six short texts totalling slightly over 1,000 words.

As an equal number of correlating positive codes for overall focus, tone and messages were created and available for coding, and computer-aided qualitative analysis was conducted on both typical (negative) media articles as identified in quantitative analysis and disconfirming (positive) articles, these findings can taken as reliable reflections of media discourse and confirm the findings reported in quantitative analysis and human qualitative analysis.

Conclusions

This extensive analysis of mass media news, current affairs, talk shows and lifestyle media shows that these primary sources of what are claimed and widely seen as fact, truth and reality predominantly portray men as violent and aggressive thieves, murderers, wife and girlfriend beaters, sexual abusers, molesters, perverts, irresponsible, deadbeat dads and philanderers, even though, in reality, only a small proportion of men act out these roles and behaviours.

In the large sample of news, current affairs and lifestyle media content analysed, almost 70 per cent of all reporting and comment on men and male identity was negative and more than 80 per cent of portrayals of men and male identity were unfavourable. Violence and aggression are overwhelmingly the most frequent representations associated with men and boys, portrayed in a daily barrage of reports of criminal acts, including armed robberies, assaults, murder, sexual abuse and assaults on women; domestic violence, harassment and discrimination in work. Men and boys are also widely represented as irresponsible, risk-taking, commitment-phobic, insensitive, undomesticated, out of touch with their feelings and poor communicators.

With the exception of a small minority of positive media portrayals of male heroes such as war veterans, firefighters and rescuers, and an equally small percentage of portrayals of men as good fathers, husbands and citizens, the only males presented positively are men and boys who have been feminized, such as metrosexuals and males who exhibit 'a feminine side'. In short, the only good in men, according to most discourse reflected and propagated in mass media, are traits identified as female. Maleness is widely represented as innately and culturally evil, and characteristics of masculinity are principally portrayed as undesirable and anachronistic – notably aggression, violence, sexual predaciousness and promiscuity, competitiveness and traditional body image.

As well as highly negative portrayals in mass media discussion of serious issues such as violence, family involvement, fatherhood and work, men are trivialized and objectified in populist media content such as the 'Hunk of the month' and 'Man without his shirt' sections in women's magazines, and treated as the butt of jokes in newspaper cartoons and TV 'sitcoms' such as *Frasier*.

Negative representations of men and male identity are not only a quantitative phenomenon – i.e. outnumbering positive portrayals which, in isolation, may not prove anything. Qualitative analysis also conducted as part of this study shows highly negative messages concerning men and male identity are communicated through influential quality media as well as popular press (University of Queensland, 1992); are contributed by credible sources such as academics and best-selling authors (see Figure 6.12); and are couched in semiotically significant (i.e. persuasive) language as discussed in Chapter 5. In-depth text analysis techniques reveal that, tonally, mass media content frequently contains emotional charged vitriol and invective against men and male identity, and balance is not provided through oppositional (i.e. male supportive) views in all but a few cases.

It can be concluded from this study that men are widely demonized, marginalized, trivialized and objectified in mass media. These findings support and expand those of Nathanson and Young (2001) and others, who have reported 'misandry' and denigration of men in modern societies.

Some media writers recognize the prevalence of negativity in mass media portrayals of men. Andrew Bock (2003) reports that 'media that appeal to women are more likely to portray men as bungling, incompetent fall guys in the workplace and in relationships'. Bock also alleges that articles in print media contain more prejudicial generalizations about men partly because women dominate the field of writing about relationships, as is shown in this study. 'Biases run many ways across the media, but an overriding bias in modern media seems to run away from positive images of men' Bock says (2003, p. 13). Similarly, Alan Close (2003, p. 51) in his 'In the male' column in the *Sydney Morning Herald Good Weekend* magazine, responded to a woman columnist lamenting that 'all the decent men are either married or gay' by saying:

> It's an example of the systemic dismissal men have suffered for decades, from insidious images of dumbcluck husbands and inept fathers on TV to the pernicious suspicion that any man seen in public with a child must be a potential pederast. It's a sobering reminder of how accepted this degradation of men has become.

In a major opinion feature in the *Sydney Morning Herald*, Miranda Devine (2003) sympathetically summarized the plight of men today. Devine cited:

- The Oxford University research finding outlined in *Adam's Curse* by the genetics professor, Bryan Sykes, that the male Y chromosome is disintegrating and destined for extinction (although this finding has been contradicted in other research).
- British psychotherapists' description of the 'Atlas syndrome', the male equivalent of 'superwoman' which, it was said, is setting impossible ideals for men to live up to as breadwinners, workers, 'super-dads', perfect husbands and other roles.
- Men's Line counselling service data which report that 80 per cent of 30,000 calls from men in two years of operation were about family and relationship problems, particularly distress over lack of access to their children, with many men suicidal.
- Surveys which have found that at least one in ten men feel they have been discriminated against by the Family Court.

- Confusing new images of masculinity such as metrosexuals. Devine asked: 'What is the average man to make of ads for hair-removal treatments in which a woman recoils from the embrace of a hairy chested man in the before shot and, in the after shot when he is hairless, she can't keep her hands off him?' (p. 17).

Devine acknowledged 'there are very negative images of men at the present time . . . anger at broken relationships, coupled with a masculine ideal they have no hope of meeting and an epidemic of man-bashing in popular culture, leads to challenged self-worth at best for men. At its extreme, it can lead to the kind of tragic murder-suicide we witnessed in Sydney this week' (2003, p. 17) (referring to a father who killed his three children and himself).

A further important conclusion that can be drawn from this media content analysis is that the most frequent and generalized representations of men identified – men as violent aggressors frequently committing domestic violence, child abuse, sexual assault and other violent crimes – are *misrepresentations*. Woods (1998) and a number of other researchers challenge many of the so-called facts presented by mass media in relation to domestic violence and child abuse. Woods says that 'using data from reputable sources such as the United States Bureau of Justice Statistics, and major research studies, we find that the "demonizing" of the male is certainly not justified'. He cites longitudinal research conducted by Strauss and Gelles in 1975 and again in 1985. The National Family Violence Survey in the US (Straus and Gelles, 1986), one of the largest studies of family violence undertaken, reported that women are just as likely to perpetrate violence on men as men on women. Further, the researchers found that, between 1975 and 1985, the rate of violence by men against women decreased, while the rate of violence by women against men increased.

Tomison (1996) has reported that most physical abuse of children is perpetrated by women, with the single largest group of child abusers being mothers. Other studies support this claim. A US National Incidence of Child Abuse and Neglect study in 2000 reported that 'where maltreatment of children led to death, 78 per cent of the perpetrators were female' (Hilton, 2000).

Clare (2000) reports that in 1981, 43 per cent of children living in households with a mother only were abused, compared with 18 per cent of children who were abused in the population overall. Abuse by single mothers' male partners or casual acquaintances was not identifiable in this study, but it did suggest that single mothers living alone with children committed or were party to abuse more frequently than occurred in dual-parent families.

While these studies were conducted across a number of different cultures and socio-economic groups and investigated different types of domestic violence, which makes comparison problematic, they consistently contradict claims that men are responsible for domestic violence. Recent Australian statistics directly comparable with Australian media content analysis cited in this chapter confirm this misrepresentation of men. In 2001–2, there were 30,500 substantiated cases of child abuse or neglect in Australia, involving 25,600 children aged between 0 and 17 years. Physical abuse and emotional abuse or neglect each comprised 27 per cent of these, while sexual abuse comprised 14 per cent of cases. Information collected by community services authorities indicates that the incidence of abuse or neglect was higher in one-parent families (Australian Bureau of Statistics, 2003, p. 52). Analysis shows that in more than 88 per cent of 23,000 Australian one-parent families, children under 15 were under the care of their mother (20,300), compared with just 11 per cent of children under 15 (2,700) in the care of their fathers (Australian Bureau of Statistics, 2003, p. 28). If men were the predominant child abusers, sole-parent children in the care of women should have a lower rate of abuse than families where men were present. But, instead, the contrary is true.

Despite these research statistics, an editorial in *The Australian* (2003) reported that a Queensland Crime Commission study found 45 per cent of females and 10 per cent of males had been abused and stated, 'offenders are almost universally male'. The claim and many others about male-perpetrated domestic violence are simply wrong, say researchers such as Woods (1998).

Statistics on domestic violence are hotly contested, with various studies using different definitions of violence and agencies suggesting that reported violence is only the 'tip of the iceberg', arguing that many instances remaining unreported. However, Woods (1998) notes that under-reporting is more likely to occur among men, as police do not take complaints of 'husband-bashing' seriously in most cases and many men are reluctant to admit that they have been battered or abused. There are few if any support agencies or refuges for men to go to as there are for women, so reporting offers little benefit. The man often has few options but to return home.

Claims in relation to domestic violence are also skewed by the definitions employed. Hilton (2000) cites a brochure on domestic violence which states that 'watching' a person can constitute the crime of stalking. He also comments on a brochure distributed by the Centre for Women and Families which informs readers that 'embarrassing a person in public or private', criticizing or 'withholding approval, appreciation or affection' can constitute 'dating violence'. That the definition is applied to men as perpetrators is clear from the text and the distribution which specifically addressed women. Hilton notes: 'It used to be called free speech, constructive criticism or free choice.' This latter definition of violence – 'withholding approval, appreciation or affection' – begs challenge as it suggests that a man breaking off a relationship or even declining sexual activity could constitute the offence of 'dating violence'. In simple terms, it suggests that men could be charged for *not* dating and *not* having sex with a woman.

These concerns and research contradicting claims of men being perpetrators of most or all child abuse and domestic violence are not cited to repudiate justifiable concerns of women over violence committed by men against them and children. Whatever level of violence against women and children is perpetrated by men, it is unacceptable and initiatives to reduce domestic violence are commendable. But men suffer in three ways in relation to discourse on domestic violence: 1) they are demonized as the perpetrators of most or even all violence; 2) all men are implicated and placed under a 'cloud of suspicion' by generalizations about male violence against women and children; and 3) it is assumed that violence is not done to men and little or no attention is paid to claims that it is.

Generalizations including those in relation to male violence and others cited in this study, such as women are better communicators than men and claims that the world would be peaceful and a better place if women were in charge, are allowed to pass unchallenged in popular and academic discourse reported in mass media. Statements of superiority in reverse (i.e. suggestions that men are better than women) are defined as sexism and viewed as 'politically incorrect' and even illegal in some cases. This analysis shows that gender discrimination in language and discourse cited by Weatherall (2002) has reversed, or at least applies to both genders but is recognised only in the case of offences against women.

Notwithstanding the validity and international relevance of this extensive study of media content, additional analysis of a range of leading international media in the UK, US and Asia was conducted to further explore international trends in mass media portrayals of men and male identity and is reported in Chapter 7.

7
The Ongoing International Media Debate on Men

Content analysis in a selection of leading international mass media conducted since the 2003–4 study reported in Chapter 6 confirms overwhelmingly negative portrayals of men and male identity and shows this trend to be consistent across developed Western societies, including the UK, US and Australia. If anything, the research suggests there is an escalation in the trends of gynocentric and feminist focus in discourse about men and negative portrayals of men and male identity. Furthermore, there is evidence of this negative discourse reaching a point where it is causing educated, sensitive, supportive men – not only reactionary men's groups – to express concern and increasingly to speak out. What happens when men take exception to or challenge the negative diatribe against them is interesting in itself for what it reveals about gender politics today.

In exploring and confirming international trends, analysis focused on a random selection of content from leading newspapers and networks including *The Times*, *Telegraph*, *Guardian*, the BBC and ITV in the UK, and the *New York Times*, *Observor*, magazines such as *Maxim* and NBC in the US, as well as global media such as *The Economist* and *TIME* magazine. Few could argue that issues prominent in such media are unimportant or unrepresentative. These media were selected as they are widely regarded as mainstream news and current affairs media in the world's largest media centres.

The making and remaking of male identity continues

The pervasiveness of misandry in mass media and the social impact that it can have were the subject of an 'op ed' article by the US columnist John Tierney in the *New York Times* (18 June 2005). Tierney began his column titled 'The Doofus Dad' reporting that, after watching *The Simpsons*, his six-year-old son turned and asked him: 'Why are dads on TV so dumb?'

Tierney went on to report on a study by the National Fatherhood Initiative in the US that found fathers are eight times more likely than mothers to be portrayed negatively on network television – a finding that echoes those reported in Chapter 6 and those of Nathanson and Young (2001) and others reported in Chapter 5.

Notwithstanding the irony that she effectively launched the mediated hyper-reality of metrosexuals in 2003, Marian Salzman, along with her co-authors Ira Matathia and Amy O'Reilly, published a book in late 2005 titled *The Future of Men*. Again we see the trend noted in Chapter 6 of women writing and theorizing on men! In the book, Salzman, who is an executive vice-president at the leading advertising agency J. Walter Thompson in New York, acknowledges that men have become 'the butt of every joke' and an easy target for mockery in the media and she calls for media advertising to provide 'smart, positive portrayals of the modern man' (Murray-West, 2005).

Despite their constructive admonition to the media to stop mocking and trivializing men, Salzman et al. (2005) outline their 'new *new man*' and provide an insight into the growing industry involved, in concert with mass media, in the making and remaking of men. They advocate that, instead of being metrosexuals (men who are self-aware to the point of narcissism and feminized), men need to become *über*-sexuals. According to Salzman et al., *über*-sexuals project 'M-ness', which they describe as 'a masculinity that combines the best of traditional manliness (strength, honour, character) with positive traits traditionally associated with females (nurturance, communicativeness, cooperation)'. Elsewhere in Salzman et al.'s descriptions and prognostications which have been widely propagated in mass media are references to 'My-ness' 'emmo boys' and 'femme-y' men (Mount, 2005). Of course, women have faced similar labelling, such as the Bridget Jones 'thirtysomething and single' phenomenon referred to as 'singletons'. But, whereas gender debate urges women towards autonomy, to be 'whatever they want to be' and to bring out their inherently good femaleness, men are being told that they need a major makeover – physically, culturally and socially.

Salzman et al.'s book has been extensively reported in the US and the UK. The *New York Times* (10 October 2005) noted the authors' admission that metrosexuals risk being 'sad sacks who seem incapable or retaining their sense of manhood in postfeminist times'. However, confirming the extent of the re-branding of male identity, it went on to report that 'a flurry of articles about metrosexuals appeared... in publications all over the world, including in the *New York Times, The Economist, The Financial Times* in London and *The Boston Herald* (Newman, 2005).

Mark Simpson, who originally coined the term 'metrosexual', claims that metrosexuality is an ongoing media creation – even if it has been re-branded *über*-sexuality by some. Writing in *The Times*, he points out that mass media publish 'coquettish, semi-naked pictures of such modern male heroes as Gavin Henson, David Beckham and Freddie Ljungberg, not to mention the shaved, pumped pectorals of the entire Chelsea squad' (Simpson, 2005).

The American writer and academic Thomas de Zengotita, in his book *Mediated*: How the Media Shapes Your World and the Way You Live in It (as reviewed by Harris, 2005), says that mass media have obfuscated authenticity and spontaneity, leaving people acting out an endless chain of clichés. In his review of the book, John Harris says Zengotita's theory 'comes into its own when it grapples with the myth that drives so many men to distraction':

> images of washboard stomachs, expensive shirts and airbrushed girlfriends play their own role in men's self-alienation, but it's surely here that we encounter one of modern masculinity's most dysfunc-tional aspects – the drive to avenge all that creeping inadequacy by affecting the behaviour of the alpha male. (*Guardian*, 10 August 2005)

A 'snapshot of British men' conducted by consumer research company Mintel reports that one in seven 25–44-year-old men are 'anxiety-ridden' over pressures to conform to images of the 'alpha male'. Harris (2005) cites a cover of *Men's Health* magazine that 'screams "get a summer body. Your six-pack starts here"' and says 'elsewhere, the usual impossible imperatives apply – be groomed, designer-dressed, comprehensively sport and tech literate, fond of beer but also suitably toned'.

Even the normally conservative London *Times* has taken to publishing a 'Men's style' section with photographs and text urging men to 'get chic', wear 'slick clothes' and advocating that 'there's always a need for fancy accessories'. Under a photo of a male torso with pronounced abdominal muscles, a typical edition of *The Times* offered 'the products that will help you turn into a new man' (12 August 2005).

A *New York Times* arts/cultural review headlined 'Hollywood's He-men are Bumped by Sensitive Guys' reported that 'romantic and action heroes like Bruce Willis, Arnold Schwarzenegger, Sylvester Stallone, Harrison Ford and Kevin Costner [have] been replaced by Tobey Maguire,

Orlando Bloom, Leonardo DiCaprio, Ryan Gosling and Jake Gyllenhaal' (*New York Times*, 1 July 2004, A1).

Another *New York Times* article in 2005 noted that it is hard to tell gay men from straight men, and commented that 'the newly styled Backstreet Boys, hoping for a comeback, look an awful lot like the stars of *Queer Eye for the Straight Guy*'. The same article also noted that the movie 'heartthrob' Brad Pitt had changed his appearance to a more feminine style (*New York Times*, 19 June 2005, section 9, p. 1).

Under the headline 'I'm a Man, not a Metrosexual', Robert Elms wrote in *The Times*:

> we now have a plethora of magazines, newspapers articles and even TV shows telling us what to wear, the tone is set by professional 'stylists'. So we get male models instead of role models, fashion instead of clothes, design instead of tailoring, glitz instead of élan. It's all gone a little fey. There seems to be a prevailing wisdom that insists that it's only our gay brethren who know how to cut a dash. (Elms, 2005)

There are signs that men are becoming concerned, frustrated and increasingly angered by the trivialization, objectification and marginalization that they see and hear. Tom Cox has written about the media's manufacture of metrosexuals and the 'new man', saying 'we shrug off such nauseating labels in our easy-going way – but don't let that fool you. Inside, we're not so relaxed about how things have turned out. We're burning with manly rage. Or gently simmering anyway' (*Telegraph*, 4 August, 2005).

The veteran BBC news journalist Michael Buerk caused an uproar in British media when he spoke out on men and male identity in an article published in *Radio Times* (August 2005) in which he asserted that 'our society is becoming a femocracy in which men and masculinity are being marginalized . . . Men are being edged out of the family, the workplace and wider society. The game of life is increasingly being played by women's rules; success and failure measured by women's criteria . . . In this feminized society, men who act like women are clearly preferred to men who act like men' (cited by Carol Midgley, *The Times*, 17 August, 2005, p. 24; *Telegraph*, 16 August 2005; *Guardian*, 18 August 2005).

Even if one does not agree with Buerk, the outrage expressed at his comments is puzzling given that, far from being an emotional men's rights activist, Buerk is a journalist with a distinguished 30-year career and a reputation for being a cool, dispassionate and thorough reporter as evidenced by his internationally acclaimed reports of the 1984 Ethiopian famine which inspired Live Aid. Carol Midgley, reviewing his statements in *The Times*, demonstrated Buerk's point about the marginalization of men and the misandry that infects so much mass media discourse on men with her retort: 'He's just a man, so who really cares what Buerk thinks?'

A number of men – and women – do care it seems, although their voices are a minority in mass media hell-bent on making money out of turning men into fashion victims and caught in the grip of feminist editorial zeal. A letter to the editor from one man read: 'Michael Buerk's comments about the all-pervading influence of women in society is a cry of despair – not a moan'. He concluded: 'We have lost sight of male virtues... keep talking, please, Mr Buerk' (*Telegraph*, Letters, 18 August 2005).

Marian Salzman supports what Buerk is saying – albeit for her own reasons – commenting that men must adapt if they are to reassert themselves in a world increasingly defined and dominated by femininity (Midgley, 2005).

Writing in the *Telegraph* (Health, 4 August 2005), Tom Cox refers to articles in the US magazine *Maxim*, warning that 'mantrophy', a disease which causes men to become more feminized, is propelling them towards extinction and points to UK surveys which show that men and women are tired of media images of well-groomed, feminine-looking men. A number of writers note that women do not like the trend towards the feminization of men any more than men do. In the New York *Observor*, Rachel Elder stated that she and her sex loath what she called 'whimpsters' (Mount, 2005). Salzman says, 'women too want men to assert themselves as confident, vital, masculine partners. They want "real" men back' (Midgley, 2005).

California Governor Arnold Schwarzenegger's admonition 'don't be a girlie man' is increasingly being quoted and becoming symbolic of men's – and some women's – opposition to the media-propagated campaign to reconstruct men in feminized ways.

The advertising industry's own research confirms the emptiness and falsity of mass media creations which it had a major part in propagating. As well as Marian Salzman's research for J. Walter Thompson, the global agency Leo Burnett released its *Man Study* (2005), which found that 60 per cent of men surveyed rejected both metrosexual and retrosexual (traditional hegemonic masculinity) images and 74 per cent believe that images of men in advertising are out of touch with reality. In a review of the research headlined 'The Myth of the Male', a leading advertising industry magazine confessed: 'Thousands of men were interviewed for the *Man Study* and it was found that metrosexuality is largely a media creation' (Veldre, 2005). The same point is made by the Australian social analyst David Chalke in citing yet another label, 'Noughties Man', in a newspaper article: 'I think the metrosexual was a fanciful invention of the media' (*The Australian*, 20 July 2005, p. 3).

Leo Burnett's global planning director for beauty care brands, Linda Kovarik, acknowledges in relation to men: 'Our research revealed that they are as deep and complex as women, but they're often portrayed very stereotypically as insensitive and one-dimensional' (Veldre, 2005). The same article quoted the chairman and CEO of Leo Burnett, Tom Bernardin, who further confirms the feminization of societies as well as the marketing objectives of many mass media messages:

With the world tending increasingly feminine, more and more of the social constructs men have taken for granted are either teetering or have been outright dismantled. As a result, there's never been a better time or a more relevant time to reassess the state of masculinity particularly as it affects buying patterns in global marketing. (Veldre, 2005)

In addition to the global trend of feminization of male identity, slurs and invective against men that would not be tolerated in relation to women are openly expressed in major mass media. For instance, following a tabloid newspaper report of an affair between the actor Jude Law and his nanny, Jemima Lewis wrote in *The Telegraph* that 'evolution has not yet caught up with the sexual revolution. Try though they might to disguise it with moisturizer and displays of hands-on parenting, most men remain cave-dwellers at heart'. In the same edition, Kathy Lette commented: 'the only time a woman can ever change a man like [Jude Law] is out of a nappy, as a baby' (*Telegraph*, Opinion, 24 July 2005).

Fatherhood and child custody are hot issues in many countries. A media 'event' which demonstrated the concerns of even powerful men at all levels of society was Bob Geldof and Bruce Willis, without prompting, raising their concerns over the impact of divorce on men as fathers in a 2005 interview with Michael Parkinson. Willis drew spontaneous applause from the live *Parkinson* audience when he said: 'I just don't understand, particularly in this country, that if two people get divorced, they fall out of love, why the guy loses his children as well as the person he loves.' Geldof said that divorce was too easy and broke families apart. Parkinson agreed with both, saying, 'It's a problem isn't it?' Willis continued:

> 'I believe in commitment and . . . I hope to God that we'll stay married for the rest of my life but if it doesn't work out, then you get half of this and you get the kids and if I want to see the kids I have to ask permission to go see the kids. I think that that is really . . . ' (*Parkinson*, ITV 1, 12 February 2005)

Geldof has also championed the subject in press interviews such as a major profile written by the leading UK journalist and author Ginny Dougary published in *The Times Magazine* and other international media shortly after the Live 8 concert. On the subject of his divorce from Paula Yates, Geldof said:

> I was thrown up against this thing, that my wife didn't love me any more. And I was bereft beyond belief but I understood that she had to go now because she didn't love me . . . and it was like this great joy went out of my life. But I didn't understand why my children went. What had I done? Why did the supreme joy of my life have to go as well? Then people say 'Oh, he's against women'. No, I'm against a law being prejudiced towards women and against men. (Dougary, 2005)

Demonization of men also continues in mass media globally. For instance, claims that one woman in three worldwide is subjected to violence or sexual abuse have been widely circulated (e.g. Associated Press globally syndicated article, 11 October 2005; *New York Times* major news story, 12 October 2005). This figure, quoted by the United Nations in its State of World Population 2005 report, includes poor, uneducated and violent societies, but a Women's Safety Survey in Australia claims that one woman in four experiences domestic violence in her lifetime even in such an educated peaceful Western society. While not denying violence is perpetrated by men and abhorring such behaviour, it is significant that the primary research on which such claims are based is rarely if ever cited. Michael Gray, a government statistical officer writing in an e-journal of social and political debate, says the Women's Safety Survey study was not subjected to peer review, data were gained from voluntary participation rather than a valid sample and violence included generalized, low-level incidents such as 'verbal abuse' (Gray, 2005) – factors which raise serious questions over the validity and reliability of the data.

Also, the data do not separate violence perpetrated by women against women. Furthermore, Gray says some claims of male violence are based on intervention orders which, he says, require low levels of evidence and are often granted simply because they are uncontested.

Demonization, marginalization, trivialization and objectification of men continue to be manifested in leading Australian mass media which have been monitored since the 2003–4 study reported in Chapter 6. *Good Weekend* magazine (22 January 2005), published in the *Sydney Morning Herald* and Melbourne's *Age* newspapers, presented a four-page feature entitled 'So Who Wants to be a Father?' examining Australia's falling birth rate – down to 1.74 children per woman compared with a rate of 2.1 needed to maintain a stable population. In a continuation of the trend identified in Chapter 6, the feature was written by a woman, Leslie Cannold, a fellow at the Centre for Applied Philosophy and Public Ethics at the University of Melbourne. Given that the feature was about fathering, Cannold, with no subjective experience of the topic, would interview men who are fathers, right? Wrong. Despite beginning with an introduction stating that 'men are overlooked in debates about Australia's plummeting birth rate', the four-page feature did not include a single interview with or comment from a man.

After describing the anxiety and anguish of women who want to have children, Cannold declared that the falling birth rate was a 'male problem'. She concluded: 'The sort of bloke in short supply is the sort who doesn't throw up at the thought of love or even commitment, but looks quite capable of pulling off both should the need arise'. There's that word again, *commitment*. Commitment is clearly identified in this, like many other texts on men, as wanting to father children with a particular woman. If he chooses for some reason not to do this, he is commitment-phobic. Never mind that he might be a firefighter, a policeman, a soldier, a CEO responsible for the jobs of thousands, or even an aid or charity worker. Never mind that she may be a contributing factor to his reluctance. Those, or other possibilities, were not considered by Cannold.

The quoted comment of one childless woman, Sharon, was particularly revealing. Cannold reported that she 'eventually packed her boyfriend, Martin, off to therapy in the hope that he might deal with his fatherhood "issues"' (2005, p. 18). The clear message is that if a man decides not to have or puts off having children, he needs therapy. This raises two issues. First, whatever happened to choice? Feminism has campaigned strongly for women to have choice in how they live their lives, but it seems men are not permitted to exercise choice in

how they live theirs. This point, and the possibility of other contributing factors to some men's avoidance of fatherhood, were raised by a
man in a letter to the editor of *Good Weekend* magazine published two
weeks later:

> Did Leslie Cannold ever think to ask men why they are fatherhood-
> phobic? Maybe a visit to the local pub where many fortysomething
> men have sorry tales to tell of wives who initiated divorces would
> be revealing. All they are left with are bitter memories and the size-
> able financial burden of child support. No wonder the current crop
> of potential fathers is wary. (*Sydney Morning Herald, Good Weekend*
> magazine, 12 February 2005, Letter to the editor, p. 8)

The *Sydney Morning Herald* trumpeted its 27–28 August 2005 weekend
edition as 'The Men's Issue' on the front page masthead. Readers
might have been tempted to think, at long last, some serious reporting
on men. Not so. 'The Men's Issue' comprised a profile of Barry
Humphries, aka Dame Edna Everage (a man dressed as a woman),
and a satirical two-page insert magazine feature titled 'For What is a
Man?' by the comedic actor Jonathon Biggins, who drew conclusions
such as:

> We've reached a point where traditional male strengths are no longer
> required: there aren't that many more wild animals left to kill, food
> production is automated or already done by women, and any heavy
> lifting can easily be handled by machines – or by big girls with a keen
> interest in V8s and the music of k.d. lang. The future success and genetic
> diversity of the species could be effortlessly guaranteed if every male
> was simply raised to the point of puberty, sent off to the sperm bank
> for a quick visit and then goodbye, thanks for coming. (*Sydney Morning
> Herald, Good Weekend* Magazine, 27 August, pp. 68–70)

A half-page feature in a weekend newspaper lift-out section headlined 'An Alien at My Table' explored fathers' relationships with their
daughters – again, as is so common on the topic of fatherhood,
written by a woman (*Sydney Morning Herald*, 12–13 February 2005,
Spectrum, p. 5). At least the author of this article, Emily Maguire, interviewed men and quoted some of them. But the question has to be
asked of intellectual and mass media discourse on men's issues: where
are the men authoring their own narratives of the self in modern
societies?

Mark Simpson asks a telling question in discussing Marian Salzman et al.'s *The Future of Men* (2005):

> Can you imagine what would happen if a man published a book called *The Future of Women* in which he said that women must dedicate themselves more to men and their children? (Simpson, 2005)

Concern over boys falling behind in education continues. An Australian Institute of Family Studies conference in 2005 heard a research report finding that boys are less ready for school at age four and five because they lag behind girls in language skills and they continue to trail behind girls in most years of school (*Sydney Morning Herald*, 10 February 2005, p. 2). International research by the Dutch psychologist and researcher Martine Delfos, aired at a number of conferences in 2005, has supported studies showing that boys' learning can be enhanced by taking account of gender differences and providing class stimuli attuned to the needs of boys and not only girls (Delfos, 2005).

In a special colour magazine titled '40 Years – the Sexual Revolution' distributed by a leading daily newspaper, Greg Callaghan, co-author of *Men Inside Out*, summarized the plight of modern men:

> middle-aged men are being marooned by devastating divorces ... girls are beating the pants of us men from kindergarten to university, our sperm counts are in trouble, we're plagued by sexual self-doubt and resorting to pharmaceutical reinforcements, our male role models have turned to celebrity chefs and landscape gardeners, and a few of us unfortunates have been branded deadbeat dads. ('40 Years: The Sexual Revolution', *The Australian*, 2005, p. 14)

Differences across countries and cultures

It is important to note that research reported in this book relates to Western societies and to recognize that its conclusions in relation to men and male identity may not apply in other cultures such as Asian, Eastern European, Middle Eastern and African countries. Mass media models differ markedly between countries and cultural differences affect audience interpretations and effects of media content. While further research in non-Western societies is necessary to draw reliable conclusions about other societies, a sample of leading Asian newspapers and TV networks was analysed during 2003 and 2004 to explore whether globalization has resulted in the same or similar trends emerging. This preliminary analysis found that many of the same issues appear to be prominent in mass media in Asia, particularly in developed or rapidly developing Asian societies such as Singapore and Malaysia.

For example, a television debate broadcast on *Channel News Asia*, a major Singapore-based South-east Asian network, was controversially entitled 'Women have evolved, but men have not'. Men and women speakers agreed that women in Asia have evolved significantly over the past few decades – particularly in developed countries such as Singapore, Hong Kong, Japan and Malaysia – and that women have much more power and independence than in the past. But, equally, women and men speakers rejected the implication of the title and agreed that men have evolved also. One woman stated: 'Most women have partners and women cannot be independent and build careers as well as have children without the co-operation of their men' (*Channel News Asia*, 17 July 2003).

Other examples of prominent Asian media articles on topics and themes consistent with mass media content analysed in this study were:

- 'Civil Service Flexi-hours Get More Flexible' – a feature reporting on a new 'pro-family' scheme to allow men and women to work flexible work hours without loss of career status and opportunity (*The Straits Times*, Singapore, 7 May 2004, p. 3).
- 'Ireland Helps Women Balance Job and Family' – a report republished in Asian media from Dublin on the 'Celtic Tigress', a term used for the surge of women into Ireland's workforce during the 1990s and recent initiatives by companies to offer flexible work arrangements for women (*The Straits Times*, 18 March 2004, p. 12).
- 'Having a Baby? Here's a Bonus from the Bosses' – a feature reporting that private firms in Singapore, while not offering paid maternity leave to women, are offering bonuses such as cash or gift vouchers to department stores (*The Straits Times*, 29 March 2004, p. 3).
- 'What Mums in Europe Really Want' – a one-and-a-half-page feature on motherhood and parenting issues such as maternity leave, reviewing practices and trends in Europe. As with many similar media features in western media, paternity leave and the needs of fathers was not addressed (*The Straits Times*, 13 March 2004, pp. 32–3).
- 'It's Not Just a Man's World' – a column reporting that, while men have dominated executive positions in the civil service in Singapore in the past, 11 of 26 deputy secretaries are now women. The article also reported on the appointment of the first woman permanent secretary (*The Straits Times*, Insight column, 8 May 2004, p. H16).

- 'Singapore Women Hold All the Cards' – a feature reporting that women hold more credit cards than men by a ratio of five to three and that many women are spending as much or more than men on credit cards (*The Straits Times*, 28 May 2003, p. 3).
- 'Be Fair, Dear Man' – a full-page feature on male beauty, asking why men should not hide dark circles under their eyes or add colour to pale lips. The 'metrosexual' is a mass media representation in Asia too! (*The Star*, Malaysia, 11 December 2003, Lifestyle, p. 10).
- 'Keep Talking, I'm Listening' – a column by a man talking about fatherhood, proposing that parents including fathers should spend time talking to and listening to their children (*The Straits Times*, 8 October 2003, p. L6).
- 'Meet the New Exhausted Super Dad' – a profile on a Singapore stay-at-home dad who carries out most of the domestic duties in his home (*The Sunday Times*, Singapore, 5 October 2003, p. 10).
- 'MP Aims to Turn out Family-friendly Men' – a report on a prominent Singapore politicians starting a men's club to nurture men as husbands and fathers (*The Straits Times*, 13 July 2004, p. H3).
- 'What Women Really Want' – a major TV programme on domestic violence examining the causes and calling for tougher action to curb male violence (*Channel News Asia*, 16 March 2004).
- 'Living in Fear of Rape' – a major feature reporting on rape of women in Iraq (*Sunday Times*, World section, 20 July 2003, p. 15).
- 'Fight Sex Crimes' – a front page report calling for a major public campaign to reduce sex offences by men in Malaysia (*The Star*, Malaysia, 12 May 2004, pp. 1, 10).

One article from India published internationally reported on violence against men. A London *Telegraph* article filed from India and published in several countries including Australia (an example of the globalization of mass media) reported that a group called the All-India Front Against Atrocities by Wives had been formed in India to demand laws to protect husbands against maltreatment by their wives. The organization claimed to have 40,000 abused husbands as members in 400 branches. A police officer quoted said there had been 6,700 cases of marital harassment registered in Delhi during 2002–3, of which 10 per cent were 'women harassing and beating up their husbands'. Also, it reported that a common complaint was wives making false allegations against their husbands which take years to sort out in the legal system (*Telegraph*, London, reprinted in *The Age*, 14 October 2003, p. 8).

A limited examination of some Asian mass media content suggests that the 'work/family collision', men's role as fathers, domestic violence, sex crimes and male body image including metrosexuality are widely discussed in many countries and men are mostly represented negatively in this discourse. Mark Simpson openly boasts that his creation, the metrosexual, has gained global interest in mass media in Russia, India, China and Mexico (Simpson, 2005).

Further international study of representations of men and male identity is necessary to understand better the lot of men in non-Western societies – and the position of women in these societies also warrants attention, particularly in less developed nations. But it seems we are not as different as is often claimed. Around the world, humans search for their identity – personal, social and political. People seek freedom and choices. Around the world there are abuses and inequities and women *and* men suffer. The question begged is can we not seek to reduce suffering and injustices for both women and men? Can we not look beyond gender differences to see and share our common humanity?

John Harris (2005) writing in the *Guardian* sums up research findings succinctly. He says we live in 'a world in which men and women are just about as worried and alienated as each other'.

8
Personal, Social and Political Implications

A final key question to ask in this research inquiry is, what do the findings mean – or as researchers like to challenge, so what? What are the implications of the extensive demonization, marginalization, trivialization and objectification of men and male identity in mass media? As discussed in Chapter 4, the answers hinge on whether media images and messages are *reflecting* social attitudes (the humanist view) or *causing* or *influencing* them (the behaviourist view), or a combination of the two (Shoemaker and Reese, 1996, pp. 31–2).

As well as considering the extent to which mass media content might reflect societal attitudes as well as or instead of causing them, discussion of the implications of this research must also be cognizant of the limitations of content analysis which have been openly acknowledged in framing this research. Notwithstanding recognition of the importance of discourse and research techniques for analysing discourses and texts, there is a move away from the view that discourse is transparent and that texts can be taken in themselves to reveal meaning. Hermes (1995, p. 148) warns that 'cultural studies often makes the mistake of assuming that "texts are always significant"'. Poststructuralist theory holds that 'neither the . . . subject who produces the texts, nor the researcher, is the final arbiter of meaning' in any text being read. Davies and Gannon (2005) propose that it is the task of researchers 'to develop concepts they find in . . . texts as a source of creative possibilities' . . . the point of a . . . poststructuralist analysis is not to expose the hidden truth in all its simplicity, but to disrupt that which is taken as stable/unquestionable truth'. This study involved empirical research rather than poststructuralist analysis, but drawing conclusions and citing possible implications of the empirical data gathered are informed by poststructuralist theory.

Clatterbaugh (1998, pp. 42–3) also warns that 'we should be reasonably clear that we are not talking about men when we are talking about images, stereotypes or norms'. He notes two ways of studying men: examining male behaviours, attitudes and abilities on the one hand and images, stereotypes, norms and discourses on the other.

This study has examined images, stereotypes, norms and discourses represented in mass media and, therefore, cannot directly report implications in relation to attitudes or behaviour. Fully understanding the implications of the negative representations of men and male identities reported will require further research such as audience studies using surveys, interviews, focus groups or even experiments, ethnographic techniques and clinical psychology methods.

However, postmodernism and poststructuralist thinking informs us of the important constitutive force of discourse. As cited in Chapter 1, Foucault points to the significance not only of the origin of discourses (i.e. what they reflect), but their power effects and the types of knowledge they produce and institutionalize (Woods, 1999). And mass media are recognized as playing an important and, according to many, growing role in discourse in contemporary societies (Grossberg et al., 1998; Curran, 2002). The decline in influence of the Church, the family, trade unions, work and local neighbourhoods which has occurred in most Western societies has reduced alternative sources of discourse for many audiences and left them more reliant on mass media (Grossberg et al., 1998; Curran, 2002, p. 23).

As discussed in Chapter 4, mass media almost certainly do a lot of both reflecting societies and causing effects in societies (Lull, 2000, p. 165; Gauntlett, 2002, p. 254). Furthermore, as argued in Chapter 4, even when mass media reflect what people are saying or doing, by their selection of certain information, and their amplification of that information to large audiences, mass media fuse the processes of reflecting effects and causing effects. They often are engaged in both simultaneously.

To some extent, the difference is only one of timing. A 'media as mirror' view must see the issues raised in this book and the problems discussed in the following as here and now. A 'media as manufacturer' of social effects view sees these as issues and problems in the making. In either case, they are issues and problems that must be addressed.

Because of the mass media's relatively narrow selection of information and viewpoints to 'broadcast', and the nature of news and news-related media content which of itself does not only reflect what people are already saying, doing and thinking (if it did, it would not be news), the potential for mass media to cause effects remains a key concern of researchers (e.g. Bryant and Zillman's 600-page *Media Effects: Advances in Theory and Research*, 2002).

A further important concept in relation to the likely impact and implications of mass media representations (in addition to those outlined in Chapter 4) is the notion of intertextuality (Kristeva, 1980). Kristeva refers to the construction of meaning from texts on two axes: a horizontal axis connecting the author and reader of a text, and a vertical axis on which the text is connected to other texts (1980, p. 69). This is particularly relevant in the case of mass media representations. Few if any people connect with only one media text. Most read one or more newspapers and several magazines, listen to radio and watch three to four hours of television each day according to media research (Barr, 2000). Therefore, most consume numerous media texts and are likely to encounter a multitude of representations of men and male identities. Kristeva (cited in Culler, 1981, p. 105) says, 'every text is from the outset under the jurisdiction of other discourses which impose a universe on it'. This points to the likelihood of the cumulative effects of mass media representations. Drawing on Kristeva's theory of intertextuality, it can be concluded that sustained negative portrayals of men and male identity, as identified in this study, are likely to have long-term cumulative effects as well as an immediate impact.

Transmission of meaning and, therefore, the implications of the findings of this study, are also informed by Eco's (1965) concept of 'aberrant decoding' – audiences' capability to decode texts using different codes from those used to encode them. Eco (1981) describes texts as 'open' or 'closed' and says that aberrant decoding is most likely to occur with open texts. Exemplars of open texts, which have a wide range of possible meanings, are literary works which use metaphor and symbolism and poetic expression. Eco believes aberrant decoding is less likely or unlikely to occur with closed texts. Mass media texts tend to be closed because they are written to formulaic journalistic styles and produced to programming standards which are widely followed. While Eco believes that diverse decodings can occur with mass media texts when they are broadcast to heterogeneous audiences, media increasingly target and package their content for specific demographic groups (eg. men's and women's magazines). Hence, Eco's views on audience decoding further suggest that mass media content can have significant effects.

These factors, together with the sheer pervasiveness of mass media today, their audience reach and the volume of content to which audiences are exposed, make mass media representations socially, cultural and politically significant. It is pertinent that this analysis is not based on a small sample, but on 1,799 articles and programme segments discussing men and male identities from a selection of 21 media over a six-month period in Australia, plus more than 500 articles randomly selected from major media in the UK, US and Asia – a total of almost 2,300 media articles and programme segments. Mass media content identified in this study speaks to societies on a massive scale. In Australia alone media studied reach an audience of 20 million,[1] and many are reached daily. Worldwide, international programs and content analysed reach an estimated audience of over 100 million.

As Lull (2000, p. 266) says, 'people navigate endless archipelagos of cultural representation'. Similarly, Lash (1990, p. 24) observes: 'We are living in a society in which our perception is directed almost as often to representations as it is to "reality"'. What media representations of men and male identity found in this study might mean for men and boys, women and girls and societies are explored in the following concluding sections.

Implications for men and boys

From both a humanist perspective in which mass media content provides a site of discourse where one can examine reflected societal attitudes and culture, and from a behaviourist view which sees mass media as a major source of societal influence, this study suggests alarming implications for men and boys growing up.

A significant number of mass media articles contributed by writers external to the media on subjects such as domestic violence and fatherhood indicate that viewpoints propagated on these subjects are reflective of at least some elements of society. In particular, analysis of sources contributing the most negative discourse on men and male identity shows that these views are reflective of intellectual and academic thinking. For instance, leading commentators and writers on fatherhood and related child support issues included Australian Anti-Discrimination Commissioner Pru Goward; the 'fatherhood consultant' and author,

---

[1] Total audience is derived from total circulation/audience of daily, weekly and monthly media as shown in Table 8.1, minus duplications inherent in counting weekend editions and insert magazines of newspapers (i.e. only incremental circulation on weekends has been counted). Audience is different to population as some people are reached by more than one medium.

Adrienne Burgess; Trish Bolton, cited as a tutor in media and communications at Swinburne and Monash Universities; and Sian Prior who has worked as a lecturer and media trainer at the Performing Arts School, Deakin University and the Royal Melbourne Institute of Technology. In this sense, mass media cannot be directly 'blamed' for the views

Table 8.1 Circulation/audience of mass media analysed in 2003–4 Australian study

Media	Daily	Weekly/Weekend	Monthly	Frequency
The Australian	453,000	910,000		*5 x daily + 2 x wknd*
Sydney Morning Herald	879,000	1,333,000		*5 x daily + 2 x wknd*
The Age	689,000	1,022,000		*5 x daily + 2 x wknd*
The Telegraph	991,000	1,216,000		*5 x daily + 1 x Sat*
Sunday Telegraph		1,958,000		*Sunday*
Sunday Age		648,000		*Sunday*
Australian Women's Wkly			2,735,000	*Monthly*
Ralph			545,000	*Monthly*
FHM			462,000	*Monthly*
Cosmopolitan			956,000	*Monthly*
The Bulletin			293,000	*Weekly*
Australian Family Circle			489,000	*Monthly*
Nine News	1,490,000	2,100,000		*5 x daily + 2 x wknd*
A Current Affair	1,400,000			*5 x daily*
60 Minutes	1,790,000			*Sunday*
Oprah	1,000,000			*5 x daily*
Frasier	1,100,000			*5 x daily*
Queer Eye...		1,528,000		*1 x weekly*
Good Weekend magazine		1,906,000		*In Sat SMH & Age*
The Australian magazine		924,000		*In Sat Australian*
Sunday Magazine		2,130,000		*In Sunday Tele*
TOTAL AUDIENCE	**9,792,000**	**15,675,000**	**5,480,000**	

Roy Morgan Research readership data for 12 months to March, 2003 and OZTAM TV ratings data for weeks of 30 March–5 April 2003 and 2–8 November 2003.

expressed and one must consider the implications of these negative views of men being held in societies. That highly negative views of men are held in intellectual and academic fields is arguably of more concern than the potential for mass media communication of these views to influence society, as it indicates that these attitudes already exist at an influential level. University lecturers, trainers, writers and senior political appointees frame education and social policy for future generations.

In addition, by their amplification of selected viewpoints and frequent communication to large audiences, mass media are likely to have significant negative impact on the self-identity and self-esteem of men. Femiano and Nickerson (2002) argue that media propagated male stereotypes are powerful because:

> they affect our expectations of what men should and should not be like. They are damaging because they narrow our notions of what men can be and do. They affect women's expectations of men in relationships and men's expectations of other men in work settings or in friendships. Media stereotypes have extra impact because they create images based on these assumptions, helping to shape men's own views about how they should act and how successful [or unsuccessful] they are as men.

Looking through mass media as a lens or prism, men in contemporary Western societies are presented with a misandric world that devalues, marginalizes, demonizes, objectifies and tries to change them. The effects could be far-reaching. In exploring the potential effects of mass media representations, it is important to examine what they don't say as well as what they do. From this perspective, mass media are not representing valued and respected roles for men. This study has shown that, through industrial, economic, technological and social change, men today are denied access to many traditional roles and identities which they previously took on. While this may be seen as a progressive step for societies and men in some respects, discourse which demonizes, marginalizes, trivializes and objectifies them denies or at least limits access to the materials and opportunities to construct positive new identities. Costello (2000) says: 'Our culture is just not doing what cultures are supposed to do, providing the myths and stories and beliefs and values that give people a sense of place, or purpose, or meaning, or belonging'. The images of men reflected and refracted through mass media certainly provide little positive material for men to construct strong 'narratives of the self'.

While further research is required to identify how men feel about their treatment and position in modern society and what effects discourses might have on them, interviews among educated management-level men in Australia conducted by Connell and Wood (2005) around the same time as this study found 'uncertainty or provisionality . . . concerning the position of men in the world'. They reported one man saying, 'men's positions are more threatened, and men are perhaps more vulnerable, and women are on the ascent'. Connell and Wood concluded 'there is not the rock-solid confidence in men's position in the world that their actual power and wealth might imply and that an earlier generation of businessmen might have shown' (2005, p. 360). If this is the state of affairs with educated, allegedly powerful businessmen (many in the Connell and Wood study have MBAs and hold senior executive positions), what is the effect on men who are poor, less educated and with little access to power?

From their study in North America, Nathanson and Young raise serious questions about the long-term impact on men of such mass media representations:

> What is happening to men as a result of this massive assault on their identity? How do men feel about being portrayed over and over again as psychotic or sinister thugs? What does it mean for a group of people to be identified as a class of victimizers? We will not know the full effect of all this misandry for many years . . . In the meantime, one thing is certain: attacking the identity of any group of human beings per se is an extremely dangerous experiment. (2001, p. 248)

A number of social researchers, psychologists and health professionals warn of specific negative social impacts. Woods (1999) says that 'the hegemonic discourse of the "flawed male" can only lead to the experience of social exclusion for many young men, an experience that is known to lead to disastrous consequences for the well-being of individuals and communities'. Macdonald et al. (2000) conclude from their studies in the health field: 'We would suggest that there is a strong element of negativity in our culture about men which cannot contribute to positive mental health and we must actively pursue cultural initiatives which promote in boys and men a positive sense of self'. Ultimately, some researchers warn that widespread denigration of men and male identity, and policies in education, health, work and child custody and support framed by those attitudes, will lead to increased family breakdown, male health problems and even a further increase in male suicide.

This study seeks to avoid generalized claims of a crisis and inciting moral panics, believing such approaches are unhelpful and often unjustified. Throughout, this book has recognized that some men hold positions of power and enjoy privilege, and also that women face inequities – sometimes at the hands of men. But widespread generalizing and universalizing about male power and privilege and the evils of traditional masculinity occurs, as has been cited, and needs to be destabilized. Generalizations such as 'men hold all the power' and 'it's a man's world', while not completely without foundation, are dated, misleading like all generalizations, and socially destructive. Equally, views such as that of Webb (1998) who claims that traditional masculinity is redundant and needs to be 'junked', while containing elements of 'truth', fall into the trap of generalizing and are extreme in that they recognize no good in men or masculinity at all. This is a position also taken by pro-feminist academics such as Connell (1995a) and Edgar (1998), who urge men to discard traditional masculinity and evolve instead to feminist-dominated gender studies notions of what they should be – usually involving, as Edgar's concluding chapter title says 'Reshaping masculinity'.

Most writers agree that men will benefit from change in many respects – for example, flexible work regimes to allow more time with their partners and children and a wider range of accepted male identities. But the direction and degree of change advocated in discourse contains an underlying devaluation of manhood and maleness. Edgar (1998) cites Clive James who, in his memoir, *Unreliable Memories*, recounts a turning point in his life where he asks himself (in Edgar's words) 'whether he wants to join in the construction of a typical masculine self, or whether he wants to take off on some utterly different project of self' (p. 219). The words 'utterly different project of self' imply that only outright rejection of traditional manly and masculine characteristics is acceptable – i.e. traditional manliness and masculinity have no value and no redeeming qualities which should be retained. All traditional male characteristics are denigrated and rejected.

Significantly, feminism has not denounced any of the wide range of femininities that exist and, instead, advocates that women can be whatever they want to be – professional careerists, jet fighter pilots, astronauts, housewives, strippers, prostitutes, or 'girlies' wearing mini-skirts and boas. Third Wave feminism has celebrated traditional feminine values and traits as well as opened up new 'narratives of the self' for women. If men are to be 'liberated' and afforded the same autonomy that women claim, and there is no logical reason that they should not be, then they need to be allowed to be what *they* want to be. Imperfect that may be at times, but social equity suggests that men should be allowed to write themselves into existence and be given voice in the discourse that forms the scripts that other men use to write themselves into existence.

Boys (men in the making) are potentially affected in two ways by mass media representations of male gender. Commenting on the direct effects on boys, John Marsden, author of *The Boy You Brought Home*, (2002b), said in an interview:

> Teenage boys are among the most maligned in society. The media portrays them as either drug-crazed, illiterate, unemployable, suicidal, failures at school, sex criminals or vandals. So adults tend to treat them more suspiciously and that causes them (unconsciously) to become angry or frustrated or alienated. (Bock, 2003).

As well as direct effects, social learning theory informs us that boys look for role models and benefit from positive role models as they grow up. Research by Bandura (1977), Bandura and Walters (1963), Brewer and Wann (1998), applied studies such as Gibbs (1991) and reviews by Wells-Wilbon and Holland (2000) report that positive and relevant role models contribute significantly to learning and personality development. Ideally, role models and mentors, such as fathers, grandfathers, uncles and friends should exist in the physical world. But, in addition, mediated images of men serve as exemplars and role models for boys and mass media portrayals shape their perceptions of what it means to be a man. Edgar (1997, p. 54) concludes in relation to mass media images: 'it's unavoidable that our cultural self-definitions are forged against this shining crucible of glamorous manhood'.

This study has shown that there is comparatively little by way of positive representations of men in mass media for boys to use as role models. Furthermore, the representations of men that they see promise a future offering derision, marginalization, devaluation, demonization and confusing choices between social and sexual identities. A key question for women as well as men is whether they want their sons growing up in an environment of such criticism and misandry.

Nathanson and Young (2001, p. 144) conclude from their formal analysis of mass media:

> At a time when virtually all positive sources of masculine identity have been sexually desegregated, some boys and men will inevitably turn to the remaining negative ones. Because traditional sources of identity for men have been severely undermined or even attacked by a society preoccupied almost exclusively with the needs and problems of women, many men are left with whatever sources happen to be supplied by popular culture.

On a wider social scale, Bradford (1999) concludes in a report on boys in the UK:

> The consequences of having large numbers of young men who are under-educated, unemployable and who hold little responsibility in society are potentially explosive – and a tragedy for the individuals concerned as well as the community in which they live.

Marian Salzman, populariser of the 'metrosexual' craze and co-author of *The Future of Men* (2005), says: 'We used to worry about teenage girls losing their voice . . . but now I'm feeling very worried about 15-year-old boys' (cited in Mount, 2005). She says the young working-class male is the most demoralized in the new female-oriented society, having few strong role models to admire apart from sport figures. As C. S. Lewis wrote in *The Abolition of Man*: 'We castrate and bid the geldings be fruitful'.

Implications for women and girls

While the research findings outlined in this book are most directly a matter of concern for men, there is a compelling argument that the issues raised also have major implications for women and girls. Men are the husbands, partners, lovers, fathers, grandfathers, uncles, brothers, sons and friends of women. Every woman is connected to at least one man, and many women interact with and have strong emotional links to a number of men. In a broad sense, addressing the needs and concerns of men and boys, and the inequities they face, will benefit women through creating healthier, happier, better socialized males who can interact with them and societies in constructive and positive ways.

In a more specific sense, many women are concerned about their husbands and partners, their brothers and sometimes their fathers coming to grips with change in a modern world. The physical and mental health, self-esteem and happiness of men are important to many women. In particular, women who are mothers of sons have much to think about and strong reasons for creating societies in which men and women can each build positive identities and live productive and fulfilling lives.

An implication of the findings that the majority of thought leaders in debate on men, men's roles and male identity are women – particularly prominent women in academic, political and social positions – and that they hold mostly negative views of men, is that these views will 'infect' young women and girls, thus perpetuating and extending the inequities and problems cited. Just as men are mentors for boys, prominent women are mentors for girls, creating potential for the demonization, marginalization, trivialization and objectification of men and male identity to continue and even escalate as new generations of young women grow up where such discourses are the 'norm' and acceptable.

Stereotypes of men are also likely to affect women's expectations of men and lead to problems in relationships, Femiano and Nickerson (2002) warn.

And, while not supported by empirical data at this stage, negative anti-male discourses on subjects such as child custody, child support, fatherhood and domestic violence may influence men away from marriage and family commitment. Anecdotal evidence cited in this study such as letters to the editor by men show some men disillusioned with and turning away from current family structures and arrangements.

Implications for societies

As far as mass media content reflects or mirrors social attitudes, the discourses on men and male identity identified in this book reveal substantial anti-male gender bias in societies where such media content is produced, with all the social equity issues that this entails. Gender bias against women undoubtedly exists in these societies also. But to the extent that mass media reflect societies, this study shows that gender bias is not a one-way street; it disaffects men as well. And the extent and nature of content analysed shows that this gender bias against men is not trivial.

Furthermore, in 'broadcasting' predominantly negative images and identities of men, mass media simultaneously have the potential to influence or create social attitudes towards men and boys and propagate discourse that contributes to ideology. Nathanson and Young (2001, p. 200) define ideology as 'any systematic re-presentation of reality in order to achieve specific social, economic or political goals'. The research summarized in this book shows a systematic re-presentation of reality – not necessarily intentional or pre-planned, but systematic in the sense of its regularity, consistency, language and method of classification (eg. generalizing about male violence). In this view, mass media content is ideology creation.

Nathanson and Young warn of the potential for mass propagated ideologies to become 'quasi-religious worldviews' (2001, p. 209) which gain considerable and sometimes unchallengeable influence in societies. The shift of focus and resources from boys to girls in education and national multi-million dollar taxpayer-funded campaigns against 'male domestic violence' are examples of how gender discourse shapes social and political policies and reality. In their discussion of the 'quasi-religiosity' of ideologies once they come to dominate discourse, Nathanson and Young take the analogy further and argue that anyone speaking against them is seen as a heretic. Paglia (2003b) refers to this tendency to protect and propagate ideologies in a modern social context as the 'self-defeating tyranny of political correctness' which provides a form of censorship that silences critics and alternative views.

This study confirms that, while men may not be 'silenced now . . . just as women were silenced in the past' (Nathanson and Young, 2001, p. 67), they do not have a dominant or even equal voice in discourse in relation to their identity, roles and family issues. The comparatively small number of men given space in the mass media to discuss men's perspective on issues such as fatherhood, the relatively small number of positive representations of men and male identity overall, and the hostile and sometimes hysterical reaction to views expressed by men confirm that a new dominant ideology has taken hold and become a worldview.

Notwithstanding their theoretical grounding in postmodernism and poststructuralism which seek to reject meta-narratives, modern feminism and gender studies have created a new meta-narrative or master narrative of men. That narrative, in summary, is males are valued members of societies only if they are 'feminized' (i.e. become like women) and those who cannot be rehabilitated and reconstructed are evil and to be condemned and dealt with harshly, if not dispensed with altogether.

What is happening is not a de-gendering of societies, as is often proposed, but a re-gendering where female is increasingly privileged and male is condemned for reconstruction.

Mass media are of particular significance in social study because, while they are often unjustifiably blamed for social effects, they reflect intellectual and academic discourse, as shown in media content analysis reported, propelling it into the public domain and popularizing viewpoints, as well as representing popular discourse. In other words, mass media are where intellectual and popular discourse come together and interact. When intellectual and popular discourse coalesce and align on an issue, as this research shows they do on male gender identity, they form unassailable notions.

The highly negative representations of men in areas such as father-hood, domestic violence and child abuse and the imbalance in discourse are likely to lead to an imbalance in data that inform policy-making. The result of such an imbalance is highly likely to be imbalanced policies. Hood (2001), in examining child abuse and professional intervention, reported that focus on men as the perpetrators of child abuse had influenced policy and legislation and noted that there were negative implications for all men: 'Child-care centres and schools have designed programs to ensure lone men are supervised in the company of children and adolescents at all times.' She added: 'the feminist construction of men as responsible for child abuse has had consequences for the rela-tionship of non-abusive men with children. A side-effect has been to cast a shadow over the interaction of all men with all children' (2001, p. 108).

In turn, imbalanced discourse, policies and legislation are likely to trigger resentment, frustration and anger among men – there are signs that they are already doing so. Nathanson and Young warn that the highly negative discourse on men, with its influential effects on indi-vidual men and social and political policy, will contribute to 'the growing polarization between increasingly segregated communities of rage' (2001, p. 63). Increased polarization of men and women is an undesirable outcome that will further destabilize families, communities and social cohesion, and driving men into 'communities of rage' is a highly destructive and dangerous potentiality which will have repercus-sions for men, women and societies.

Macdonald et al.'s (2000) conclusions suggest that the negative mass media representations of men shown in this study will ultimately have a catastrophic social and even financial cost to communities through deteriorating male mental and physical health, as well as personal cost to individuals – men, women and children.

As much as they may wish to challenge some assertions – and that is their right – academics in cultural studies and gender studies, grounded in poststructuralist and feminist thinking, need to engage with the research presented in this book. Not to do so would be inconsistent with the fundamental principles of poststructuralism and postmodernism, a key tenet of which is engaging with alternative and even contradictory discourses to destabilize and disrupt a single view or truth (Davies and Gannon, 2005). Feminism has advanced considerable theory on gender including male gender – e.g. men seek power, including power over women; all men are beneficiaries of this power; patriarchy is a constructed manifestation of male power which men actively maintain; male violence is perpetrated by men to maintain power over women. Less theoretically grounded discourses also make claims such as men are less sensitive, less caring, less emotional and less commitment orientated than women and that the world would be a peaceful place if women were in charge. One body of doctrine such as patriarchy should not simply be replaced by another body of doctrine. Gender theorists operating within a framework of poststructuralism and postmodernism must actively engage alternative discourses and allow 'free play' in the concepts of gender and views advocated. In so doing, they will inevitably find there is much less black and white and much more grey than some texts and theories suggest.

Mass media need to advance beyond their traditional defensiveness and review their editorial policies and structures in relation to social issues. While men may dominate positions overall in societies, media content on social and family issues is overwhelmingly dominated by women's voices and perspectives and, while this book has strenuously avoided media-bashing, the biases revealed in this research should be examined closely by media proprietors, editors, journalists and in media studies.

Perhaps it is idealistic, but the ultimate wish is that we all be humans first, and women and men second.

Appendix A
Coding List

Issue Categories and Issues (Classifications/Categorisation)

Code Issue/category

Article type
1. News article
2. Feature article
3. Editorial
4. Column
5. Letter to the editor
6. TV news
7. TV current affairs
8. TV lifestyle/drama

Sources
9. Male author/columnist
10. Female author/columnist
11. Male academic/researcher
12. Female academic/researcher
13. Man – other
14. Woman – other
15. Men's organization
16. Women's organization
17. Research study/organization
18. Government body/official
19. Judge/lawyer
20. Police
21. Other

Men profiles (overall themes)
22. Hero
23. Leader
24. Protector
25. Good provider
26. Good father
27. Good/loving husband/partner
28. Good citizen *(e.g. celebrated doctor, charity worker, rescue worker, teacher, etc.)*
29. Handyman *(including competent handyman, problem solver, etc.)*
30. Villain *(include criminals, fraudsters, conmen, etc.)*

31. Power abuser *(include leaders found corrupt or any stories about male power)*
32. Workaholic
33. Aggressor *(include attackers, murderers, rapists, thugs, etc.)*
34. Pervert *(include paedophiles, sexual abusers, peeping Toms, etc.)*
35. Philanderer *(include cads, promiscuity, playing around, leaving for other women)*
36. Deadbeat dad
37. Incompetent fool or lazy *(subject of ridicule, foolish, not doing housework, not doing share with children, being incompetent at domestic duties, etc.)*

Work and career
38. Career success
39. Career/business failure
40. Pay/earnings
41. Promotion and achievement
42. 'Boys' Club'/discrimination
43. 'Glass ceiling' for women
44. Redundancy/job loss
45. Working hours
46. Work vs. family/lifestyle

Violence and aggression
47. Crime general *(non-violent including fraud, corruption, corporate crime, theft, etc.)*
48. Violent crime *(including murder, bashings, attacks, 'gunman')*
49. Domestic violence (DV) *(bashing, attacks, etc. in the home or relationships)*
50. Sexual abuse *(rape, assault, molestation, stalking, paedophilia)*
51. Fights/brawls/thuggery
52. Gangs
53. Boys' violence *(in gangs, in schools, under-age crime)*
54. Militarism *(include men cause/promote war or are warlike, conquestorial)*
55. Risk-taking behaviour *(include drunken driving, speeding, dare-devil behaviour)*

Competition/competitiveness
56. Will to win
57. Male competitiveness benefits *(e.g. leading to efficiency, success, discovery, etc.)*
58. Male competitiveness causing harm *(e.g. lack of co-operation, destructive ego)*
59. Acceptance of failure / 'good sport'
134. Non-acceptance of failure / 'bad sport'*
60. Teamwork and cooperation
    * *Added after initial pilot testing.*

Physical health
61. Disease generally
62. Heart disease/heart attacks
63. Cancer
64. Prostrate cancer
65. STD (sexually transmitted diseases)
66. Alcohol/drinking

67. Smoking
68. Drug abuse
69. Preventative medicine *(including visiting doctors, health checkups, etc.)*

Mental health
70. Nervous breakdown
71. Stress and stress-related diseases
72. Depression
73. Mental instability/insane *(include court findings of mentally unfit or temporarily insane)*

Suicide
74. Young male suicide
75. Older male suicide
76. Female suicide
77. Male suicide attempts *(i.e. unsuccessful)*
78. Female suicide attempts *(i.e. unsuccessful)*

Education
79. Boys education needs/programmes
80. Teaching methods for boys
81. School facilities for boys *(including sport, games and exercise areas)*
82. Discipline problems
83. Academic performance
84. School completion
85. University attendance

Fatherhood and family
86. Father role/involvement *(all references to the role or importance of fathers, fathers' time with children, what fathers do or don't do with their children)*
87. Deadbeat dads *(fathers who dessert, don't pay child support, ignore their children)*
88. Single/lone parent families
89. Family Court
90. Child custody
91. Child support
92. Property settlement
93. Paternity leave
94. Househusbands
95. DNA paternity tests

Commitment and responsibility
96. Family commitment
97. Work/career commitment
98. Mateship *(standing by your mates, loyalty)*
99. Community/national commitment *(include military heroes, male rescue workers, firemen)*
100. Commitment phobic
101. Desertion/walking out

Communication
102. Talking
103. Expressing feelings/emotions
104. Non-verbal communication
105. Listening

Social behaviour
106. Gentleman
107. Family man
108. Sensitive/SNAGs *(Sensitive New Age Guys)*
109. Metrosexuals
110. Ockerism
111. Machismo
112. Mates
113. Blokes
114. Lads
135. Chauvinism*
   * *Added after initial pilot testing.*

Sexuality
115. Heterosexual
116. Homosexual/gay
117. Bisexual
118. Men's 'Feminine side'
119. Sex drive *(any articles on libido, male sex drive and energy, etc.)*
120. Sexual activity *(include attitudes towards, conduct of as well as prowess at sex (ie. skill, tenderness, ability to satisfy partners)*
121. Paedophilia *(including 'toy boy' representations as well as girl victims)*
122. Pornography

Body image
123. Body-building *(e.g. references to 'six packs', muscles, toning, 'hunks' and photos of same)*
124. Waxing/hair removal *(photos or stories)*
125. Male fashion *(clothes, dress, shoes)*
126. Male make-up/beauty products
127. Traditional masculinity *(references to or images of physical aspects of traditional masculinity – e.g. rugged, hairy, muscular, tough, strong, etc. Behavioural aspects under 'Social Behaviour')*

Domestic involvement
128. Cooking
129. House cleaning
130. Child care
131. Gardening
132. Handyman
133. Househusband

Messages

Table A.1 Favourable and unfavourable messages analysed

No.	Positive	No.	Negative
1	Balance work / personal / family	1	Work-focused
2	Share power / rights / opportunities	2	Power-focused / obsessed
3	Strong, active but non-aggressive	3	Aggressive
4	Law-abiding responsible citizens	4	Criminals
5	Protectors/carers/gentle/not violent	5	Violent
6	Sexually responsible/considerate	6	Sexual abusers/predators
7	Sensitive	7	Insensitive, out of touch with feelings
8	Good communicators	8	Poor communicators / women better
9	Well-rounded / balanced humans	9	Sex / sport / cars / mates focussed
10	Commitment-oriented and responsible	10	Commitment-phobic / lack commitment
11	Treat women equally / with respect	11	Chauvinists/oppressors/ misogynists
12	Intelligent and capable	12	Stupid or incompetent
13	Do their share domestically	13	Don't do their share / lazy domestically
14	Paternal and care for children	14	Not committed to / caring for children
15	Care for their health	15	Do not take care of health/risk taking
16	Fathers deserve equal child rights	16	Don't deserve / can't be trusted with equal child rights
17	Strong, rugged, traditionally masculine appearance	17	Groomed / waxed / feminine appearance
18	Traditional men / 'blokes' behaviour	18	SNAGs / Metrosexuals / show 'feminine side'
19	Considerate sensual lovers	19	Inconsiderate/ineffective lovers
20	Boys need special/more attention	20	Boys do not/girls need more attention

Appendix B
Quantitative Media Analysis Methodology

CARMA International is a global research firm specializing in Computer Aided Research and Media Analysis (of which its name is an abbreviation). The company, established in Washington, DC in 1984 and with offices in the US, UK, Europe, Japan, Asia Pacific headquartered in Australia, India and South America, developed proprietary software for media content analysis (primarily quantitative) and is a recognized leader in this field of research.

The CARMA® system utilizes an Oracle database with customized data entry screens, menus and functions for conducting media content analysis. The CARMA® proprietary database also includes media circulation and audience data for each country.

CARMA® provides fields for media analysts to enter a range of coding data including:

- Date
- Headline
- Media name
- Media type (newspaper, magazine, radio, TV, online, etc.)
- Article type (news, feature, editorial, opinion column, letter to the editor)
- Prominence of mention (e.g. headline, first paragraph, prominent, passing)
- Issues categories and issues (categories/classifications assigned by coders)
- Messages (positive and negative)
- Sources quoted
- Byline (i.e. author name)
- Photos or illustrations
- Tone.

CARMA International conducts media content analysis for companies and for government agencies, not-for-profit organizations and academic institutions.

Methodology

A list of issues categories and issues (categories/classifications), messages and sources to be analysed (the coding list) is set up in the CARMA® system before content analysis is undertaken. Issues and messages are categorized by key words and phrases and sources by names or title descriptions. Content analysts then enter data about articles in the fields according to the criteria set up in the coding list.

The CARMA® system captures and analyses mainly *quantitative* content analysis data including the volume, frequency and type of reporting of each category and issue, message, source and media. The system can also calculate total audience reached by articles from circulation and audience ratings data. CARMA® also allows collection and processing of some *qualitative* data such as leading messages and calculates an average **Favourability Rating** of articles, media and sources based on a total cumulative score of coding data. The method of calculating the CARMA® Favourability Rating is outlined below. This overall rating of articles was used in this study as it is a more sophisticated and specific than a simple positive/negative/neutral categorisation (Note: this is particularly relevant where articles contain a mixture of positive, negative and sometimes neutral content).

Technical Specs

The CARMA® system utilizes an Oracle V. 8-10 database with customized data entry screens and fields for media analysis. Data is queried using Business Query™ and analysed using Business Objects™ or SPSS™ software. Data is also exported into Microsoft Excel® for further detailed analysis including development of pivot tables and charts and graphs for reporting.

Calculation of favourability ratings using CARMA®

Each article begins at 5.0 on the scale of 1 to 10 (i.e. neutral).

1. **For PROMINENCE of mention** (add up to maximum of 2 points):

a. HEADLINE mention of name – add 0.5 if favourable; subtract 0.5 if unfavourable;
b. PRIORITY/TARGET MEDIA – if the article is in a high circulation or target media, add 0.5 if the article favourable; subtract 0.5 if unfavourable;
c. PROMINENCE – if the mention is prominent taking account of (i) page number (e.g. pages 1,2,3, A1, A2, etc.); (ii) size or length of the article (medium to large); and (iii) the subject has more than a passing mention; add 0.5 if favourable; subtract 0.5 if unfavourable;
d. PHOTO or LOGO – if there is a photo or logo of or related to the subject, add 0.5 if the article is favourable, or subtract 0.5 if unfavourable;

2. **For favourable or unfavourable SOURCES**, add or subtract up to a maximum of one point (1.0) as follows:

a. ONLY A FAVOURABLE SOURCE quoted – add 1.0;
b. ONLY AN UNFAVOURABLE SOURCE quoted – subtract 1.0;
c. EQUAL NUMBER OF FAVOURABLE AND UNFAVOURABLE SOURCES – no change;
d. MORE FAVOURABLE THAN UNFAVOURABLE SOURCES quoted – add 0.5;
e. MORE UNFAVOURABLE THAN FAVOURABLE SOURCES quoted – subtract 0.5;

3. **For favourable or unfavourable MESSAGES,** add or subtract up to a maximum of one point (1.0) as follows:

a. ONLY POSITIVE MESSAGES in an article – add 1.0;
b. ONLY NEGATIVE MESSAGES in an article – subtract 1.0;
c. EQUAL NUMBER OF POSITIVE and NEGATIVE MESSAGES – no change;
d. MORE POSITIVE THAN NEGATIVE MESSAGES in an article (or more prominent) – add 0.5;
e. MORE NEGATIVE THAN POSITIVE MESSAGES in an article (or more prominent) – subtract 0.5;

4. **For the OVERALL TONE** of an article, add or subtract to a maximum of one point (1.0) as follows:

a. If the article is substantially POSITIVE overall in tone and angle with positive messages or content in addition to those already counted, add 1.0;
b. If the article is substantially NEGATIVE overall in tone and angle with negative messages or content in addition to that already counted, subtract 1.0;
c. If the article has NO OTHER POSITIVE OR NEGATIVE characteristics beyond those already counted – no change.

The Favourability Rating is then **totalled and scaled out of 100** in the CARMA® system.

Appendix C
Intercoder Reliability Assessment

Lombard et al. (2004) note that there are 'literally dozens' of different measures or indices of intercoder reliability. Popping (1988) reported 39 different 'agreement indices'. However, Lombard et al., Neuendorf (2002) and a number of other researchers agree that the following indices are the most reliable and important:

	Level of Measurement
• Per cent agreement (a basic assessment)	(Nominal)
• Scott's *pi* (π)	(Nominal)
• Cohen's *kappa* (κ)	(Nominal)
• Holsti's coefficient of reliability	(Nominal)
• Spearman's *rho*	(Ordinal – rank order)
• Pearson's correlation coefficient (r)	(Internal or ratio)
• Lin's concordance correlation coefficient (r_c)	(Interval or ratio)

The relatively complex formulae for calculating these reliability indices are provided in Neuendorf (2002). Manual calculation requires familiarity with statistics and considerable time – no doubt the reason that most content analyses do little more than assess percentage agreement (if that), as reported by Riffe and Freitag (1997 and Lombard et al. (2003).

A number of software programs help calculate intercoder reliability assessment, including statistics programs such as SPSS, which can assess Cohen's *kappa* (κ) and Simstat from Provalis Research which can calculate a number of intercoder reliability statistics. Also, specialist software programs have been and are being developed for this purpose including Popping's AGREE (1984) and Krippendorf's Alpha 3.12a, although the latter is a beta (test) program and not available widely (Lombard et al., 2004). An American company, SkyMeg Software, in consultation with academics from Cleveland State University, has developed PRAM (Program for Reliability Assessment of Multiple Coders) which can calculate reliability statistics for each of the most recommended indices. PRAM is still in development and an academic version alpha release 0.4.4 available as at January 2004 was found to contain some minor 'bugs' and 'clunky' features. However, release notes on the program state that all coefficients have been tested and verified by Neuendorf's students at Cleveland State University.

In this study, intercoder reliability of a sub-sample was assessed before further coding was undertaken using PRAM (Program for Reliability Assessment with Multiple Coders) (SkyMeg Software, 2003). The program, which analyses coding data exported to Microsoft Excel® templates, provides reliability statistics for each variable assessed on a scale of 0–1 where one is 100 per cent agreement or co-variation.

PRAM is described by Neuendorf (2002, p. 241) as providing 'the full complement of intercoder reliability statistics'. Further information is available at: http://www.geocities.com/skymegsoftware/pram.html.

Intercoder reliability testing was conducted on 41 variables analysed (20 positive messages; 20 corresponding negative messages; and overall favourability rating of articles).

An intercoder reliability sub-sample of 100 articles was selected with ten drawn randomly from each of ten categories (crime, work, sexuality, health, etc.) and coded by two coders (the primary coder and secondary coder). Sub-sample size was informed by Neuendorf (2002, p. 159) who states: 'the reliability sub-sample should probably never be smaller than 50 and should rarely need to be larger than about 300'.

'Blind coding' of the intercoder reliability sub-sample was conducted by the two coders (ie. neither coder saw the coding of the other prior to completion) to minimize what researchers term 'demand characteristic' – a tendency of participants in a study to try to give what the primary researcher wants or to skew results to meet a desired goal.

Intercoder reliability was assessed for:

1. Messages – the primary unit of analysis (20 positive messages and 20 corresponding negative messages) coded as present or not in articles. (Messages analyzed are listed in the coding list shown in Appendix A); and
2. The overall 'favourability/unfavourability' rating of articles towards men calculated using the CARMA® cumulative scoring method as outlined in Appendix B.

Neuendorf (2002, p. 143) says that 'most basic textbooks on research methods in the social sciences do not offer a specific criterion or cut-off figure and those that do report a criterion vary somewhat in their recommendations'. However, Neuendorf cites Ellis (1994) as offering a 'widely accepted rule of thumb'. Ellis states that correlation coefficients exceeding 0.75–0.80 indicate high reliability (1994, p. 91). In relation to specific statistics, Frey, Botan and Kreps (2000) declare 70 per cent agreement (0.70) is considered reliable. Popping (1988) suggests 0.80 or greater is required for Cohen's *kappa* which he cites as the optimal (i.e. strictest) measure, while Banerjee et al. (1999) propose that a 0.75 score for Cohen's *kappa* indicates excellent agreement beyond chance. Riffe, Lacy and Fico (1998), without specifying the type of reliability coefficient, recommend high standards and report that content analysis studies typically report reliability in the 0.80–0.90 range.

Neuendorf (2002) notes that it is clear from a review of work on reliability of content analysis that reliability coefficients of 0.90 or greater are acceptable to all and 0.80 is acceptable in most situations. Furthermore, Neuendorf notes that the 'beyond chance' statistics such as Scott's *pi* and Cohen's *kappa* are afforded a more liberal criterion.

Table C.1 provides a summary of the average intercoder reliability score generated by PRAM for the 40 messages tracked and analysed in this study (20 positive messages and their 20 corresponding negative forms) across the 100 articles in

Table C.1 Summary of average intercoder reliability assessment of coding of 20 positive messages and 20 negative messages analysed in sub-sample of 100 articles using PRAM (Program for Reliability Assessment of Multiple coders)

Messages 1–20 (Positive and Negative)	Reliability Score
Percent Agreement	0.997
Holsti's co-efficient of reliability	0.997
Scott's *pi* (π)	0.861
Cohen's *kappa* (κ)	0.862
Spearman's *rho*	1.000
Pearson's Correlation Co-efficient (r)	0.966
Lin's Concordance Correlation Co-efficient (r_c)	0.894

the sub-sample. This shows reliability ratings in the high to very high range, with the lowest being 0.861 (where 1.0 is 100 per cent agreement or covariance).

Table C.2 summarizes intercoder reliability for the overall favourability/unfavourability rating of articles in this study generated by PRAM. This shows reliability ratings between 0.797 and 0.999 – equal to or well in excess of the acceptable reliability rates proposed by media researchers.

In an independent review of PRAM, Lombard (Temple University), Synder-Duch (Carlow College, Pittsburgh) and Campanella Bracken (Cleve State University, Ohio) state that they found PRAM results for Holsti's coefficient of reliability 'not trustworthy'. However, they confirm that, as with other indices, coefficients of 0.90 or greater are 'nearly always acceptable' and 0.80 or greater is acceptable in most situations. Furthermore, they confirm that higher criteria can be used for indices known to be liberal (ie. per cent agreement) and lower criteria can be used for indices know to be more conservative such as Cohen's *kappa*, Scott's *pi* and Krippendorff's *alpha* (Lombard et al., 2003 and 2004).

A sample of a PRAM report from which data summarized in Table C.2 is drawn is provided in Table C.3.

Table C.2 Summary of intercoder reliability assessment of overall 'favourability/unfavourability' rating of 100 articles in the sub-sample using PRAM (Program for Reliability Assessment of Multiple coders)

Overall Rating of Articles	Reliability Score
Percentage agreement	0.860
Holsti's co-efficient of reliability	0.860
Scott's *pi* (π)	0.797
Cohen's *kappa* (κ)	0.798
Spearman's *rho* (ρ)	0.944
Pearson's Correlation Coefficient (r)	0.975
Lin's Concordance Correlation Coefficient (r_c)	0.999

Table C.3   PRAM intercoder reliability assessment report
Variable 41 - Overall Rating of Articles (favourability score out of 100)

Percent Agreement	Variable 41	Average
Coder Pair:		
1,2	0.86	0.86
Average	0.86	0.86
Holsti's Coefficient of Reliability		
Coder Pair:		
1,2		0.86
Average		0.86
Scott's *pi*		
Coder Pair:		
1,2	0.797	0.797
Average	0.797	0.797
Cohen's *kappa*		
Coder Pair:		
1,2	0.798	0.798
Average	0.798	0.798
Spearman's *rho*		
Coder Pair:		
1,2	0.944	0.944
Average	0.944	0.944
Pearson's Correlation Coefficient(r_c)		
Coder Pair:		
1,2	0.975	0.975
Average	0.975	0.975
Lin's Concordance Correlation Coefficient *(r)*		
Coder Pair:		
1,2	0.999	0.999
Average	0.999	0.999

Appendix D
Media Sample

Newspapers (news, current affairs and lifestyle)	Readership (weekday/weekend)
• *The Australian* (national daily newspaper)	453,000/910,000
• *Sydney Morning Herald* (daily newspaper – Sydney)*	879,000/1,333,000
• *The Age* (daily newspaper - Melbourne)*	689,000/1,022,000
• *Telegraph* (daily tabloid newspaper – Sydney)	991,000/1,216,000
• *Sunday Telegraph* (Sunday newspaper – Sydney)*	1,958,000
• *Sunday Age* (Sunday newspaper – Melbourne)*	648,000

* Included colour insert magazines *Good Weekend* in *The Sydney Morning Herald* and *The Age* (1,906,000); *The Australian Magazine* in the *Weekend Australian (924,000)* and *Sunday Magazine* in the *Sunday Telegraph* (2,130,000).

Basis of selection of sample newspapers

The Australian, Sydney Morning Herald and *The Age* have been identified as the three highest rated 'quality' press in Australia, according to a University of Queensland Journalism Department survey (1992). Further, one is the leading national newspaper; one is the leading daily newspaper in Australia's largest city (Sydney); and one is the leading daily newspaper in Melbourne, Australia's second largest city. The *Daily Telegraph* was identified as the leading tabloid in the UQ survey (with a more working-class and 'popular' market). The *Sunday Age* (Melbourne) was identified as the leading weekend newspaper in Australia. The *Sunday Telegraph* (Sydney) is the highest readership Sunday newspaper in Australia. This sample was constructed to include the most influential newspapers and provide a balance geographically, between week day and weekend, and between major publishers (University of Queensland Journalism Department survey conducted by Quadrant Research, 1992 and Roy Morgan Research readership data, 12 months to March, 2003 published in *The Australian*, 23 May 2003, p. 18).

Magazines (current affairs, men's, women's and lifestyle)	Audited Circulation
• *Australian Women's Weekly* (national monthly women's magazine)	2,735,000
• *Ralph* (international monthly men's magazine)	545,000
• *FHM* (international monthly men's magazine)	462,000
• *Cosmopolitan* (international monthly women's magazine)	956,000

- *The Bulletin* (national weekly current affairs   293,000
  magazine)
- *Australian Family Circle* (national monthly family   489,000
  magazine)

Basis of selection of sample magazines

These comprise the highest circulation current affairs magazine in Australia (*The Bulletin*); the highest circulation magazine overall in Australia and the highest circulation women's magazine *(Australian Women's Weekly)*; the highest circulation young women's magazine (*Cosmopolitan*); the two highest circulation men's magazines (*FHM* and *Ralph*); and the highest circulation specialist family magazine (*Family Circle*) (Roy Morgan Research published in *B&T Weekly*, 30 May 2003).

TV news, current affairs and talk shows	Audience (Weekday/Weekend)
• Nine News (national TV news)	1.49 m / 2.1 m
• *A Current Affair* (national TV current affairs)	1.4 m
• *60 Minutes* (international TV current affairs)	Australia only – 1.79 m
• *Oprah* (international TV talk show)	Australia only – 1.0 m approx
• *Frasier* (international TV drama)	Australia only – 1.1 m approx
• *Queer Eye for the Straight Guy*[1]	Australia only – 1.528 m

Basis of selection of sample TV programmes

Based on 2002 and March-April 2003 ratings data, Nine News was, at the time, the highest rating TV news in Australia; *A Current Affair* and *60 Minutes* were the two highest rated current affairs shows in Australia (and *60 Minutes* is a highly influential programme internationally). *Oprah* has been consistently one of the highest rating talk show dealing with social issues and problems (and also a popular and credible international TV programme). *Friends, Frasier* and *Everybody Loves Raymond* were the top-rating TV lifestyle drama shows in 2002-2003 (not including home renovation and sports programmes) as well as popular internationally. *Frasier* was selected as it features gender-related themes and prescriptive narratives, with *Frasier* being a male psychiatrist hosting a radio show advising callers on relationships and personal matters. It was originally intended to analyse *Sex and the City* because of its specific gender themes, but this programme was not on air during the study period. *Queer Eye for the Straight Guy*, launched in Australia 29 September 2003, was the highest-ever rated show on NBC cable channel Bravo in the US with 7 million viewers and has a specific male gender focus. Hence it was included in the study (OZTAM ratings data from ratings weeks 30 March–5 April 2003 and 2–8 November 2003 and US TV Ratings, 2002).

---

[1] From 29 September 2003 when it started on air in Australia.

References

Adorno, T. (1991). *The Culture Industry: Selected Essays on Mass Culture*. London: Albert Britnell and Routledge.

Adorno, T. and Horkheimer, M. (1972). *Dialectic of Entertainment*. New York: Herder and Herder. (Original work published 1947.)

Allen, R. (1985). *Speaking of Soap Operas*. Chapel Hill, NC: University of North Carolina Press.

Arndt, B. (2003, 20–21 December). The kids' project. *Sydney Morning Herald*, Spectrum, pp. 4–7.

Australian Bureau of Statistics (2003). *Australian Social Trends 2003*. Canberra: Commonwealth of Australia.

Australian, The (2003, 13 May). Editorial, p. 10.

Babbie, E. (1986). *Observing Ourselves: Essays in Social Research*. Belmont, CA: Wadsworth.

Baker, R. and McMurray, A. (1998). Contact fathers' loss of school involvement. *Journal of Family Studies*, 5(2), 201–214.

Bandura, A. (1977). *Social Learning Theory*. Englewood Cliffs, NJ: Prentice Hall.

Bandura, A. and Walters, R. (1963). *Social Learning and Personality Development*. New York: Holt, Rinehart and Winston.

Banerjee, M., Capozzoli, M., McSweeney, L. and Sinha, D. (1999). Beyond kappa: A review of interrater agreement measures. *Canadian Journal of Statistics*, 27 (1), 3–23.

Bankart, C. (2005, April). Book review in *Men and Masculinities*, Vol. 7, No. 4, pp. 434–7.

Bardikian, B. (1997). *The Media Monopoly*. Boston, MA: Beacon Press.

Barker, C. (2004, March). Evolution: no stranger to good grooming, the metrosexual is the new kid in town. *The Australian Way*, p. 14.

Barner, M. (1999). Sex-role stereotyping in FCC-mandated children's educational television. *Journal of Broadcasting and Electronic Media*, 43, 551–564.

Baron-Cohen, S. (2003a). *The Essential Difference: Men, Women and the Extreme Male Brain*. Cambridge: Allen Lane and Penguin UK-Perseus.

Baron-Cohen, S. (2003b, 9 May). On the far side of the male brain. *Australian Financial Review*, Review, 3. Extract from *The Essential Difference*.

Barr, T. (2000). *newmedia.com.au*. Sydney: Allen and Unwin.

Barthes, R. (1972). *Mythologies*. New York: Hill and Wang.

Barthes, R. (1977). Death of the author: Structural analysis of narratives. In *Image, Music, Text*. London: Fontana.

Baumgardner, J. and Richards, A. (2000). *ManifestA: Young Women, Feminism, and the Future*. New York: Farrar, Straus and Giroux.

Beale, B. (2001, 8 May). Gender is the plight. *The Bulletin*, pp. 27–30.

Beavis, A. (2002). Foreword. In H. Mackay, *Media Mania* (pp. 9–11). Sydney: University of New South Wales.

Beck, U. (2002). A life of one's own in a runaway world: Individualisation, globalisation and politics. In U. Beck and E. Beck-Gernsheim (p. 26). London, Sage.

Belkin, L. (2003, 26 October). The opt-out revolution. *New York Times Magazine*. Retrieved 10 October 2005 from http://www.nytimes.com/2003/10/26/magazine

Berelson, B. (1952). *Content Analysis in Communication Research*. New York: Hafner.

Berger, M., Wallis, B. and Watson, S. (Eds.) (1995). *Constructing Masculinity*. New York: Routledge.

Betcher, R. and Pollock, W. (1993). *In a Time of Fallen Heroes: The Recreation of Masculinity*. New York: Atheneum.

Beynon, J. (2002). *Masculinities and Culture*. Buckingham: Open University Press.

Bibler, K., Sears, T. and Trudinger, D. (1999). Pre-match entertainment: introduction. In K. Bibler, T. Sears and D. Trudinger (Eds). *Playing the Man: New Approaches to Masculinity*. Sydney: Pluto Press.

Biddulph, S. (1994). *Manhood: An Action Plan for Changing Men's Lives*. Sydney: Finch Publications.

Bilton, T., Bonnett, K., Jones, P., Skinner, D., Stanworth, M. and Webster, A. (1996). *Introductory sociology* (third edn.) London: Palgrave Macmillan.

Blakenhorn, D. (1996). *Fatherless America: Confronting Our Most Urgent Social Problem*. New York: HarperCollins.

Blood, W. (1989). Public agendas and media agendas: Some news that may matter. *Media Information Australia*, No. 52, May.

Bly, R. (1990). *Iron John: A Book about Men*. Reading, MA: Addison-Wesley.

Bock, A. (2003, 19 September). Dumb and dumber stereotypes take the heart out of boy's hopes. *The Sydney Morning Herald*, p. 13.

Bourdieu, P. (1990). *In Other Words: Essays towards a Reflexive Sociology*. Cambridge: Polity Press.

Bradford, W. (1999). *Raising Boys' Achievement*. Kirklees: Education Advisory Service (cited in West, 2002b)

Braver, S. and O'Connell, D. (1998). *Divorced Dads: Shattering the Myths*. New York: Tarcher/Putnam.

Breen, M. (Ed.). (1998). *Journalism Theory and Practice*. Sydney: Macleay Press.

Brewer, K. and Wann, D. (1998). Observational learning effectiveness as a function of model characteristics: Investigating the importance of social power. *Social Behaviour and Personality*, 26(1), pp. 1–10.

Brod, H. (1987). The case for men's studies. In H. Brod (Ed.), *The Making of Masculinities: The New Men's Studies* (pp. 39–62). Boston: Allen and Unwin.

Brod, H. and Kaufman, M. (Eds.). (1994). *Theorising Masculinities*. Thousand Oaks, CA: Sage Publications.

Broderick, D. (2003, 20–21 December). Men lose on Y-front [Review of the book *Adam's Curse*]. *The Weekend Australian*, Books, p. 10.

Bryant, J. and Zillman, D. (2002). *Media Effects: Advances in Theory and Research*. New Jersey: Lawrence Erlbaum Associates.

Bryman, A. (1988). *Quantity and Quality in Social Research*. London: Unwin Hyman.

Burgess, A. (1997). *Fatherhood Reclaimed: The Making of the Modern Father*. UK: Vermilion.

Burgess, A. (2004, 29 July). Children in the undertow of divorce. *The Sydney Morning Herald*, p. 13.

Busby, L. (1975). Sex-role research on the mass media. *Journal of Communication*, 25 (4), 107–131.

Butler, J. (1995). Melancholy gender/refused identification. In M. Berger, B. Wallis, and S. Watson (Eds.), *Constructing masculinity* (pp. 21–36). New York: Routledge.

Butler, J. (1999). *Gender Trouble: Feminism and the Subversion of Identity*. New York: Routledge.

Cairnes, M. (2003, 3 October). Women mean good governance, which means good business. *The Age*, p. 13.

Cannold, L. (2004, 27 July). Choices a hurdle for new feminism. *The Sydney Morning Herald*, p. 11.

CARMA International (2003). Is free enterprise self-destructing? An analysis of the public profile of business in leading Australian and Asian media. Sydney.

Carpenter, S. (2000). Biology and social environments jointly influence gender development. *Monitor on Psychology*, Vol. 31, No. 9, October. Retrieved 1 June 2004, from http://www.apa.org/monitor/oct00/maccoby.html.

Castells, M. (1997). *The Power of Identity*. Oxford: Blackwell.

Chaney, D. (1994). *The Cultural Turn*. London: Routledge.

Clare, A. (2000, 24 September). Female power and the forgotten father. *Sunday Telegraph Magazine* London. Extract from *On Masculinity: Masculinity in Crisis*. Retrieved 12 March 2003, from http://au.geocities.com/dadsaustralia/forgotten.htm

Clatterbaugh, K. (1998). What is problematic about masculinities. *Men and Masculinities* Vol 1, No 1, 24–45.

Close, A. (2003, 28 June). No good men? The *Sydney Morning Herald,* Good Weekend, p. 51.

Cohan, S. and Hark, R. (Eds.). (1993). *Screening the Male: Exploring Masculinities in Hollywood Cinema*. London: Routledge.

Coltrane, S. and Messineo, M. (2000). The perpetuation of subtle prejudice: Race and gender imagery in 1990s television advertising. *Sex Roles*, 42, 5–6, 363–389.

Connell, R. (1995a). *Masculinities*. Sydney: Allen and Unwin.

Connell, R. (1995b). Masculinity, violence and war. In M. Kimmel and M. Messner (Eds.). *Men's Lives* (third edn.) (pp. 125–30). Boston: Allyn and Bacon.

Connell, R. (2000). *The Men and the Boys*. Sydney: Allen and Unwin.

Connell, R. and Wood, J. (2005). Globalisation and business masculinities, *Men and Masculinities*, Vol. 7, No. 4, April, pp. 347–64.

Cook, J. (1980). The interpretive tradition. In M. Alvarado and O. Boyd-Barrett (1992). *Media education: An Introduction* (pp. 155–67). London: British Film Institute.

Costello, T. (2000, 17 October).The youth suicide myth. *The Age*. Retrieved 12 March 2003, from http://au.geocities.com/dadsaustralia/youthmyth.htm.

Cox, E. (1995). Boys and girls and the costs of gendered behaviour. Proceedings of the Promoting Gender Equity Conference, Ministerial Council for Education, Employment, Training and Youth Affairs, Canberra.

Craig, S. (1993). Selling masculinities, selling femininities: multiple genders and the economics of television. *The Mid-Atlantic Almanac* 2.

Culler, J. (1981). *The Pursuit of Signs: Semiotics, Literature, Deconstruction*. London: Routledge and Kegan Paul.

Cunningham, S. and Turner, G. (1993). *The Media in Australia: Industries, Texts, Audiences*. Sydney: Allen and Unwin.

Curran, J. (2002). *Media and Power*. London: Routledge.

Curran, J. and Gurevitch, M. (Eds.). (1996). *Mass Media and Society*. London: Edward Arnold.

Dale, D. (2000, 15 January). Television ratings data. In *The Sydney Morning Herald*, p. 15.

Daly, M. (1984). *Pure Lust: Elemental Feminist Philosophy*. London: Beacon Press.

Das, S. (2003, 23 September). So, what planet? *The Age*, Agenda, p. A3, 6.

Davies, B. (1993). *Shards of Glass*. Sydney: Allen and Unwin.

Davies, B. and Gannon, S. (2005). Feminist/Poststructuralism. In C. Lewin and B. Somekh, (Eds.). *Research Methods in the Social Sciences* (Chapter 35, pp. 318–25). London: Sage.

De Beauvoir, S. (1997). *The Second Sex*. Trans. H. Parshley. London: Vintage. (Original work published 1949.)

De Lauretis, T. (1987). *Technologies of Gender: Essays on Theory, Film, and Fiction*. Indianapolis: Indiana University Press.

Delfos, M. (2005, 5 April). About boys: The core of the matter. Paper presented to a boys' education conference, Melbourne.

Denzin, N. and Lincoln, Y. (Eds.). (1994). *Handbook of Qualitative Research*. Thousand Oaks, CA: Sage Publications.

Devine, M. (2003, 18 September). The pain of the modern male eunuch. *Sydney Morning Herald*, p. 17.

Devine, M. (2004, 9 September). The rise of the women warriors. *Sydney Morning Herald*, p. 15.

Dougary, G. (2005, 25 June). Preacher man. Profile of Bob Geldoff, *The Times Magazine*, cover story. Republished (2005, 23 July). The devil in Saint Bob. *Sydney Morning Herald, Good Weekend* magazine, pp. 25–29.

Douglas, A. (1990). *Terrible Honesty: Mongrel Manhattan in the 1920s*. New York: Farrar, Straus and Giroux.

Drago, R. (2003, 13 March). Working time preferences in couple households. Paper presented to Melbourne Institute of Applied Economic and Social Research.

Dressingandpehl GbR and Verbi GmbH. (2004). MAXqda. [Computer Software]. Retrieved 19 July 2004, from http://www.winmax.de.

Drewniany, B. (1996). Super Bowl commercials: The best a man can get (or is it?). In P. M. Lester (Ed.), *Images that Injure: Pictorial Stereotypes in the Media* (pp. 87–92). Westport, CN: Praeger.

Eckert, P., and McConnell-Ginet, S. (1992). Think practically and look locally: language and gender as community-based practice. *Annual Review of Anthropology*, 21.

Eco, U. (1965). Towards a semiotic inquiry into the television message. In. J. Corner and J. Hawthorne (eds.) (1980), 131–50. Hodder Arnold.

Eco, U. (1981). *The Role of the Reader*. London: Hutchinson.

Edgar, D. (1997). *Men, Mateship, Marriage*. Sydney: HarperCollins.

Edwards, D. (1997). *Discourse and Cognition*. London: Sage.

Elasmar, M., Hasegawa, K. and Brain, M. (1999). The portrayal of women in US prime time television. *Journal of Broadcasting and Electronic Media*, 44, 1, 20–34.

Ellis, L. (1994). *Research Methods in the Social Sciences*. Madison, WI: WCB Brown and Benchmark.

Elms, R. (2005, 20 September). I'm a man, not a metrosexual. *The Times*. Retrieved 13 October 2005 from http://www.timesonline.co.uk/article/0,,20029–178954,00.html.

Embser-Herbert, M. (2004, 19 May). Women's abuse of prisoners a symptom of access to power. *Sydney Morning Herald*, Opinion, p. 17 (reprinted from *The Washington Post*).

Faludi, S. (1991). *Backlash: The Undeclared War against Women*. London, Vintage.

Faludi, S. (2000). *Stiffed: The Betrayal of Modern Man*. London, Vintage.

Family Court of Australia. (2003, 16 October). Submission Part B, Statistical Analysis to the House of Representatives Standing Committee on Family and Community Affairs Inquiry into Joint Custody Arrangements in the Event of Family Separation.

Fausto-Sterling, A. (1995). How to build a man. In M. Berger, B. Wallis, and S. Watson (Eds.). *Constructing Masculinity* (pp. 127–34). New York: Routledge.

Femiano, S. and Nickerson, M. (2002). How do media images of men affect our lives? Retrieved 25 June, 2004 from Center for Media Literacy website http://www.medialit.org/reading_room/article39.html.

Ferguson, T. (2004, 10 April). Masculinity is redundant. *The Age*, Insight, p. 9.

Fiske, J. (1989). *Understanding Popular Culture*. Boston, MA: Unwin Hyman.

Fiske, J. (1995). *Television Culture*. London: Routledge.

Flood, M. (2003). Fatherhood and fatherlessness. Discussion Paper No. 59, November. Australia Institute.

Flood, M. (2004). *The Men's Bibliography: A Comprehensive Bibliography of Writing on Men, Masculinities and Sexualities* (ninth edn.). Retrieved 13 April 2004, from http://www.anu.edu.au/~a112465/mensbiblio/mensbibliomenu.html.

Foucault, M. (1972). *The Archeology of Knowledge and the Discourse on Language*. New York: Harper and Row.

Foucault, M. (1977). *Language, Counter-memory, Practice*. Bouchard, D. F. (Ed.). New York: Cornell University Press.

Foucault, M. (1978). *The History of Sexuality: An Introduction*. New York: Pantheon Books.

Foucault, M. (1980). The history of sexuality: an interview.*Oxford Literary Review*, 4:1.

Foucault, M. (1998). *The Will to Knowledge: The History of Sexuality, Vol. 1, The Care of the Self* (R. Hurley, Trans.). London: Penguin.

Frey, L., Botan, C. and Kreps, G. (2000). *Investigating Communication: An Introduction to Research Methods* (second edn.). Boston, MA: Allyn and Bacon.

Friedan, B. (1997). *The Feminine Mystique*. New York: W. W. Norton. (First published 1963.)

Fuss, D. (1989). *Essentially Speaking: Feminism, Nature and Difference*. London: Routledge.

Garfinkel, H. (1967). *Studies in Ethnomethodology*. Cambridge, MA: Polity Press.

Gauntlett, D. (2002). *Media, Gender and Identity*. London: Routledge.

Geraghty, C. (1991). *Women and Soap Opera: A Study of Prime Time Soaps*. Cambridge: Polity Press.

Gibbs, C. (1991). Project 2000: Why black men should teach black boys. *Dollars and Sense*, February/March, pp. 18–28.

Giddens, A. (1991). *Modernity and Self-identity: Self and Society in the Late Modern Age*. Cambridge: Polity Press.

Gilens, M. (1996). Race and poverty in America: Public misconceptions and the American news media. *Public Opinion Quarterly*, 60, 515–41.

Gill, R. (1993). Justifying injustice: Broadcasters' accounts of inequality in radio. In *Readings of Texts in Action* (pp. 75–93). London: Routledge.

Glaser, B. and Strauss, A. (1967). *The Discovery of Grounded Theory: Strategies for Qualitative Research*. Chicago: Aldane.

Goffman, E. (1976). *Gender Advertisements. Studies in the Anthropology of Visual Communication*. New York: HarperCollins.

Goodwin, F. (1992, May). Conduct disorder as a precursor to adult violence and substance abuse: can the progression be halted? Paper presented to American Psychiatric Association Annual Convention.

Gray, M. (2005). Domestic violence – a statistical 'shock and awe' campaign? *Online Opinion*. Retrieved 16 October 2005 from http://www.onlineopinion.com.au.

Grbich, C. (2004). *New Approaches in Social Research*. London: Sage.

Greenberg, B. (1980). *Life on Television: A Content Analysis of US TV Drama*. Norwood, NJ: Ablex.

Greer, G. (1999). *The Female Eunuch*. London: Flamingo (HarperCollins). (Original work published 1971.)

Grossberg, L., Wartella, E. and Whitney, C. (1998). *Mediamaking – Mass Media in a Popular Culture*. London: Sage.

Grosz, E. (1990a). Contemporary theories of power and subjectivity. In S. Gunew (Ed.), *Feminist knowledge: critique and construct* (pp. 59–120). London: Routledge.

Grosz, E. (1990b). Conclusion: a note on essentialism and difference. In S. Gunew (Ed.), *Feminist Knowledge: Critique and Construct* (pp. 332–44). London: Routledge.

Grosz, E. (1994). *Volatile Bodies: Toward a Corporeal Feminism*. Sydney: Allen and Unwin.

Grunig, J. and Hunt, T. (1984). *Managing Public Relations*. Chicago: Holt, Rinehart and Winston.

Guilliatt, R. (2001, 26 August). The Y front. *The Sydney Morning Herald*, Good Weekend, pp. 18–22.

Gunter, B. (1995). *Television and Gender Representation*. London: John Libbey.

Gurevitch, M., Blumler, J. and Weaver, D. (1986, May). The formation of campaign agendas in the US and Britain: A conceptual introduction. Paper presented to the annual conference, International Communication Association, Chicago.

Habermas, J. (1989). *The Structural Transformation of the Public Sphere*. Cambridge: Polity. (Original work published 1962.)

Hagenbaugh, B. (2002, 21 October). Women more recession-proof than men. *USA Today*, p. 1.

Hall, S. (1973). Encoding/Decoding. Reprinted in S. Hall, D. Hobson, A. Lowe and P. Willis (Eds.), *Culture, Media, Language* (pp. 26–7). London: Hutchinson.

Hall, S. (1977). Culture, media, and the ideological effect. In J. Curran, M. Gurevitch and J. Woollacott (Eds.), *Mass Communication and Society* (pp. 332–3). London: Edward Arnold.

Hall, S. (1980). Encoding/decoding. In Centre for Contemporary Cultural Studies (Ed.), *Culture, Media, Language: Working Papers in Cultural Studies, 1972–79* (pp. 128–38). London: Hutchinson. (Original work published in 1973 as *Encoding/Decoding in Television Discourse*)

Hall, S. (1990). Cultural identity and diaspora. In J. Rutherford (Ed.), *Identity: Community, Culture, Difference* (pp. 222–37). London: Lawrence and Wishart.

Hall, S., Hobson, D., Lowe, A. and Willis, P. (Eds.). (1980). *Culture, Media, Language*. London: Hutchinson.

Hammersley, M. (1992). *What's Wrong with Ethnography? Methodological Explorations.* London: Routledge.

Hansen, A., Cottle, S., Negrine, R. and Newbold, C. (1998). *Mass Communication Research Methods.* London: Macmillan.

Harris, J. (2005, 10 August). Driving us to nuts. *The Guardian.* Retrieved 12 August 2005 from http://www.guardian.co.uk/print/0,3858,5258811–103677,00.html.

Haussegger, V. (2003, 14 March). Wanted: a way out of the unbearable lightness of modern coupling. *The Sydney Morning Herald*, Opinion, p. 11.

Hawes, T. and Thomas, S. (1995). Language bias against women in British and Malaysian newspapers, *Australian Review of Applied Linguistics*, 18 (2).

Hawthorne, B. (2000). Non-resident fathers struggle with the system. Retrieved 10 July 2003 from MHIRC website http://www.menshealth.uws.edu.au/publications.html.

Hawthorne, B. (2002). Australian non-resident fathers: missing in action. Paper presented to Australian Institute of Family Studies conference.

Hearn, J. (Ed.) (1993). Researching men and researching men's violence'. Research Paper No. 4.BD7, University of Bradford. Retrieved 14 April 2004, from http://www.europrofem.org/o2.info/22contri/2.04en/4en/viol.42en_vio.htm.

Hedges, L. and Nowell, A. (1995). Sex differences in mental test scores, variability and numbers of high-scoring individuals, *Science*, July 7, 41–45.

Herman, E. and Chomsky, N. (1988). *Manufacturing Consent.* New York: Pantheon Books.

Hermes, J. (1995). *Reading Women's Magazines: An Analysis of Everyday Media Use.* Cambridge: Polity.

Hijams, E. (1996). The logic of qualitative media content analysis: a typology. *Communications*, 21, 93–109.

Hilton, J. (2000). *Presumed Guilty: The Invisible War against the Working-class Male.* Sydney: International Press Publications.

Hirst, J. (2004, 6 August). Dads bear the burden of proof. *The Australian*, p. 13.

Hoff Sommers, C. (2000). *The War against Boys.* New York: Simon and Schuster.

Hood, M. (2001). Men and child protection: Developing new kinds of relationships between men and children. In B. Pease and P. Camilleri (Eds.), *Working with Men in the Human services.* Sydney: Allen and Unwin.

Horkheimer, M. (1972). *Critical Theory.* New York: Herder and Herder.

House of Representatives Standing Committee on Education and Training. (2002, October). Boys: getting it right. Report on the inquiry into the education of boys. Commonwealth of Australia.

Humm, M. (1997). *Feminism and Film.* Edinburgh: Edinburgh University Press.

Internet Industry Association. (2004). Letter introducing the tenth Anniversary Annual Meeting, 1 December.

Irigaray, L. (1996). *i love to you.* New York: Routledge.

Jackson, J. (1998). Explore the strengths and weaknesses of classical content analysis: content analysis and objectivity, language and metaphor. Retrieved 1 May 2004, from http://www.spinworks.demon.co.uk/pub/content2.htm.

Kalis, P. and Neuendorf, K. (1989). Aggressive cue prominence and gender participation in MTV. *Journalism Quarterly*, 66, 148–154, 229.

Kaplan, A. (1983). *Women and Film: Both Sides of the Camera.* London: Methuen.

Kaplan, G. and Rogers, L. (1990). The definition of male and female: biological reductionism and the sanctions of normality. In S. Gunew (Ed.). *Feminist Knowledge: Critique and Construct* (pp. 205–28). London: Routledge.

Katz, E. (1977). Looking for trouble: social research on broadcasting. Presentation to British Broadcasting Corporation, London.

Katz, E. (1995). Advertising and the construction of violent white masculinity. In G. Dines and J. Humez (Eds.), *Gender, Race and Class in Media* (p. 133). London: Sage.

Katz, E. and Lazarsfeld, P. (1955). *Personal Influence*. New York: Free Press.

Kaufman, M. (Ed.). (1987). *Beyond Patriarchy: Essays by Men on Pleasure, Power and Change*. Toronto: Oxford University Press.

Kessler, S. and McKenna, S. (1978). *Gender: An Ethnomethodological Approach*. New York: Wiley.

Kidder, K. (2004). American masculinities: a historical encyclopaedia. Retrieved 10 May 2004, from www.referenceworld.com/mosgroup/masculinity/mstudies.html.

Kimmel, M. (1987). *Changing Men: New Directions in Research on Men and Masculinity*. Newbury Park, CA: Sage.

Kimmel, M. (2002). *The Common Review*, Vol. 1, No. 3, Spring. Book Reviews.

Kimmel, M. and Messner, M. (Eds.). (1995). *Men's Lives* (third edn.). Boston, MA: Allyn and Bacon. Reprinted Pearson Education Australia.

Kimura, D. (1992). Sex differences in the brain. Reprinted as e-book, *Scientific American: Sex Differences in the Brain*. Retrieved 14 May 2004, from www.ebookmall.com/alpha-titles/Scientific-American-Sex-Differences-in-the-Brain.

Kimura, D. (1999). Sex differences in the brain. In *Scientific American Presents*, Special Issue: Men: The Scientific Truth about Their Work, Play, Health, and Passions, Summer, Vol. 10, No. 2, 26.

Kipnis, A. (1991). *Knights without Armour: A Practical Guide for Men in Quest of Masculine Soul*. Los Angeles: Tarcher.

Kirkham, P. and Thumim, J. (Eds.). (1993). *You Tarzan: Masculinity, Movies and Men*. London: Lawrence and Wishart.

Kirkham, P., and Thumim, J. (Eds.). (1995). *Me Jane: Masculinity, Movies and Women*. London: Lawrence and Wishart.

Klapper, J. (1960). *The Effects of Mass Communication*. New York: Free Press.

Kristeva, J. (1980): *Desire in Language: A Semiotic Approach to Literature and Art*. New York: Columbia University Press.

Kristeva, J. (1981). Woman's time (A. Jardine, Trans.). *Signs* 7 (1) reprinted.

Kruk, E. (1993). *Divorce and Disengagement: Patterns of Fatherhood within and beyond Marriage*. Halifax, NS: Fernwood Publications.

Langley, W. (2003, November). Rebel with a cause. *Australian Women's Weekly*, pp. 106–12.

Lash, S. (1990). *The Sociology of Postmodernism*. London: Routledge.

Lee, V., Chen, X. and Smerdon, B. (1996). *The Influence of School Climate on Gender Differences in the Achievement and Engagement of Young Adolescents*. Washington, DC: American Association of University Women Education Foundation.

Lemish, D. and Tidhar, C. (1999). Still marginal: women in Israel's 1996 television election campaign. *Sex Roles*, 41, 389–412.

Lingard, B. (2003, 10 October). Doing research in education: A consideration of the issues. Paper presented to Education Research Conference, University of Western Sydney.

Lombard, M., Snyder-Duch, J. and Bracken, C. (2004). Practical resources for assessing and reporting intercoder reliability in content analysis research projects. Retrieved 28 April 2004, from www.temple.edu/mmc/reliability.

Lombard, M., Synder-Duch, J. and Bracken, C. (2003). Content analysis in mass communication: assessment and reporting of intercoder reliability. *Human Communication Research*, 29, 469–472.

Lovdal, L. (1989). Sex role messages in television commercials: an update. *Sex Roles*, 20, 715–724.

Lovell, T. (1980). *Pictures of Reality*. London: British Film Institute.

Low, J., and Sherrard, P. (1999). Portrayal of women in sexuality and marriage and family textbooks: A content analysis of photographs from the 1970s to the 1990s. *Sex Roles*, 40, 309–318.

Lull, J. (2000). *Media, Communication, Culture*. Cambridge: Polity Press.

Lyotard, J. (1979). *The Postmodern Condition: A Report on Knowledge* (G. Hennington and B. Massumi, Trans.). Manchester: Manchester University Press.

Mac An Ghaill, M. (1994). *The Making of Men: Masculinities, Sexualities and Schooling*. Buckingham: Open University Press.

Maccoby, E. (1999). *Two Sexes: Growing up, Coming Together*. Cambridge, MA: Harvard University Press.

Macdonald, J. (1999, October). A salutogeneic approach to men's health. Paper presented to the third national men's health conference, Alice Springs.

Macdonald, J. and Crawford, D. (2002). A population health approach to preventing male suicide: the need for positive cultural images of men. Paper presented to the ninth Suicide Prevention Australia Conference, 21 June.

Macdonald, J., McDermott, D. and Di Campli, C. (2000). Making it OK to be Male. Paper presented to the eighth National Australian Suicide Prevention Conference, Sydney.

MacDonald, M. (1995). *Representing Women: Myths of Femininity in the Popular Media*. London: Arnold.

Macnamara, J. (1993). Public relations and the media: A new influence in 'agenda setting' and content. Unpublished Masters thesis, Deakin University, Geelong, Australia.

Macnamara, J. (2005). Representations of men and male identities in Australian mass media. Unpublished doctoral thesis, University of Western Sydney.

Maio, K. (1991). *Popcorn and Sexual Politics*. Santa Cruz, CA: Cross Press.

Mansbridge, J. (1995). What is the feminist movement? In M. Feree and P. Martin (Eds.). *Feminist Organizations: Harvest of the Women's Movement* (pp. 27–34). Philadelphia: Temple University Press.

Marcuse, H. (1972). *One Dimensional Man*. London: Sphere.

Mariani, P. (1995). Law and order science. In M. Berger, B. Wallis, and S. Watson (Eds.), *Constructing Masculinity* (pp. 135–56). New York: Routledge.

Marsden, J. (2002a, 6–7 July). The boys are all right. Extract from *The Boy You Brought Home. The Sydney Morning Herald*, Spectrum, pp. 4–5.

Marsden, J. (2002b). *The Boy You Brought Home*. Sydney: Pan Macmillan.

Mayring, P. (2000). *Qualitative inhaltsanalyse. Grundlagen und Techniken* (seventh edn.). Weinheim: Psychologie Verlags Union. (Original work published 1983.)

Mayring, P. (2003). Qualitative content analysis. Forum Qualitative Sozialforschung/Forum Social Research. Online journal, 1, (2). Retrieved 18 December 2003, from http://qualitative-research.net/fqs/fqs-e/2-00inhalt-e.htm.

McCombs, M. (1977). Agenda setting function of mass media. *Public Relations Review*, 3 (4), 89–95.

McKay, J. and Huber, D. (1992). Anchoring media images of technology and sport. *Women's Studies International Forum* 15 (2), 205–218.

McKay, J. and Middlemiss, I. (1995). Mate against mate, state against state: a case study of media constructions of hegemonic masculinity in Australian sport. *Masculinities*, Vol 3, No 3, Fall, pp. 28–45.

McKee, A. (2004). A beginner's guide to textual analysis. Retrieved 13 April 2004, from http://www/enhancetv.com.au/articles/article3_1.htm.

McLuhan, M. (1964). *Understanding Media: The Extensions of Man.* New York: McGraw-Hill.

McQuail, D. (1984). With the benefit of hindsight: Reflections on uses and gratifications research. *Critical Studies in Mass Communication* 1 (2), VA: Speech Communication Association, 177–193.

McQueen, D. (1998). *Television – A Media Student's Guide.* London: Arnold.

McQueen, H. (1977). *Australia's Media Monopolies.* Camberwell, Victoria: Widescope.

Merchant, C. (1980). *The Death of Nature: Women, Ecology, and the Scientific Revolution.* New York: Harper and Row.

Messner, M. (1988). Sports and male domination: the female athlete as contested ideological terrain. *Sociology of Sport Journal* 5 (3), 197–211.

Messner, M. (1992). *Power at Play: Sports and the Problem of Masculinity.* Boston, MA: Beacon Press.

Messner, M. and Sabo, D. (Eds.). (1990). *Sport, Men and the Gender Order: Critical Feminist Perspectives.* Champaign, IL: Human Kinetics Books.

Messner, M., Duncan, M. and Jensen, K. (1990). Separating the men from the girls: the gendering of televised sport. Paper presented at a meeting of the North American Society for the Sociology of Sport, Denver, CO.

Messner, M., Duncan, M. and Jensen, K. (1993). Separating the men from the girls: the gendered language of televised sport. *Gender and Society*, 7, 121–137.

Michelson, J. (1996). Visual imagery in medical journal advertising. Unpublished Master's thesis. Cleveland State University, Ohio.

Midgley, C. (2005, 30 August). Future perfect: how to be a 'real' man again. Interview with Marian Salzman, cover story. *The Times*, p. 24.

Miles, M. and Huberman, M. (1994). *Qualitative Data Analysis.* Newbury Park, CA: Sage.

Miranda, C. (2003, 26 September). Car yards gear up for a feminine image shift, *The Daily Telegraph*, Sydney.

Mitchell, J. (1971). *Woman's Estate.* Harmondsworth: Penguin.

Mitchell, J. (1974). *Psychoanalysis and Feminism.* Harmondsworth: Penguin.

Modleski, T. (1991). *Feminism without Women: Culture and Criticism in a Postfeminist Age.* New York: Routledge.

Moi, T. (1985). *Sexual/Textual Politics: Feminist Literary Theory.* London: Menthuen.

Moloney, J. (2000, 23 September). Why men are running a poor second in the gender race. *The Sydney Morning Herald*, p. 11.

Morley, D. and Chen, K. (Eds.) (1996). *Stuart Hall: Critical Dialogues in Cultural Studies.* London: Routledge.

Mosco, V. (1995). *The Political Economy Tradition of Media Research*, Module 2, Unit 4 of the MA in Mass Communications. University of Leicester.

Mount, H. (2005, 12 August). The future is übersexual. *The Telegraph*, London. Retrieved 15 September, 2005 from http://www.health. telegraph.co.uk/core/content/displayPrintable.jhtml?xml=/arts/.

Mumford, L. (1998). Feminist theory and television studies. In C. Geraghty and D. Lusted (Eds.). *The Television Studies Book* (pp. 114–30). London: Arnold.

Murray-West, R. (2005, 22 August). Adland pulls plug on man's lustful ineptitude. *The Telegraph* (UK), Health. Retrieved 16 September 2005 from http://www.health.

Nathanson, P. and Young, K. (2001). *Spreading Misandry: The Teaching of Contempt for Men in Popular Culture*. Quebec: McGill-Queen's University Press.

Neuendorf, K. (2002). *The Content Analysis Guidebook*, Thousand Oaks, CA: Sage Publications.

Neuman, W. (1997). *Social Research Methods: Qualitative and Quantitative Approaches*. Needham Heights, MA: Allyn and Bacon.

Newbold, C., Boyd-Barrett, O., and Van Den Bulck, H. (2002). *The Media Book*. London: Arnold, Hodder Headline Group.

Newman, A. (2005, 10 October). In time of studied ambiguity, a label for the manly man. *The New York Times*. Retrieved 13 October 2005 from http://nytimes.com/2005/10/10business.

O'Connor, P. (1983). *Men and Midlife*. Melbourne: Sun Books.

O'Donnell, H. (1999). *Good Times, Bad Times – Soap Operas and Society in Western Europe*. Leicester: Leicester University Press.

Only losers get married. (2004, 15 July). *The Times*, p. 6.

Organisation for Economic Co-operation and Development (OECD). (2003). *Education at a Glance*.

OZTAM TV and Radio Ratings (2003). Retrieved weekly 1 July–20 December 2004, from http://www.oztam.com.au.

Paglia, C. (2003a). *Gender Whores*. Retrieved 28 October, 2003, from http://www.salon.com/it/col/pagl/1999/02/10pagl.htm.

Paglia, C. (2003b) Camille Paglia on political correctness. Extract from *Vamps and Tramps*, pp. 35, 431. Retrieved 28 October 2003, from http://www.dimensional.com/~randl/camille.htm.

Patton, M. (1990). *Qualitative Evaluation and Research Methods* (second edn.). Newbury Park, CA: Sage.

Patton, M. (2002). *Qualitative Evaluation and Research Methods*. (third edn.). Newbury Park, CA: Sage.

Pavlik, J. (1987). *What Research Tells Us*. Newbury Park, CA: Sage.

Pocock, B. (2003). *The Work/Life Collision*. Annandale, Sydney: The Federation Press. Extract retrieved 26 March 2004, from www.federationpress.com.au/ books/Pocock.htm.

Popping, R. (1984). AGREE, a package for computing nominal scale agreement. *Computational Statistics and Data Analysis, 2*, 182–185.

Popping, R. (1988). On agreement indices for nominal data. In W. E. Saris and I. N. Gallhofer (Eds.), *Sociometric Research: Volume 1, Data Collection and Scaling* (pp. 90–105). New York: St Martin's Press.

Reddy, M. (1979). The conduit metaphor – a case of frame conflict in our language about language. In A. Ortony (Ed.), *Metaphor and Thought* (pp. 284–324). Cambridge: Cambridge University Press.

Regidor, C. (2003a, 10 April). What women want: world domination. *Daily Telegraph*, p. 30.

Regidor, C. (2003b, 16 October). Don't you love those idol hours. *Daily Telegraph*, p. 24.

Riffe, D. and Freitag, A. (1997). A content analysis of content analyses: Twenty-five years of *Journalism Quarterly*. *Journalism and Mass communication Quarterly*, 74, 873–882.

Riffe, D., Lacy, S. and Drager, M. (1996). Sample size in content analysis of weekly news magazines. *Journalism and Mass Communication Quarterly*, 73, 635–644.

Riffe, D., Lacy, S. and Fico, F. (1998). *Analysing Media messages: Using Quantitative Content Analysis in Research*. Mahwah, NJ: Erlbaum.

Riffe, D., Lacy, S., Nagovan, J. and Burkum, L. (1996). The effectiveness of simple and stratified random sampling in broadcast news content analysis. *Journalism and Mass Communication Quarterly*, 73, 159–168.

Ripley, A. (2005, 28 March). Who says a woman can't be Einstein? *Time*, pp. 55–61.

Roberson, J. (2005). Fight!! Ippatsu!!: Genki energy drinks and the marketing of masculine ideology in Japan, *Men and Masculinities*, Vol. 7, No. 4, April, pp. 365–84.

Robinson, P. (2003, 23 May). Women at top would prevent corporate calamity, says expert. *The Sydney Morning Herald*, p. 4.

Robson, C. (1993). *Real World Research: A Resource for Social Scientists and Practitioner Researchers*. Oxford: Blackwell.

Rosen, M. (1973). *Popcorn Venus*. New York: Avon Books.

Rubin, G. (1984). The traffic in women: notes on the political economy of sex. In R. Reiter (Ed.). *Pleasure and Danger: Exploring Female Sexuality* (pp. 267–319). New York: Routledge and Kegan Paul.

Sabo, D. and Curry Jansen, S. (1992). Images of men in sport media; The social reproduction of gender order. In S. Craig (Ed.), *Men, Masculinity, and the Media* (pp. 169–84). London: Sage.

Saco, D. (1992). Masculinity as signs: Poststructuralist feminist approaches to the study of gender. In S. Craig (Ed.), *Men, Masculinity and the Media*. Newbury Park, CA: Sage.

Salzman, M. (2005). *The Future of Men*. New York: Palgrave Macmillan.

Sargent, L. (1981). *Women and Revolution*. Boston, MA: South End.

Sartre, J. (1958). *Being and Nothingness: An Essay on Phenomenological Ontology*. London: Methuen. (Original work published 1943.)

Sarup, M. (1988). *An Introductory Guide to Poststructuralism and Postmodernism*, New York: Harvester Wheatsheaf.

Schirato, T. and Yell, S. (1999). The new men's magazines and the performance of masculinity. *Media International* Australia, 92, August.

Sedgwick, E. (1995). Gosh, Boy George, you must be awfully secure in your masculinity. In M. Berger, B. Wallis and S. Watson (Eds.), *Constructing Masculinity* (pp. 11–20). New York: Routledge.

Segal, L. (1987). *Is the Future Female?* London: Virago.

Segal, L. (1990). *Slow Motion: Changing Masculinities, Changing Men*. London: Virago.

Seger, L. (2004). How to evaluate media images of women. Retrieved June 25, 2004 from Center for Media Literacy website http://www.medilit.org/reading_room/article44.html.

Seidler, V. (1994). *Unreasonable Men: Masculinity and Social Theory*. London: Routledge.

Seymour-Smith, M. (1998). *The 100 Most Influential Books Ever Written*. Secaucus, NJ: Citadel Press.

Shannon, C. and Weaver, W. (1949). *A Mathematical Model of Communication*. Urbana, IL: University of Illinois Press.

Sheridan, S. (1990). Feminist knowledge, women's liberation and women's studies. In S. Gunew, *Feminist Knowledge: Critique and Construct* (pp. 36–55). London: Routledge.

Shoemaker, P., and Reese, S. (1996). *Mediating the Message: Theories of Influences on Mass Media Content*. White Plains, NY: Longman.

Silverman, D. (1993). *Interpreting Qualitative Data: Methods for Analysing Talk, Text and Interaction*. London: Sage.

Silverman, D. (2000). *Doing Qualitative Research*. London: Sage.

Simpson, M. (2005, 31 August). Narcissists unlimited. *The Times*, Viewpoint, p. 26.

SkyMeg Software. (2004). Program for Reliability Assessment of Multiple Coders'. Alpha release 0.4.4. [Computer Software]. Retrieved 7 January 2004, from http://www.geocities.com/skymegsoftware/pram/html.

Smith, S. (1972). The image of women in film: some suggestions for future research. *Women and Film*, 1, 13–21.

Smyth, B. (Ed.). (2004) *Parent–Child Contact and Post-Separation Parenting Arrangement*. Australian Institute of Family Studies. Research Report No. 9.

Soccio, L. (1999). From girl to woman to grrrl: (sub)cultural intervention and political activism in the time of postfeminism'. In *Invisible Culture*, Issue 2 (an electronic Journal for Visual Studies). Retrieved 3 May 2004, from http://www.rochester.edu.in_visible_culture/issue2/soccio/htm.

Sommer, H. (2003). Equality for Australian families. DADs Australia Web site. Retrieved July 7, 2003, from http://geocities.com/dadsaustralia.

Stacey, J. (1990). *Brave New Families: Stories of Domestic Upheaval in Late Twentieth-century America*. New York: Basic Books.

Stewart, J., Schwebel, A. and Fine, M. (1986). The impact of custodial arrangement on the adjustment of recently divorced fathers. *Journal of Divorce*, 9 (3).

Stirling, L. (1987). Language and gender in Australian newspapers. In A. Pauwels (Ed.). *Women and Language in Australian and New Zealand society* (pp. 108–28), Sydney: Australian Professional Publications.

Strauss, A. and Corbin, J. (1990). *Basics of Qualitative Research: Grounded Theory Procedures and Techniques*. Newbury Park, CA: Sage.

Strauss, M. and Gelles, R. (1986). Societal change and change in family violence from 1975 to 1985 as revealed by two national surveys. *Journal of Marriage and the Family*, 48, 465–479.

Strinati, D. (1995). *An Introduction to Theories of Popular Culture*. London: Routledge.

Sullivan, R., Craig, J. and Howard, S. (2000, 24–26 July). Family futures: issues in research and policy. Paper presented to the seventh Australian Institute of Family Studies conference, Sydney.

Summers, A. (1975). *Damned Whores and God's Police: The Colonisation of Women in Australia*. Ringwood: Penguin.

Summers, A. (2003). *The End of Equality*. Sydney: Random House.

Summers, A. (2004, 21 July). Labor brings women in from the cold. *The Sydney Morning Herald*, p. 13.

Sykes, B. (2003). *Adam's Curse: A Story of Sex, Genetics and the Extinction of Men.* London: Bantam.

Sykes, B. (2004). *Adam's Curse: a Future without Men.* New York: W. W. Norton.

Tacey, D. (1997). *Remaking Men: The Revolution in Masculinity.* Melbourne: Viking.

Tasker, Y. (1998). *Working Girls: Gender and Sexuality in Popular Cinema.* London: Routledge.

Teese, R. and Polesel, J. (2003). *Undemocratic Schooling.* Melbourne University Press.

Tester, K. (1994). *Media, Culture, and Morality.* London: Routledge.

The Economist (2005, 4 June). Sex changes, pp. 55–6.

Times Mirror Center for People and the Press survey. (1994, 16 March). *Los Angeles Times.*

Tinsley, H. and Weiss, D. (1975). Interrater reliability and agreement of subject judgements. *Journal of Counseling Psychology,* 22.

Tomison, A. (1996). Protecting children: Updating the national picture. *Child Welfare Series,* 16. Canberra: Australian Government Publishing Service.

Tuchman, G. (1978). The symbolic annihilation of women by the mass media. In G. Tuchman, K. Kaplan, A. Daniels, and J. Benet (Eds.). *Hearth and Home: Images of Women and the Media* (pp. 3–17). New York: Oxford University Press.

University of Queensland Journalism Department. (1992). Survey of 1,068 journalists conducted by Quadrant Research. Funded by Australian Research Council.

University of Western Sydney (2003, 11–12 October). (Re)visioning education. Paper presented to Education Research Conference, Parramatta, Sydney.

Van Tiggelen, J. (2005, 21 May). Here come the men in black. *Sydney Morning Herald, Good Weekend* magazine, pp. 20–5.

Van Zoonen, L. (1994). *Feminist Media Studies.* London: Sage.

Vance, C. (1995). Social construction theory and sexuality. In M. Berger, B. Wallis and S. Watson (Eds.), *Constructing Masculinity* (pp. 37–56). New York: Routledge.

Veldre, D. (2005, 1 July). The myth of the male. *B&T* magazine, p. 5.

Vilain, E. (2003, October). *Molecular Brain Research.*

Warren, A. (1988). *Gender Issues in Field Research.* Newbury Park, CA: Sage.

Watkins, P. (1996). Women in the work force in non-traditional jobs. In P. M. Lester (Ed.), *Images that Injure: Pictorial Stereotypes in the Media* (pp. 69–74). Westport, CN: Praeger.

Watson, I., Buchanan, J., Campbell, I. and Briggs, C. (2003). *Fragmented Futures – New Challenges in Work Life.* Sydney: Federation Press.

Watson, J. (2000). *Male Bodies: Health, Culture and Identity.* Buckingham: Open University Press.

Weatherall, A. (1996). Language about women and men: an example from popular culture. *Journal of Language and Social Psychology.* 15 (1), 59–75.

Weatherall, A. (2002). *Gender, Language and Discourse.* Hove: Routledge.

Weaver, J. B. III (1991). Are slasher horror films sexually violent? A content analysis. *Journal of Broadcasting and Electronic Media,* 35, 385–392.

Webb, J. (1998). *Junk Male.* Sydney: HarperCollins.

Weigman, R. (1994). Feminism and its mal(e)contents. *Masculinities: Interdisciplinary Studies on Gender,* Vol. 2, No. 1, Spring, 1–7.

Wells-Wilbon, R. and Holland, S. (2000). Social learning theory and the influence of male role models on African American children in PROJECT 2000. *The*

Qualitative Report, Volume 6, Number 4, December, 2001. Retrieved 23October 2004, from http://www.nova.edu/ssss/QR/QR6–4/wellswilbon.html.

West, P. (1995, February). Giving boys a ray of hope: masculinity and education. Discussion Paper for Gender Equity Task Force, Sydney.

West, P. (1996). *Fathers, Sons and Lovers: Men Talk about their Lives from the 1930s to Today.* Sydney: Finch Publishing.

West, P. (1999, October). The way forward for men. Paper presented to conference Men: the way forward, Moe, Victoria.

West, P. (2002a). It ain't cool to like school: why are boys underachieving around the world and what can we do about it? Report of research study funded by The King's School and University of Western Sydney. Retrieved 15 March 2003, from http://www.menshealthweekaustralia.org/mhirc.htm.

West, P. (2002b, 13 October). Being a boy in many countries around the world: a bird's eye view. Paper presented to Australian Boys Education Conference. Sydney.

Wheldall, K. (2003, December). Positive teaching for boys. *MultiLit® Moments,* Macquarie University, Vol. 2, Issue 3.

Whittier, N. (1995). *Feminist Generations: The Persistence of the Radical Women's Movement.* Philadelphia: Temple University Press.

Wilbur, K. (1996). *A Brief History of Everything.* Boston: Shambhala Publications.

Wilson, E. (1975). *Sociobiology: A New Synthesis.* Cambridge, MA: Harvard University Press.

Windschuttle, K. (1998). Cultural studies versus journalism. In M. Breen (Ed.), *Journalism Theory and Practice* (pp. 17–36). Sydney: Macleay Press.

Windschuttle, K. (2000). The poverty of cultural studies. *Journalism Studies,* (UK), 1, 1. February. Retrieved 20 April 2004, from http://www.sydneyline. com/Poverty%20ofMediaTheory.htm.

Winter, M., and Robert, E. (1980). Male dominance, late capitalism and the growth of instrumental reason, *Berkeley Journal of Sociology,* Vol. 24/25, 249–280.

Wolf, N. (1991). *The Beauty Myth: How Images of Beauty Are Used against Women.* New York: William Morrow.

Woods, M. (1998). Domestic violence and the demonising of men. *Jumbunna.* University of Western Sydney.

Woods, M. (1999, October). Masculinities and discourse. Paper presented to the third National Men's Health Conference, Sydney.

Woods, M. (2001). Men's health at the beginning of the new millennium: trends and black holes. Paper presented at the 4th Australian National Men's Health Conference, Sydney.

Woodward, K. (Ed.) (1997). *Identity and Difference.* London: Sage/Open University.

Index